A Family of Brothers

A Family of Brothers

Soldiers of the 26th New Brunswick Battalion in the Great War

J. Brent Wilson

GOOSE LANE EDITIONS and
THE GREGG CENTRE FOR THE STUDY OF WAR AND SOCIETY

Edited by J. Marc Milner.
Cover design by Kerry Lawlor.
Page layout by Chris Tompkins.
Front Cover: Captain Frederick F. May and enlisted men of the 26th New Brunswick Battalion, East Sandling Camp, England, July 1915. Harold Wright Collection.
Frontispiece: Soldiers of the 26th New Brunswick Battalion on board the troopship S.S. *Caledonia*, June 13, 1915. 1989.140.2, New Brunswick Museum
Printed in Canada.
10 9 8 7 6 5 4 3 2 1

We acknowledge the generous support of the Government of Canada, the Canada Council for the Arts, and the Government of New Brunswick.

Goose Lane Editions
500 Beaverbrook Court, Suite 330
Fredericton, New Brunswick
CANADA E3B 5X4
www.gooselane.com

New Brunswick Military History Project
The Brigadier Milton F. Gregg, VC,
Centre for the Study of War and Society
University of New Brunswick
PO Box 4400
Fredericton, New Brunswick
CANADA E3B 5A3
www.unb.ca/nbmhp

Library and Archives Canada Cataloguing in Publication

Wilson, J. Brent, author
A family of brothers : soldiers of the 26th New Brunswick Battalion in the Great War / J. Brent Wilson.

(New Brunswick military heritage series ; 25)
Includes bibliographical references and index.
Co-published by: New Brunswick Military Heritage Project.
ISBN 978-0-86492-923-5 (softcover)

1. Canada. Canadian Army. Battalion, 26th--History. 2. World War, 1914-1918--Regimental histories--Canada. 3. Soldiers--New Brunswick--Biography. I. New Brunswick Military Heritage Project, issuing body II. Title. III. Series: New Brunswick military heritage series ; 25

D547.C2W55 2018   940.4'1271
C2016-907608-3

RECYCLED
Paper made from recycled material
FSC
www.fsc.org   FSC® C103567

Dedicated to the soldiers who served in the
26th New Brunswick Battalion during the Great War.

Contents

Introduction

On May 17, 1919, The 26th New Brunswick Battalion, C.E.F.,[1] returned home after being overseas for more than four years. During that time, 5,719 soldiers, many of them New Brunswickers, served in its ranks. As such, the 26th Battalion was the single largest concentration of Great War soldiers from the province to fight on the Western Front.

The details of the 26th's war are well known, especially through the richly detailed regimental history, *New Brunswick's "Fighting 26th": A History of The 26th New Brunswick Battalion, C.E.F. 1914-1919*, by S. Douglas MacGowan, Harry (Mac) Heckbert, and Byron E. O'Leary. What is less familiar is who these soldiers were and what they experienced. To that end, this book describes the basic history of the "Fighting 26th," and provides an in-depth examination of how these soldiers endured the war. What emerges is a story about how ordinary men, many of them young, unmarried, and living at home when they enlisted, found a place in history and experienced one of the greatest and most tragic events of modern times. The tale will enable us to understand better not only how an infantry battalion functioned at the front in the Great War, but also how the war affected New Brunswick as a whole both during and after the conflict.

---

1   The battalion went through a few names changes during the war. To avoid confusion, I have used the original name throughout the book.

The book views the war through the eyes of the troops by drawing heavily on the letters and diaries they wrote. Hundreds of these letters were printed, often verbatim, in provincial newspapers, especially early in the war before censorship limited their publication. The book also makes use of the few post-war memoirs written by soldiers of the 26th. As well, to provide the wider context needed to understand more specific personal experiences, the book draws on numerous primary documents, including the unit's war diaries, Daily Part II Orders, and after-action reports, soldiers' personnel files, which are now available online at the website of Library and Archives Canada, and unit nominal rolls. Finally, the story is also based on field work conducted by the author, including numerous tours of the battlefields and travels throughout New Brunswick, particularly to visit local cemeteries, churches, schools, and cenotaphs, to help us see these soldiers within their family and community settings.

Nevertheless, some important parts of the story are either missing or underreported, mainly because the records do not exist. Many of the men in uniform who supported the fighting forces remain largely anonymous: little is known, for example, about the day-to-day activities of Major James Pringle and his quartermaster staff, the medical officer and his assistants, the paymaster, and the orderly room staff; they, too, made a significant contribution to the battalion's war.

The book follows a chronological format, beginning with the raising of the battalion in the late fall of 1914, followed by the long period of preparation in New Brunswick and Britain, and then its time at the Western Front in Belgium and France starting in mid-September 1915 and concluding with the Armistice on November 11, 1918. The survey then follows the battalion's little-known time in Germany as part of the Allied occupation force and longer interlude in a small town in central Belgium, the return home in May 1919, and then, more briefly, the lives of the battalion's soldiers in the post-war years. Two thematic chapters step outside this chronological timeframe, however, to examine important subjects that are often overlooked. The first focuses on the soldiers' life at the front, especially before and after major battles during periods of more routine trench warfare, and while the troops were at rest behind the lines—a longer period than is generally understood.

The second thematic chapter looks at the experiences of the large number of troops who left the battalion, either temporarily or permanently, especially as casualties. This chapter also examines the thousands of men — the majority of the soldiers of the 26th — who joined the battalion as reinforcements beginning in the fall of 1915: who they were, how they arrived, and how they fitted in.

In the end, *A Family of Brothers* hopes to present a more complete story of the men of New Brunswick's only infantry battalion to serve at the Western Front during the worst war Canada has ever experienced.

Chapter One

Raising the Battalion and Going Overseas

On September 15, 1915, the 26th New Brunswick Battalion of the Canadian Expeditionary Force (CEF) crossed the English Channel to join the fighting in the trenches of the Western Front. Over the next three years and two months, the 26th served as the province's only front-line battalion, fighting in most of the Canadian Corps' major battles and suffering almost five thousand casualties. None of this could have been foreseen as the battalion underwent a slow transformation from newly raised infantry force to a well-organized, well-trained combat unit.

Recruitment and Mobilization

On October 19, 1914, only two weeks after the First Contingent sailed from Canada and while fighting in France and Belgium raged on, its outcome still very much in doubt, the decision to raise a Second Contingent was announced. It became clear that one of the new infantry units would come from New Brunswick. On October 25, Lieutenant-Colonel James L. McAvity was directed to recruit a battalion headquartered at the Saint John Armoury. Following the CEF's practice of numbered battalions, the new unit was designated the 26th New Brunswick Battalion.

Born in Saint John in 1867, James McAvity was a successful businessman and veteran militia soldier. He had enlisted in the 8th Hussars in 1881 as a

Lieutenant-Colonel James L. McAvity, first commanding officer
of the 26th Battalion. Harold Wright Collection.

trumpeter and worked his way through the ranks. He was commissioned
as a lieutenant in the 62nd Battalion "Saint John Fusiliers"[2] in 1888, and
by December 1909 he had become lieutenant-colonel, in command of the
unit. During the early days of the Great War, he had organized troops from
his regiment for both home defence and service overseas with the First
Contingent. With thirty-five years of service in the provincial militia and
strong local connections, he was the obvious choice to command the 26th.

In early November 1914, recruiting for the 26th Battalion began through-
out the province. To stimulate interest and organize recruiting meetings in
Saint John, a special committee was set up that included Mayor J.H. Frink.
Recruiting officers and staff were also appointed elsewhere in the province.
In the Restigouche district, for example, Captain A.E.G. McKenzie, a local
lawyer, politician, and adjutant of the 73rd (Northumberland) Regiment,

2   In May 1900, the battalion was redesignated the 62nd Regiment "St. John Fusiliers."

took over recruiting with an office in Campbellton. McKenzie was assisted by Lieutenants Harry Ferguson and Godfrey ("Goog") Mowat, also from the 73rd. All three became officers in the 26th, with McKenzie appointed as major and second-in-command at the end of the month.

As men signed up, they were sent on to Saint John in groups of ten or twelve to receive their equipment and begin training. Initial response was slow, however, and some became concerned that the unit might be cancelled. Although there were more than sixty thousand men of eligible age in the province, the requirements for infantry service were strict, and not everyone who volunteered was selected. Successful volunteers had to be between eighteen and forty-five; men under age twenty-one needed permission from their parents; married men needed permission from their wives; and all had to pass a medical examination. During the mobilization phase, the unit enrolled 1,630 recruits, but 524 were later rejected for various reasons.

Newspapers urged men to enlist by appealing to their patriotism and stressing the urgency of the moment. The Saint John *Daily Telegraph* made it clear that the war was Canada's war: "We are fighting for our soil, our homes, our women and children as surely as are the chivalrous sons of France or the glorious remnant of the army of Belgium...knowing that if France and England fall our turn will come next." The papers also referred to the men's cultural heritage as descendants of Loyalists, Acadians, Scots, and Irish, pointing to the need to protect the lands and homes their ancestors had gained at such a high cost. The *Daily Telegraph* wrote that, "to suggest that there will be difficulty in recruiting the eleven hundred men necessary to complete the New Brunswick regiment should be to insult the manhood of this city and province."

Recruiting meetings featured prominent speakers, including influential members of the clergy. On November 17, a large gathering at the Imperial Theatre was addressed by Bishop Edouard LeBlanc, the Roman Catholic bishop of Saint John, and Bishop John Richardson, the Anglican bishop of Fredericton. A later meeting in Fredericton in the Unique Theatre included the presentation of a four-reel film entitled "The Making of a British Soldier," which followed the career of a recruit from enlistment to "that proud moment

FOR THE EMPIRE!

BRITAIN NEEDS MEN

LORD KITCHENER SAYS:—

"TO THE PEOPLE OF THE EMPIRE:—EVERY FIGHTING UNIT WE CAN SEND TO THE FRONT MEANS ONE STEP NEARER PEACE"

WHO WILL VOLUNTEER TODAY FOR OVERSEAS SERVICE

HERE ARE THE CONDITIONS

Recruiting for the New Brunswick Regiment Must be Completed Within Ten Days

THE VOLUNTEERS	THEIR FAMILIES
THE PERIOD OF ENLISTMENT is for the duration of the war and for six months after termination if required.	SOLDIERS MAY ASSIGN any portion of their regular pay to wives or others, and such sums will be paid regularly to the persons so designated.
THE RATE OF PAY is $1.10 per day and found for seven days a week, equal to $33.00 per month.	WIVES OF VOLUNTEERS will receive twenty dollars per month separation allowance from the Canadian Government over and above the soldiers pay.
IF DISABLED, the soldier will receive a pension at such rates as may be fixed by the Government.	THE PATRIOTIC FUND will supplement this with an additional allowance as described hereafter.
IF WOUNDED OR ILL, the soldier will be well cared for and sent back to his home at the proper time.	SHOULD ANY OF THE SOLDIERS BE KILLED, their wives and children will become wards of the Canadian Government, and generous provision will be made for them.

The National Patriotic Fund Committee has decided on a basis of distribution of funds among the wives and children, and other dependents of volunteers. It is estimated that a wife on her own account requires Thirty Dollars Per Month for her maintenance. The Canadian Government provides Twenty Dollars per month of this amount and the Patriotic Fund the remaining Ten Dollars, if required. Children between ten and fifteen years of age are allowed twenty-five cents per day; from five to ten years of age, fifteen cents per day; and under five years of age, ten cents per day. Thus a wife and three children of the ages of three, seven and twelve, may receive a total monthly allowance of Forty-five Dollars, of which Twenty Dollars is payable by the Canadian Government and Twenty-five Dollars by the Patriotic Fund. This is of course in addition to the Thirty-three Dollars per month paid to the soldier, and which may be assigned by him to his family.

Besides the above, provision is made for a compassionate allowance for temporary extraordinary need such as accident, sickness, etc. In short, the whole purpose of the Patriotic Fund is so to supplement the Government allowance as to provide all reasonable comfort for the families of men on service. Such provision, in each individual case, is subject to the report of local committees, who shall consider all the circumstances of families affected, with respect to the earnings of members of such families, amounts received from former employer of the soldiers, and other sources of income.

Every reasonable provision is thus made for dependent relatives, and volunteers need have no anxiety regarding the welfare of those left behind.

The 26th New Brunswick Regiment, 2nd Canadian Overseas Expeditionary Force requires Six Hundred more men at once. The full strength must be completed in ten days. **WHO WILL ENLIST?**

Recruits Will Be Received By the Following Officers:—

MADAWASKA, VICTORIA, CARLETON—MAJ. A. A. H. MARGISON, 67th Regiment, Woodstock.

SUNBURY, YORK, CHARLOTTE—MAJ. W. H. GRAY, 71st Regiment, Fredricton.

QUEENS, KINGS, ST. JOHN—LT. COL. WETMORE, 74th Regiment, Sussex.

WESTMORLAND, ALBERT —CAPT. F. R. SUMNER, Moncton.

GLOUCESTER, RESTIGOUCHE—LT. COL. MALTBY, CAPT. A. E.G. McKENZIE, 73rd Regiment, Campbellton.

ST. JOHN CITY—LT. COL. ARMSTRONG, LT. COL. McAVITY, LIEUT. CROCKETT.

NORTHUMBERLAND, KENT—LT. COL. IRVING, 71st Regiment, Newcastle.

Recruiting advertisement for the 26th Battalion,
Saint John *Daily Telegraph*, November 23, 1914.

Soldiers of the 26th Battalion, Barrack Green Armoury, Saint John.
The photo hung in the bedroom of Private Hugh Wright, an original
member of the battalion, who stands in the second row, sixth from left.

Courtesy of Dawne McLean

when he stands the splendid 'finished product' as His Majesty passes down
the line at inspection." The unit also set up an officers' committee that sent
recruiting parties in automobiles into such smaller communities as Mace's
Bay, Chance Harbour, Musquash, Fairville, Jones' Creek, Westfield, Rothesay,
and Hampton to organize meetings. Meanwhile, Major McKenzie extended
his efforts across the Chaleur Bay into the Gaspé Peninsula, holding meetings
in places such as New Richmond, New Carlisle, Port Daniel and Chandler.
The eight men from New Carlisle brought the total from the Restigouche
district to some fifty volunteers.

Recruitment picked up toward the end of November: on November
26, ninety men enlisted in Saint John, and many others were on their way
from elsewhere. By December 1, the establishment quota of 1,150 officers
and men had been met and organized into eight companies. On January
1, 1915, the battalion was reorganized into four companies, each with four
sixty-four-man platoons, to bring it in line with the system used by the
British Army it would soon join.

Many of the original recruits were born in New Brunswick. The
personnel files of a large sample of these early recruits — 1,251 of the
original 1,302 who enlisted before May 1915 — examined by historian
Curtis Mainville reveal that more than half (691, or 55 percent) were born

in the province; others (138, or 11 percent) came from Nova Scotia and Prince Edward Island, and a small number came from Newfoundland, then still a British dominion. Another group of fifty-two came from Quebec, many of them recruited in the Gaspé by McKenzie. As in most battalions of the CEF, a large number of the recruits (334, or 26 percent) were recent immigrants from the United Kingdom, most (212) coming from England. Compared with many other Canadian units, however, especially those in the First Contingent — where over 60 percent were from the United Kingdom — the number of expatriate Britons joining the 26th was comparatively low.

About a dozen Americans, two of whom had served with the US army, also joined the 26th. As well, a number of Canadian-born volunteers listed their next-of-kin as living in the United States; some of them likely had moved there at some point, and four had also served in the US army. Other recruits had more distant birthplaces, including Denmark, Norway, and France. Private Genaro Seccia (#69900), for example, was born in Malta and had served with the Brazilian navy, while Private John Vetckalm (#70012), from Durban, South Africa, was a veteran of the Russian navy. The presence of these British and foreign nationals, especially those with army and naval backgrounds, reflected the province's proximity to the United States and its connection in general — and Saint John's more particularly — with the Imperial economy.

As these backgrounds suggest, many of the early recruits had prior military service, with 607 (48 percent) of the sample Curtis Mainville studied having declared such service on their attestation papers. Almost all of the battalion's original officers had served with the pre-war militia. Of the forty-one officers who went overseas with the unit, twenty had come from the 62nd Regiment: Lieutenant-Colonel McAvity, two majors, eight of nine captains, and nine lieutenants; the remainder came from a number of other provincial militia regiments, including the 71st, 73rd, and 74th Regiments, the 8th Hussars, and the 3rd Regiment, Canadian Garrison Artillery. Many of the rank and file with previous service had also been in the New Brunswick militia. Among the senior non-commissioned officers (NCOs), Company Quartermaster Sergeant (CQMS) Lyman

Table 1: Originals of the 26th Battalion, by Place of Birth

Place of Birth	Number	Percent of Total
New Brunswick	691	55.2
Other Maritimes	138	11.0
Nova Scotia	72	
Prince Edward Island	66	
Other Canada	64	5.1
Quebec	52	
Ontario	8	
British Columbia	4	
United Kingdom	303	24.2
England	212	
Scotland	56	
Wales	5	
Ireland	30	
Newfoundland	15	1.2
Other British possessions	16	1.2
United States	15	1.2
Other	9	0.7
Totals	1,251	100.0

Survey of a sample of 1,251 original members of the 26th Battalion
Curtis Mainville.

J. Richards (#69830) was from the 62nd Regiment. A few others, like Company Sergeant Major (CSM) John J. Hanlon (#69395), had served with the Royal North-West Mounted Police. Some of the volunteers were veterans of the South African War, including, among the officers, Majors R.H. Arnold, L.R. Murray, and James Pringle, and, among the private soldiers, Frank Buck (#69062) and Alexander Chisholm (#69107), as well as CQMS Frederick Rickwood (#69807). Of the UK-born volunteers, 108 had prior military service before moving to Canada. Several of them immediately became senior NCOs in the battalion, including Regimental

Quartermaster Sergeant (RQMS) William Pitt (#69795), CQMS William F. Mason (#69617), CQMS Edward W. Elliot (#69263), and CSM William H. Buddell (#69064). Some, like Elliot and Buddell, had also served in South Africa. More than half the recruits, however, had no prior military service.

Organization and Training

Unlike the units raised for the First Contingent, which went overseas almost immediately, the Second Contingent battalions waited in Canada for about seven months before departing. As well, unlike the First Contingent, they did not concentrate at the huge army camp at Valcartier, Quebec. Instead, the Second Contingent units spent many months undergoing individual and unit-level training, and did not engage in any formation-level exercises prior to sailing for Britain.

In Saint John, throughout the winter and early spring, the 26th carried out training under the direction of the instructional cadre of The Royal Canadian Regiment, from Halifax, according to syllabi provided weekly by the general officer commanding (GOC), 6th Canadian Division. Beginning at 9:00 a.m., the men did one hour of physical training, then an hour of squad drill, consisting of rifle exercises and bayonet fighting. Half-hour-long lectures on such subjects as discipline, cleanliness and sanitation, and care of arms followed. The morning concluded with more squad drill, followed by dinner at noon. Much of this instruction was carried out in the nearby Exhibition Building, especially when it rained, or, when weather permitted, outdoors in open spaces such as Queen Square. Afternoons were taken up with more squad, section, platoon, and, eventually, battalion drill, followed by a route march, sometimes as far afield as Fairville, several kilometres away. Musketry training, instruction in judging distances, and providing protection on the march with advance field guards, and drills for making contact with the enemy and attacking vigorously were gradually introduced. Clearly, early training focused on the offensive, mobile warfare that had characterized the opening months of the conflict.

In the New Year, the troops put their training into practice in the field, conducting infantry in attack and defence exercises at both the company and battalion levels at places around Saint John, including the Golf Links, Mahogany Ridge, Manchester Field, and Rockwood Park. Beginning in February, they practised advancing by section under covering fire. Later, they practised battalion attacks, whereby two companies would form a firing line and advance against an enemy force represented by the transport section waving flags, while the other two companies provided cover and reserves. On other occasions, two companies would act as the enemy force, defending an outpost against which the attacking force would manoeuvre across open ground. Later on, the defenders practised tracing out entrenchments, entanglements, and other fieldworks. In early March, large-scale exercises took place in Rothesay. Two companies arrived by train, while the other two moved overland, requiring thirty-seven kilometres of marching. Lieutenant Harry Ferguson from Campbellton wrote in his diary that, although a long distance, "the men are now in quite good shape and stood up to it well."

Throughout these months, the troops had to contend with winter weather. At first, it was constant rain, which had a dispiriting effect on the men. Ferguson recorded: "Wet days are not conducive to good results as they sap a man's vim and life and make him feel limp and ragged indeed." When the weather turned cold, some troops suffered from frostbite on the ears; only in late January were fur caps and greatcoats issued. Then, in early February snow began to fall and accumulate, leaving the men to trudge through several inches of it during some route marches.

By March, the field training had become more interesting, especially learning to identify targets based on the clock face and prominent objects. According to Lieutenant Ferguson, "field work seems to be more appealing to the entire 26th than close order formations," and the troops caught on quickly to the advanced training. Officer training also became more challenging, especially learning how to conduct marches on compass bearings on the Golf Links, which the officers did in groups of three. They then practised leading platoons and companies across the course, using a compass. During these later field exercises, particular attention was paid to training NCOs in the handling of small groups and patrols and in making use of ground. Troops often fired blank ammunition, sometimes at skeleton enemy targets. They also developed inter-unit competitions:

Soldiers of No. 1 Platoon, A Company, 26th New Brunswick Battalion, wear fur hats during the winter of 1914/15. Courtesy of Dawne McLean

for example, on March 11, the signals and machine-gun sections had a marching contest during their return to barracks in which they covered nine kilometres in fifty-five minutes.

In early April, the companies completed their musketry courses using small-calibre ammunition at miniature ranges in the armoury basement. By then, some of the training, particularly the drill, had become stale, especially in the cramped Exhibition Building. "It is getting a trifle monotonous beyond question of a doubt without proper adequate facilities for training troops," Ferguson wrote. "This is the discouraging feature, the lack of space to work in." His frustrations later reached a new level: "of all the damp, chilly, uncomfortable, unhealthy, unsanitary, pneumonia-breeding places, the Exhibition Building caps the climax." At the beginning of May, more emphasis was placed on the trench warfare that was taking hold on the Western Front. A staff major lectured on field entrenchments, while Major

McKenzie gave a lecture based on "notes from the Front." It was apparent, however, that advanced training for trench warfare would have to wait until they reached Britain.

While the troops prepared for war, they also interacted closely with the citizens of Saint John. According to Ferguson, "During all the time, the people of St. John have been doing all in their power to amuse and entertain the 26th Battalion, their efforts being much appreciated." On New Year's Day 1915, the mayor and city held a banquet for members of the unit at the armoury: "The spread was a marvelously good one of turkey and plum pudding, to which the men did ample justice." In February, the Daughters of the Empire donated drums to the fife and drum band. And on Saint Patrick's Day, Mrs. McAvity presented each man with a shamrock. The unit reciprocated by holding public events, including band concerts at the armoury on Sundays and afternoon tea. Local citizens also attended drumhead church services.

During its seven months in Saint John, the battalion witnessed the kinds of "growing pains" most newly formed units experienced, which sometimes affected relations with civilians. Overall, discipline was good, but some individual soldiers fell short: for example, in early February, a private was arrested for stealing money from a fellow soldier. Occasional larger-scale lapses also occurred: at the end of January 1915, a "slight mutiny" took place during dinner when men from C Company protested against their uncooked meal by leaving the table en masse and forming up on the armoury floor. Harry Ferguson, who was the company orderly officer, quelled the disturbance by getting the cooks to serve out cheese, jam, and bread.

The battalion also took steps to keep the troops active in the evenings and on weekends. The YMCA had a large space in the armoury that featured a "splendid assortment of reading material...and writing utensils." The men also played various forms of sports, including tug of war and boxing at the armoury, while companies competed against each other in soccer and baseball. Some of the boredom was broken on Sundays when the battalion attended church. When they could, the men paraded to the Anglican Stone Church on Germain Street. Sometimes a drumhead service would be held

Battalion baseball, Barrack Green Armoury, Saint John. Harold Wright Collection

at the armoury, with the band of the 62nd Regiment furnishing the music. Printed programs would be passed around, and the men would form a hollow square on three sides with the pulpit on the fourth. Some men found the services inspirational. In early April, Chaplain Bertram Hooper preached a sermon about a man's duty during wartime. Ferguson greatly enjoyed the talk, and believed it should be delivered to the masses "to awaken a sense of personal responsibility in the present crisis which seems so lacking in the average individual who is content to shrug his shoulders and let the other fellow carry the gun."

In early February, discipline was tightened. Evening passes were stopped after 10:00 p.m. and guards at the armoury were tripled, presumably to prevent soldiers from slipping out. Private Egbert M. Robertson (#69811) of Saint John commented in his diary that this was "pretty hard lines." It did not help that enforcement seemed inconsistent. A few days later, Robertson overstayed his pass, and spent the night at the YMCA without any apparent consequences. Although officers were able to stay out until much later, the conduct of the junior officers was watched closely. As Ferguson observed, "if one isn't up to scratch, he usually hears about it. The adjutant has an eagle eye."

Drinking was a common problem. Ferguson held back part of his men's monthly pay, "as it would only mean a prolonged drunk for some of my men." In March, the unit entered an intense period of unrest stemming mostly from drunkenness outside the barracks. On March 22, orders again directed that no passes would be issued to NCOs and men after 10:00 p.m. The next day, turmoil occurred after lights out: "The men got noisy and out of hand, throwing bottles about" and calling officers names. Major McKenzie ordered the general assembly blown, and the men were taken on a route march that was kept up until they had "quieted down somewhat." The troops finally returned to barracks around 5:00 a.m. after having marched about twenty-two kilometres during the night. Ferguson related how Corporal John Ashe, one of the chief disturbers, handed in his stripes without being asked for them. In the aftermath, the battalion was confined to barracks for three days, and no one was allowed out except on duty. Ferguson, who lived in a nearby apartment, noted that being confined to his lodgings made him "feel like some interned German." By March 25, the men could again leave the armoury, but only until 9:30 p.m., which Private Robertson commented was "getting a little too strict for pleasure." As part of a general tightening up of discipline, officers were now required to attend physical drill class at 7:00 a.m. for half an hour. The confined-to-barracks order was lifted, but from then on all soldiers leaving the barracks needed a pass, and they were warned that the ban would be reinstated upon the first offence being committed by a drunken soldier on the streets of the city. By March 30, order had been restored. Ferguson, however, did not see the unrest as insubordination; rather, "the men only wanted a little excitement. They're a keen bunch and I feel will make good when the time comes."

The incident, however, was not yet over, for "the Colonel is thoroughly riled." On April 1, a defaulter's parade was held, at which eighteen defaulters were lined up in front of the battalion. Lieutenant-Colonel McAvity read the militia order dealing with the discharge of drunks and incompetents, and announced that he would discharge them all and anyone else who was charged with similar offences in the future. Three were given ten days' detention and then discharged, with one soldier's mother trying unsuccessfully to plead her son's case. The rest "barely escaped" dismissal.

The event was probably symptomatic of a wider problem the battalion faced. By then, the men had been anticipating departure for overseas for many months, and the long wait had been hard on morale. Rumours about their embarkation began in early January and surfaced again in February. On March 4, Ferguson wrote: "We'll have to move soon if we're to be real soldiers.... The men have reached the stage where something novel is required to keep them interested." In early April, anticipation again built: on the ninth Ferguson noted that "the time draws very close. We can almost feel it in the air." Shortly afterwards, he reported: "We all hope for such a move as the men are itching under the continued restraint." By mid-April, the troops were tired of waiting: "If ever a bunch of men were 'fed up' with anything, the 26th are surely surfeited with the enforced delay in getting away from Canada.... They feel badly abused and are in a state of readiness for almost any mischief. One can almost liken them unto a powder barrel that an incautious maneuver might blow up at any time. They're spoiling for a fight and may declare war on St. John at any time." On April 17, their frustrations were made obvious with the departure of an Army Service Corps contingent from Saint John. Ferguson was called on to command a platoon that acted as a picket to police the wharf in West Saint John, where the troopship S.S. *Grampian* was tied up. It was extremely difficult keeping the crowds of relatives from breaking through the line to say goodbye. When the ship finally pulled away amid singing, shouting, and waving, Ferguson admitted that the wish of his men was: "If it had only been the 26th... If we could only get away from St. John, we would be able to stick most anything for a while."

The men's frustrations contributed to clashes between members of the 26th and city police. On April 26, a series of disturbances began when Private Andrew Stevens (#70106) from Carleton, New Brunswick, got into a fight with a civilian and then was arrested by the deputy chief of police, who was not in uniform. Subsequently, other soldiers, including Private Thomas Madden (#69557), an Irishman living in Saint John who was a member of the 26th guard that had arrived on the scene, intervened to free Stevens. In the process, Madden was apprehended by a police sergeant whom he struck in an effort to free himself. In the meantime, a large crowd of civilians had gathered, and they also joined in the melee. The police withdrew, summoned several other officers, and, once reinforced, advanced and arrested Madden, whereupon they retreated to the police station under attack by the crowd. In the meantime, the military guard tried to subdue other soldiers who were swearing and had become rowdy. The crowd dispersed an hour later. Madden was incarcerated and charged with resisting the police and assaulting an officer. Subsequently, Andrews was also charged.

The community was left somewhat divided by the event. In a letter to the editor in the *Saint John Globe* the next day, "A Citizen" asked how much longer "is the good name of the 26th Battalion going to be discredited in this community and in the Province generally by the actions of a few ruffians that are allowed to remain in the Battalion and by the apparent lack of enforcement of discipline which seems to have been the order of the day since the regiment was first organized." He went on to write that the blame should "rest on the shoulders of those who are properly entitled to carry it. Last night's episode was certainly not to the credit of the regiment still less of a credit was it to the Officer Commanding." Others were more sympathetic. A newspaper editorial published in the *Saint John Globe* on April 30 stated:

> The soldiers who have been stationed in St. John for the past few months have borne themselves well. They are, for the most part, sons of the province, and in them and their work we all should manifest interest and pride. Where so many men are gathered together, away from their families and friends, consumed with a commendable desire to be up and at work for which they have cast aside business and social ties, it is reasonable to expect an occasional incident such as

that of Monday evening. Generally, however, the discipline and conduct of the men under arms has been such as to bring honour to the regiment and pride to the province.

As for the officers and men of the 26th, they believed that unwarranted efforts were being made to influence public opinion against them, and they resented that only soldiers were arrested, even though the majority of the rioters were civilians. Chaplain Hooper also came to their defence publicly with his own letter to the editor of the *Saint John Globe* stating that "A Citizen" did not know what he was talking about, and pointing to the challenges the unit was facing: "When all the circumstances are considered and especially the long stay in the city where every avenue of temptation is open to the men, the officer commanding should be congratulated upon the splendid body of soldiers six months of hard work has produced. You can't make a regiment of perfectly trained and disciplined soldiers in six months, but the officers and men of the 26th have gone a good way towards that standard. And I venture to believe that their moral conduct, in so far as matters of temperance and purity are concerned, will compare well with that of any average regiment in the British service."

Steps were taken to ensure that these kinds of events did not recur. The city was divided into three sections, and each of the military units then present — the 26th and 55th Battalions, and the Railway Construction Corps — agreed to have men carry out picket duty on the streets in their zone twenty-four hours a day. The 26th also agreed to have a full platoon on standby at the armoury as a reserve in the event of serious trouble and to arrest all soldiers who were drunk and making trouble, take them to their respective headquarters, and turn them over to the police if requested. On April 29, the arrested soldiers appeared in court. After hearing several witnesses, the magistrate decided to impose strong punishment: Madden would be fined $80 or serve ten months in jail, and Stevens $20 or two months. However, after Major McKenzie, a lawyer in civilian life, argued that the police had not properly identified themselves to the soldiers and that steps had been taken to cooperate fully with the police in the future, the magistrate released both men without fines.

The incident did not end there, however. The soldiers' animosity was also being fuelled by a growing dislike for civilians who refused to join up and who soon became known to the troops as "slackers." A letter from a battalion soldier using the name "A.B.," published in the *Daily Telegraph* on May 26, noted that, when he enlisted, "it was a matter of much concern to me to observe the attitude in which the majority of civilians regarded the uniform." People could not understand why men joined up, but he believed that the "finest men of St. John" were in the battalion, and he reminded those who had not enlisted that they held their positions only because of those who had done so: "It is chiefly these men who are taking advantage of the sacrifices of those more worthy than themselves, who are holding up members of the battalion to scandal: while you would tell us that they are only a minority of the city's population, we can reply, with still more truth, that it is only a small minority of us which do the things of which we are all being accused."

Hard feelings about the soldiers' treatment lingered. In July 1915, shortly after the battalion arrived in England, Lieutenant Charles Lawson of Saint John received a copy of the *Telegraph* describing its send-off. He wrote home that they "made quite a fuss over it, but it seems to me it would have been better to treat the battalion a little better while they were in St. John and never mind the fuss after they had left." Still later, when Lieutenant Arthur Leger from Richibucto returned to New Brunswick in February 1916 to join the 165th Acadian Battalion, he spoke about how "the 26th used to get the worst end of things when they were in St. John."

Other symptoms of disciplinary problems, including desertion, began to surface. As early as January 1915, several members of the battalion had run off. Among the most widely known early deserters was Private Ralph Lindsay (#178) of Hartland, New Brunswick, a member of Captain Charles Dunfield's company. In late January, Lindsay went absent without leave (AWOL) for at least his second time. In early February, the police arrested him in Hartland. When asked why he had deserted, he said that "he had got in bad with the 'non-com' and life was no longer worth living in the regiment." Lindsay was not done, however: by late March, he was

Grave of Lance Corporal George H. McKee, the first member of the 26th Battalion to die on active service, Fredericton Rural Cemetery. Author's photo

living in Houlton, Maine, and when news reached the authorities in April that he was back in Hartland, Lindsay fled north on a freight train.

As the wait to move overseas dragged on, absenteeism and desertions occurred more frequently. In early April, a board of inquiry investigated the illegal absence of two men from A Company. Then, on April 21, another board investigated seven absentees from B Company who had been away the twenty-one days that constituted desertion. On May 11, a battalion muster parade revealed that no fewer than one hundred men were absent from the unit. Indeed, absenteeism and desertion were part of the battalion's steady decline in personnel—"wastage" in military terms. Men left the battalion under various circumstances. Some who became sick had to be discharged; others died. Among the latter was Lance Corporal George H. McKee (#69672), the first member of the battalion to die on active service. The thirty-seven-year-old resident of Fredericton died of pneumonia on April 21 and was buried in the Fredericton Rural Cemetery with full military honours. Private Peter Shaw also died of pneumonia soon afterwards, on May 22, and was also buried in Fredericton.

As a result of this ongoing wastage, the 26th had to recruit more troops. During the winter, a few new men arrived, but in the spring the battalion undertook a large drive to increase its strength before departing for Britain. During late March and April, the 26th recruited 118 men; sixty-five of these joined in Saint John, while the remainder were taken on strength throughout the province, including at Fredericton, St. Stephen, Woodstock, Sussex, Chatham, Bathurst, Dalhousie, and Campbellton. April 23 was a particularly busy day, with twenty-three enlisting in Saint John, Fredericton, and Chatham—no mean achievement considering that, by then, the 26th was competing for men with other recently created units, such as the 55th Battalion.[3] In May, another fifty men joined up, including fourteen from Prince Edward Island. On May 12, a draft of forty men from the 55th Battalion at Camp Sussex joined the 26th, helping to bring the unit up to full strength. Noticeable among these late recruits

---

3   The 55th Battalion was authorized in November 1914; in March 1915, it began recruiting throughout New Brunswick and Prince Edward Island.

were large numbers of francophones from both New Brunswick and Prince Edward Island. Relatively few of these latecomers had previous military experience; moreover, arriving so close to the battalion's departure, they would not have received the benefits of the months of training the earlier recruits had undergone.

Preparing to Leave

In early May, the 26th began preparing to depart for Britain. Soldiers were inoculated against disease, beginning with typhoid fever. They were also issued new weapons and equipment, including the Mark III Ross rifle that they would take to the front and the new Oliver equipment, which distributed the weight of their field kit more evenly on the shoulders and allowed for freer use of the arms. The battalion also began a final selection of personnel, weeding out unsuitable officers and men from among its ranks. Some officer appointments were cancelled; in their place, new officers were taken on strength, among them Captain Hugh Griffith of The Royal Canadian Regiment, who became the adjutant. Soldiers selected to remain behind were transferred to the 55th Battalion.

Rumours about the battalion's departure date continued to circulate throughout early 1915. On May 14, Ferguson noted that sailing orders from Halifax might have been cancelled owing to the sinking of the *Lusitania*, "a most fiendish exploit and one for which a day of reckoning is surely coming." A few days later rumours were again fuelled by reports of the heavy Canadian losses at the Second Battle of Ypres, which made it necessary "that we get across without very much delay." In fact, the need to send reinforcements to 1st Canadian Division in Belgium actually delayed the departure of 2nd Canadian Division units from Canada. In the meantime, training continued throughout May with route marches to keep the troops physically fit and much emphasis on infantry in the attack, semaphore signalling, firing the new Ross rifle, and smartness among the men, particularly walking briskly and erect, carrying the swagger stick, and saluting properly. As Ferguson explained, "smartness...makes a ground work upon which to build a soldier. A brisk smart appearing soldier is always a better man than a careless slovenly one." Officers also practised performing the salute with the sword: they planned to make a good impression overseas after Major Walter Brown of Saint John let it be known that he did not want them doing "the bloody march past in England like a lot of bally militiamen." Clearly, they now saw themselves as active service soldiers preparing for the front.

The prospect of departure became more real on May 21 when the unit heard that two other battalions of 5th Brigade, the 22nd from Quebec and the 25th from Nova Scotia, were ready to sail from Halifax. A few days later, Sir Sam Hughes, the minister of militia and defence, made a surprise visit to inspect the battalion. Then, in the first week of June, the men began getting ready for embarkation, with kit inspections, stowing rifles and other equipment, packing valises and kit bags, and cleaning up their barracks. On June 9, Ferguson recorded that the troopship S.S. *Caledonia* was expected shortly: "This time, it is no false alarm but a dead certainty. Thank fortune, for the men are at a point where they couldn't be held much longer at Home Guard work." On June 11, the long period of anticipation finally ended when the *Caledonia* entered Saint John harbour and tied up at the Customs Pier at Pettingill's Wharf.

Soldiers began saying their goodbyes. On June 11, Private J. Walter McIntyre (#70135), a twenty-year-old Methodist theological student from Saint John who had enlisted on March 16, 1915, got a pass and went home to spend the evening: "They all took it quite hard but I managed to get it over without any scenes." His mother and others sent him away with a box of cakes and other eatables and bottles of preserves. The next day, the battalion prepared to embark along with the Headquarters and No. 1 Section of 2nd Canadian Divisional Ammunition Column, also raised in New Brunswick. Early in the morning, a large crowd of family and friends gathered at the armoury, and the provost guard roped off the area to control the flow of visitors. At 6:00 p.m. the battalion paraded for embarkation and then marched to the pier led by the fife-and-drum band and three city brass bands. Huge crowds lined the streets, and people pushed through the ranks to hug and kiss their loved ones, breaking up the formation on several occasions. A reporter from the *Moncton Daily Times* described what he saw: "[S]oon the band could be heard playing a splendid march tune, and the

Crowds say farewell to the 26th, Duke Street,
Saint John, June 12, 1915. Harold Wright Collection

steady tramp, tramp of over two thousand feet. It was a most impressive
sight to see the soldiers coming with fine military stride. As the parade
drew closer lusty cheers went up on all sides, and some of the soldiers
responded by shouting 'Down with the Kaiser' and 'Long Live the King.'"
The reporter noticed "a woman and three young children clinging to her
skirts, walking alongside her husband. She joined him, I was informed,
just outside the barracks and walked with him to the wharf." They finally
arrived at the customs warehouse, where the troops took the opportunity
to say more goodbyes. As the ship was still not yet ready to take the men
on board, they spent the night in a damp and dirty freight shed used for
storing coal, sleeping wherever they could find a place.

On the morning of the thirteenth, the troops were up at 5:00 a.m., and the
muster roll was called one last time to check for absentees; Harry Ferguson
was relieved to find that only one member of his platoon was missing. At 6:00
a.m. the 42 officers and 1,106 men of the 26th began boarding the *Caledonia*.
By then, the crowds on both sides of the harbour had swelled to about twenty
thousand people, gathered from across the province to say goodbye to their

loved ones, some for the last time. The send-off thrilled the troops and left them with vivid memories. Soldiers lined the side of the ship, watching the spectacle and taking photos. Ferguson described the scene: "When we cast off our moorings at 11:30 a.m. the entire wharf and waterfront for nearly half a mile was literally jammed with people, not to mention dozens of tugs and small boats circling about in the water around us. As we swung out into the stream, pandemonium reigned supreme. The crowd cheered, whooped, yelled and every imaginable whistle was represented from penny toy whistles to that atmospheric wrecker of a foghorn on Partridge Island. As I scanned the crowd, I could see many a red nose and watery eyes due to excessive use of handkerchiefs, and all sorts of farewells were waved, thrown and kissed."

Some of the men left with mixed feelings about the day. In a letter written soon after arriving in England, Regimental Sergeant Major (RSM) Roy S. Edwards (#69267), from Saint John, commented: "[T]hat was sure some sendoff they gave us in St. John and I'll never forget it as long as I live." At the same time, he was mindful of what the departure really meant: "I felt both happy and sad for I am sure that every one of us realized that there were many of us in the crowd who were having their last farewell march on that same street." Private Hugh C. Wright (#70076), from Riverside in Albert County, wrote to his father about the events. After describing the scene, the twenty-year-old private closed his letter by trying to set the mind of his recently widowed father at rest: "Now father I don't want you to worry about me. I shall be alright and shall come back alright."

As the *Caledonia* made its way out of the harbour, the Partridge Island garrison turned out and bugles sounded the general salute. The ship gathered speed, and soon left behind the cheering crowds and boats and entered the Bay of Fundy. After a smooth passage around the tip of Nova Scotia, it put in at Halifax the next day. There, several other military units were taken on board, increasing the number of passengers to over eighteen hundred men together with all their weapons and equipment, including the artillery's guns, which had to be taken apart before loading.[4] Some of the men were allowed ashore, and at least one used the opportunity to try

---

4   According to Charles Lawson (letter of June 21, 1915), they sailed with a battery of heavy artillery, men from the 40th Battalion as reinforcements, twenty-five men from the Halifax Composite Battalion, and about thirty from the Cyclist Corps.

Lieutenant Harry Ferguson's snapshot of the *Caledonia* pulling away from the dock, June 13, 1915. 2009.4.2, Restigouche Regional Museum

"Invalid's Row." Soldiers on the deck of the *Caledonia* during the voyage to Britain, June 1915. 2009.4.2, Restigouche Regional Museum

to desert. According to Ferguson, "[James] Paddy Keefe…was brought back and ordered below by Sergeant-Major Buddell, whereupon Keefe cracked Buddell a pippin on the jaw. As I was standing near, I proceeded to tie myself in a knot around Keefe's neck. [CQMS] Rickwood and several others came to my assistance and in a very short time Keefe was all trussed up like a chicken ready for market."

The ship sailed the next morning to another rousing send-off. Among the best remembered well-wishers was Mrs. Wallie Logie, the wife of the battalion paymaster sergeant. She had been the first person to say goodbye to the soldiers when they boarded the *Caledonia* in Saint John. She then took the train to Halifax, where she led civilians in cheers as the battalion left there on the fifteenth. Her dedication impressed many soldiers of the 26th.

The Voyage to Britain

Hugh Wright described conditions during the nine-day passage to Britain: "We have rather crowded quarters. We are way up forward. We sleep in hammocks hung up above the tables at night and in the daytime we take them down and pile them in a corner. We are rather crowded when we eat, 10 or 11 men to a small table about big enough for six. Each table has a fellow to go and get the grub and wash the dishes." The officers fared better. Lieutenant Charles M. Lawson, a teacher at Saint John High School before the war, noted that it was "a pretty nice boat but not nearly as well fitted up as the C.P.R. boats." Three officers shared a room. In Lawson's case, he bunked with Lieutenants Frank Lockhart and Percy Sherren. Lawson and Lockhart were among the first three officers to die at the front.

The crossing was mostly uneventful. They used the southerly route to avoid ice. Initially, the weather was very cold, and the troops needed their greatcoats on deck. As they approached the Gulf Stream, it began to warm but also became windy, and with rougher seas many of the men became seasick. Ferguson described how the "down and outers" congregated on the top deck, which became known as "Invalid's Row."

The unit implemented a program aimed at keeping the men active during the crossing, beginning with reveille at 5:45 a.m., followed by stowing away hammocks and breakfast at 7:15. At 10:00 a.m., first parade was held for PT

("Physical Torture" to the troops), but activities were kept to a minimum to avoid making the men sick. Dinner was eaten at noon, and then an afternoon parade got the men on deck again for some fresh air. They also had a bathing parade using hoses to spray cold water from the ocean. The men ate their supper at 5:00 p.m. and then hammocks were drawn at 6:00. Their main amusements were playing shuffleboard and competitive sporting events such as boxing and tug of war. Church service was also held on deck. Occasionally, they saw schools of porpoises and whales. Officers gathered each evening in the music and writing room, where they talked, smoked, sang, and wrote letters. Singers from the companies also entertained them with songs, including D Company's quartet made up of four Acadia College lads. Lawson reported the men as being "happy as larks," but was concerned that this relaxed routine would make them "pretty soft for strenuous work in England."

Security on board the ship was tight. Its wireless received but did not send messages. At night the ship sailed without lights, and no smoking was allowed on deck. Sentries were posted all over to watch for enemy vessels and throughout the men's quarters to prevent fires. As they neared England, a platoon with loaded rifles was placed on the bridge deck ready to deal with any hostile aircraft or submarines. Fire and emergency drills were practised almost every day. According to Lawson,

> [w]hen the steamer's whistle blows one long and two short blasts, the bugles blow the "general assembly" and everyone makes on the double for their parade ground, a part of the deck being assigned to each unit for parade. The men fall in in order, stand at attention, and the roll is called to see that not a man is absent. Even the sick are supposed to be carried up. Next the life belts which are piled close at hand are passed out and each man puts one on.... The handling of the boats is of course done by the ship's crew who have their own drill in that.... They claim to have boats enough to accommodate all on board, but I am not so sure of that part of it.

Private Hugh Wright and other soldiers of the 26th at East Sandling Camp, England, 1915. Courtesy of Dawne McLean

Ferguson calculated that they had enough for only twelve hundred of the twenty-two hundred on board, counting the ship's crew. "If we hit a torpedo or a mine, I plainly see where somebody will have to swim."

Several stowaways were discovered, including nine deserters from The Royal Canadian Regiment from Halifax. Another was Private David E. Gibbons (#69323) of the 26th. Gibbons had come to Canada from Birmingham, England, when he was about eight years old under the aegis of Sir John Middlemore's Children's Emigration Home program for disadvantaged children. He found a new home with William and Elspeth Venning, who owned a farm in Smith's Creek in Kings County, where he was living when he enlisted in November 1914. As he was only eighteen, he was told he was too young to go overseas. When the unit embarked, he was nowhere to be found, and it was supposed he had run off. Once safely at sea, however, he emerged from a hold, looking the worse for wear. Colonel McAvity took pity on the youth, and allowed him to stay with the unit in Britain.

Orderly room garden, East Sandling Camp, England, 1915.

Harold Wright Collection

Training in Britain

Speculation about their destination ran rampant. Some believed they were bound for the Dardanelles, others thought they would land in France. Those who guessed Britain was their destination won the wager when they docked at Devonport, on England's south coast, on June 24. They were cheered and saluted by all of the vessels they passed and by people around the harbour. Over the next few days, the troops worked hard to unload their kit, including Colonel McAvity's car. They then moved by train to camp at East Sandling, in the Shorncliffe area in Kent. The English countryside impressed the Canadians. Lieutenant Lawson recorded that "the country is certainly wonderful, the flowers especially being magnificent after what we have been used to." They received an enthusiastic welcome at the stations they passed through.

Arrival at the camp was more chaotic. Lawson wrote that "they were not properly prepared for us, our huts were not furnished, and one would think they were not expecting us." According to Ferguson, the huts had no lights or sleeping accommodations, and so the tired men slept on the floor in their greatcoats. Once the quarters were sorted out, however, the men settled in. The huts were well built, many being sheathed with corrugated iron. The officers were housed three to a hut, and each was furnished with a cot, bureau, mirror, washstand, basin and pitcher, table, chairs, and electric reading lamp. Lawson's hut was equipped with a tin stove for heating, "which I am afraid would not be very efficient in cold weather. But they are certainly very comfortable, fitted with electric lights and all conveniences." They were "way ahead of anything we expected." The men's huts held up to thirty. Although more sparsely furnished, they were still very comfortable, and "compared with conditions at the Armoury in Saint John they are living like princes." Once they settled in, the 26th occupied a sizable area of the camp, accommodated in forty huts for the men, three cookhouses, six washhouses for both officers and men, one large canteen that held the corporals' mess along with reading, writing, and music rooms, as well as sergeants' and officers' messes, a drying house where the men could dry their clothes, a shooting gallery, two stables, and a wagon shed.

The troops soon made themselves at home. In front of the orderly room, RSM Edwards and Sergeant Alexander Dawson (#69209), a Scot from Aberdeen, made a large garden with a border of white stones. At the top was a sign made from gravel stones painted white, reading "New Brunswick, 26th Battalion." The garden itself consisted of red, white, and blue flowers arranged in the shape of a large maple leaf. In the centre was the word "Canada." Edwards noted in a letter printed in the *St. John Standard* that it attracted "quite a good deal of attention from passers-by, as it is right on the side of the road."

After being inspected and then addressed by Major-General S.B. Steele, the officer commanding, 2nd Canadian Division, they set to work. The schedule was rigorous: reveille at 5:00 a.m., biscuits and coffee at 6:15, first parade from 6:30 to 7:30, breakfast ended at 8:45, morning parade in heavy marching order for the day's work until 12:45 p.m., lunch at 1:00, afternoon parade from 1:45 until 5:00, dinner at 6:30, and evenings free with lights out by 9:45 p.m., except on those nights when they paraded at 7:00 for night work, returning at 5:00 a.m. On Saturdays they had a half-holiday. Sunday was set aside for divine service and sports, or passes for those who could get them.

Intensive training began, and lasted until September 12. Initially, they received a new form of training, practising the company in defence and listening to lectures on outposts, attack and defence in trench warfare, and the latest developments in field entrenchments from officers just returned from the front. They also engaged in entrenching work under the direction of Royal Engineers, who showed them trench models and then told them to "go there and do likewise," according to Ferguson. They constructed their own bay and traverse, and learned how to revet steps, parapets, and parados, place loopholes, build dugouts, brick the floor, and quickly reverse captured trenches. They also worked on trench warfare exercises, including the practical use of bombs (hand grenades). Walter McIntyre, one of the battalion's bombers, recorded how he found learning about the early jam pot bombs and how to throw them very interesting.[5] Company officers and sergeant majors were also sent on courses on the use of the machine gun and musketry. When they returned, they passed their training on to platoon commanders and NCOs. The battalion also continued practising the same kind of field work it had received in Saint John, including bayonet fighting and musketry, now on the Hythe School of Musketry ranges—particularly aiming and setting sights, and then firing over various distances, with and without the bayonet. To stay in shape, they also carried out route marches. Later on, as Lawson noted, they practised "carrying out a plan of attack on trenches as nearly as possible along the lines of the real thing."

By the end of July, the men had completed their musketry course and started brigade training, working with the other battalions of 5th Brigade on manoeuvres and trench fighting. Formation manoeuvres consisted of marching into the field, camping overnight, and engaging in sham battles. On August 13, a 4th Brigade attack on the 5th was "easily driven back." Toward the end of August, they began divisional manoeuvres lasting four days, during which they marched for two days to a local town, where they practised billeting, and then spent two days returning

---

5   The jam pot bomb was an improvised grenade consisting of a jam tin, filled with explosives and metal fragments, and fitted with a fuse that could be lit by a cigarette.

Men of the 26th practise digging trenches,
East Sandling Camp, England, 1915. 2009.4.2, Restigouche Regional Museum

to camp and conducting sham battles along the way. On a few occasions, the battalion provided the divisional rear guard. One exercise involved 2nd Canadian Division operating against an enemy force made up of different kinds of troops. These exercises approximated active service conditions as closely as possible. Private Fred A. Woodbury (#70027) of St. George described the rigours of training in a letter dated August 29, 1915: "We zig-zagged over the country and across country, sleeping wherever night took us, and also doing a lot of marching at night. We were told when we got back that the brigade officers (who, by the way, followed us by auto and horse and stayed at inns) were well pleased with our endurance, and that we covered over one hundred miles in four days, loaded as we were. That wasn't bad. I was with a scouting party the first night, and the second night on guard, so you see, I did three days and two nights with very little to eat and no sleep, on my feet and never had the harness and pack off my back all that time."

Training also progressed for specialist troops such as the scouts. Private Ray Hare (#69448) of Newcastle, New Brunswick, reported in a letter published in the *North Shore Leader* that, when he joined Lieutenant Edward Sturdee's scouting section, they underwent one hour of physical training, ran three miles (five kilometres) a day, swam, and practised map reading and sketching, compass reading, shooting with rifle and revolver, and scouting the countryside.

In July the battalion was assigned brigade duties, requiring it to supply guards and pickets for the whole brigade. Among other things, pickets were sent every evening to villages and small towns as well as to nearby Folkestone to look after the men and help the police keep order. The detachments consisted of forty-six men, broken down into four patrols that were sent along the streets near the seafront. They also helped to enforce discipline within the camp. Occasionally, they arrested and handcuffed soldiers, especially those who were drunk and rowdy. Lapses also occurred within their own ranks. On August 1, a corporal and private from the battalion on guard duty were arrested by the military police for being drunk, neglecting their duty, and, in the case of the private, insolence for calling an NCO "fellow." Nevertheless, Charles Lawson proudly wrote that, "in spite of our horrible reputation the 26th are regarded here as the most orderly battalion in the brigade, if not the division." He confided to his mother that prior to their arrival stories had circulated about the 26th: "Our reputation was spread over England and even to France. One story was that the men mutinied on board ship, killed two of their officers, were held in detention in Liverpool for weeks and then sent back to Canada. And the British as well as the Canadian troops expected that we were regular fire-eaters. The more I see of the other troops the more I think of the 26th and in most ways we have got them all beaten. Our men present a better appearance, have better physique, and are smarter than most of the others."

Periodic inspections took place. On July 17, Prime Minister Robert Borden and Minister Sam Hughes inspected 2nd Canadian Division. Among the other dignitaries were fellow New Brunswickers Sir Max Aitken (later Lord Beaverbrook) from Newcastle and Member of Parliament (and future prime minster) R.B. Bennett from Hopewell Hill in Albert County. Although it rained heavily and the troops were thoroughly soaked, "the inspection was great." According to McIntyre, about "30,000 soldiers, all Canadians, were there and everything came off very satisfactorily." During the march past by platoons, "everyone was right on and the sight was certainly one to be remembered."

The troops found different ways to relax in the evenings and weekends. The YMCA had three tents within 5th Brigade's lines, and the 26th's unit representative, Captain H.R. Hill from Saint John Hill, looked after packages sent from Canada and helped to organize entertainments nearly every night. These included concert parties from London and one show that featured conjuring, mind reading, hypnotism, and ventriloquism. "It was very interesting and funny, and was enjoyed by a large crowd of the fellows." Films were popular. Some soldiers attended campfire meetings organized by the YMCA or among themselves. Hill "proved to be a good man and a great help in keeping the men straight." According to Lawson, "[i]t is really wonderful what the Y.M.C.A. is doing over here. They seem to have an unlimited supply of money." The Salvation Army, Wesleyan Institute, and Church of England had clubs where soldiers could play games, write letters, read magazines, buy things at reasonable prices, and use the post office. Soldiers from the battalion also visited Folkestone to swim in the Channel, and those with weekend passes visited London, Canterbury, and other famous sites. Chaplain Hooper, meanwhile, attended to the men's spiritual needs, officiating at church parade at 9:00 a.m. every Sunday and holding communion three times throughout the day. Every other night, he held ten-minute services at 8:15 at the Jellicoe Club, one of the YMCA's soldiers' clubs.

The troops also met many friends from other units raised in the province. Among these were the 12th Battalion, a First Contingent unit containing many New Brunswickers that had been converted into a reserve unit, 2nd Canadian Divisional Ammunition Column, the 6th Canadian Mounted Rifles, and the reinforcing draft of the 55th New Brunswick and Prince

Edward Island Battalion.[6] In time, many men from these units joined the 26th as reinforcements.s.

Relations between officers and men were good. Walter McIntyre reported that the officers treated them to ginger beer some afternoons. Charles Lawson, who commanded No. 13 Platoon, described his troops as "certainly a fine body of men, most of the largest in the whole battalion, and make a fine appearance as well as being a splendid lot to handle."

Reminders of the war were never far away. Although 145 kilometres from the fighting in Belgium, the sound of the heavy guns firing could be clearly heard, "the sound coming along the valley which acted as a conductor," Lieutenant Ferguson explained. They also talked to wounded soldiers from hospitals located near the camp. In a letter published in the *St. John Standard*, RSM Edwards described the sobering effect these encounters had on him: "[T]o tell you candidly... things are looking a whole lot more serious over here than they are in Canada. There are several hospitals near here and some of the less serious wounded ones sometimes come up to see us and the tales they tell are almost too terrible to think of. The papers do not print half of what really does happen. They tell me that the Germans do not take Canadian prisoners if they can get a chance to shoot them, and I guess if what the boys tell us is true, that our fellows refuse to take prisoners at all, but just line them up and shoot them." Edwards also described how "some poor chaps in the hospital have their arms, legs and shoulders blown off."

Ferguson had a somewhat different reaction to these kinds of meetings, listening closely to what these "old hands" had to say about life at the front: "The talk of their experiences is very interesting to one going out after the same. Possibly some may be exaggerations, but with so many who have gone through the same thing, I doubt not but they are nearly all bona fide." Some of the wounded they met were old friends recovering from wounds. From them they learned who among their acquaintances had been killed, wounded, made prisoner, or were still alive and well. Other men looked

---

6   The 6th Canadian Mounted Rifles was raised in 1915 in Amherst, Nova Scotia. Among its recruits were many New Brunswickers, including militiamen from the 8th Hussars and 28th New Brunswick Dragoons. On June 19, 1915, a reinforcing draft of 5 officers and 250 other ranks from the 55th Battalion, training at Camp Sussex, New Brunswick, left Montreal for England.

Reverend Bertram Hooper, chaplain of the 26th Battalion.
X12559, New Brunswick Museum

upon these unfolding events with growing awareness of their meaning. On August 4, the first anniversary of the start of the war, Chaplain Hooper witnessed the divisional review by another distinguished New Brunswicker, Andrew Bonar Law, Britain's secretary of state for the colonies, who had been born in Rexton. Although Hooper found it a stirring spectacle and was immensely proud of the soldiers of the 26th, among them his son Douglas, he also found "my eyes dimmed with tears as I gazed so earnestly upon those sons of Canada and especially upon those from New Brunswick. For I thought how every one of those fine lads represented a home, father, mother, wife, sister or sweetheart, and I thought of the dear women at home praying and waiting with longing hearts for those gallant men. 'God keep you safe for me' is the prayer which goes to God by day and night for our soldier sons."

Preparing to Depart

By the end of August 1915, the battalion began preparing to move to France. The men received new equipment, including identification discs, balaclava caps, entrenching tools, gas helmets, field bandages, and web equipment that was superior to their Oliver Pattern. According to Lieutenant Lawson, "[i]t is a great improvement over what they have been wearing. It is the same as the English soldiers have. It requires considerable adjusting, but when properly fitted is very comfortable. I have considerable weight in mine now and when it is on it does not seem to be any great weight at all."

It was an anxious time for junior officers such as Lawson, since not all of them would be going to the front at the outset—some would stay in England and go to the 12th Reserve Battalion to await the call to replace casualties. Lawson was greatly relieved when he got command of No. 16 Platoon, "one of the best." "Thank goodness I have something definite at last. I have been nearly nine months practically on probation with everything uncertain." Some junior officers found ways to avoid being left behind: Lieutenant P.S. Nisbet, for example, resigned his commission and enlisted as a private; in short order, he became a platoon sergeant in B Company.

Many other changes in personnel took place. The battalion received a new adjutant, Major René Tidmus from the 27th Battalion, and a new company commander when Captain Elliot was replaced by Captain John Parks. The latter had seen a great deal of service with 1st Canadian Division in France, "and knows the game, and so will be a great help." Among the other officers leaving the battalion were Dr. L.R. Murray, the medical officer, who transferred to a hospital and was replaced by Captain Henry H. Argue, and Chaplain Hooper, who left for the ambulance corps. Lawson reported that Hooper was "very much broken up over being transferred from us. It was owing to no fault of his own, but to the fact that another man getting more pull. It is particularly hard on him as he has a son in the battalion."

In early September, the division was reviewed by King George V and Lord Kitchener, Britain's secretary of state for war. Word spread that the King was impressed by the 26th, telling Colonel McAvity that it was "as good a marching battalion as he had seen"; Kitchener made similarly complimentary remarks.

As the move to France approached, some troops became more reflective, perhaps sensing what lay ahead. Lieutenant Lawson thanked his mother for her packages: "I don't think I said half enough how thankful I am to you for all those good things, but it is hard to express sometimes just all that you feel." Thinking back to earlier times, he wrote: "Just to think, ordinarily I would now be grinding away at the old school work, and this work, though similar to it in some ways, still is somewhat different. Certainly it is great for the health anyway." He closed by writing, "Don't worry about me, I'll be all right." Waiting to depart made the troops restless. Ferguson reported that "the men won't be satisfied until they get a taste of real war," while Lawson wrote that "the sooner we get across the better." Rumours spread, especially about their destination. Reverend Hooper noted that some believed they were headed for the Dardanelles: "There are many rumours afoot on these subjects, as there were in St. John — and that is saying a good deal."

During the early days of September, the men were kept busy with sports and inspections. Finally, on September 13, the battalion's advance party, including transport, left for France. By the fifteenth, the "night of nights," Ferguson called it, "we were all fed up with eternal waiting and ripe for some excitement." That evening, some of the men stole three barrels of beer off a truck "and made merry." Then, around 7:00 p.m., the battalion marched to Folkestone, where it embarked on a ferry and later in the day landed in France at Boulogne. Among those making the crossing was the underaged Private David Gibbons who, having safely stowed away during the voyage to Britain, repeated his act and made it to France, where he was again allowed to remain with the unit.

Walter McIntyre recorded the events of this long day in some detail: "Lined up at 6 pm and marched by a roundabout way coming in to Folkestone through the toll gate. We embarked on the *Sea Bird* about 11 o'clock and after two hours run landed in Boulogne. The march from the camp in heavy marching order, blankets, and rubber sheets on top was a very hard one but the one from Boulogne to the camp was worse. We had to walk up a very steep hill and by the time we got to the top most of us were very much done out. Encamped in a field in which were tents all night but did not use the tent."

After almost eleven months of organizing and training, the men of the 26th were about to join the war.

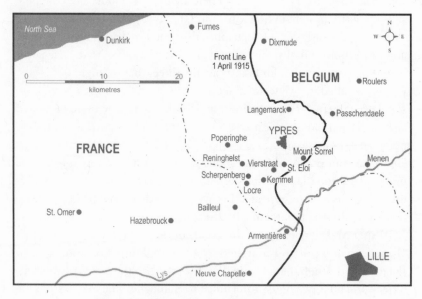

Map 1: The Ypres Salient and environs. Mike Bechthold

Chapter Two

War in the Trenches, September 1915-August 1916

In late September 1915, the 26th Battalion entered the front lines near Ypres, Belgium. Three weeks later, it undertook its first attack across no man's land in the "Crater fight." Over the next five months, the men endured a long, harsh winter moving in and out of the line. In spring 1916, they were drawn into more active operations in the Ypres Salient at the memorable battles at St. Eloi and Mount Sorrel, along with trench raids and fighting patrols. As casualties mounted, the "originals" became scarce, and newly arrived reinforcements slowly changed the character of the unit. The 26th gained valuable experience, however, so that by August 1916 when it began to prepare for its first major action on the Somme, it was a competent, battle-hardened battalion.

"Going up the line"
After arriving at Boulogne on September 15, the battalion moved toward the front over the next several days. On the sixteenth, the men were packed into boxcars and taken by rail to Wizernes, near St. Omer. From there they marched, bivouacking for the night in the field, and arrived at billets outside Hazebrouck the next day. Motor transport carried the men's blankets and packs, but it was still a difficult trek for the troops over twenty-four kilometres

of cobbled roads that were hard to walk on. Harry Ferguson noted: "rarely if ever have I been so tired." For others it was much more punishing. Ferguson wrote that, by 4:00 a.m. on the seventeenth. about half the battalion had dropped out. Among them was McIntyre, who recounted his adventure in his diary: "I stuck it till 3 o'clock Friday morning [the seventeenth] and then fell out when the string holding the rubber sheet and blanket broke and they fell off." After sleeping in the open for a few hours, he set off to find the battalion: "I was very much chafed and my feet was sore and I was generally tired out but by degrees. I managed by 9:30 pm to get within two miles of the camp. The day was very interesting indeed. Sometimes I was alone, sometimes with two or three others. It seemed strange not to be able to carry on a conversation with the people along the road but I remembered enough French to make myself understood when I needed anything. At night I slept with two others between two straw stacks. We pulled straw down and made a bed and then covered ourselves with more straw as we had no blankets or rubber sheets but we slept fine." On the morning of the eighteenth, he finally found the battalion, "scattered all over different billets." McIntyre rejoined No. 16 Platoon, where he received breakfast, and spent the remainder of the day resting and waiting for others to come up. It was not until the nineteenth that most of the battalion arrived in camp, "some without a bit of equipment, footsore and weary," according to Ferguson. Their heavy-pattern boots became the subject of general complaint, according to the brigade war diary.

By then the battalion was about sixteen kilometres from the Belgian border, and the troops could hear the guns firing and see the flash of shells bursting in the air. The troops were not impressed by France. Ferguson noted that this close to the front the country had "a deserted appearance, only bedraggled women and dirty faced kids being visible," as well as elderly men. During a trip to nearby Hazebrouck to buy some articles, he felt "considerably handicapped through my lack of knowledge of the French language."

On the nineteenth, during an inspection by senior officers, "the GOC [Lieutenant-General Edwin Alderson, commanding the Canadian Corps] gave a speech telling us that we are about to be put right into the trenches at once and that he expected us to do our best. We answered by cheers." And so, unlike those in 1st Canadian Division, 2nd Canadian Division troops received no period of apprenticeship alongside experienced British soldiers before heading into the line. Two days later, the 26th marched toward the front line, camping near Bailleul. The commanding officer, adjutant, and company commanders went forward to inspect the trenches they would soon be taking over. On the twenty-third, A Company was first into trenches, acting as the reserve company for the 22nd Battalion.

As the 26th advanced, the troops saw growing signs of the war. McIntyre wrote that "the most interesting thing of the day was the watching of a fight in the air and…the attempt to bring down an English aeroplane by the enemy." Ferguson noted the large volume of traffic on the roads: "motor lorries, ambulances, automobiles, motorcycles, cycles, guns, supply wagons, being continually on the move." On September 23, they reached their permanent billets at Scherpenberg, Belgium, about five kilometres behind the trenches, where they moved into huts that each held about thirty-three men. Here they received more new equipment, including gas helmets, which a staff officer demonstrated how to use. They were now close enough to feel the effects of long-range German artillery fire. Ferguson wrote that a windmill sitting on nearby high ground was fired at occasionally: "We would not mind if it was hit but, situated as we are, we feel much like onlookers at a family quarrel, as much in danger if not more so of the sauce pans."

Discipline was somewhat relaxed during this period. Ferguson noted that, when the battalion arrived at Bailleul, the men were not allowed out of camp in the evening; nevertheless, "several wandered through the guards returning considerably lit up. However, after sitting on a couple of them, they quieted down and went to sleep." A few days later the troops received a pay advance, and some spent their money on "oh-be-joyful," as Ferguson put it, and once again "became a trifle noisy…but quieted down without much trouble." Serious breaches, however, were met with more severe punishment. On September 19, during the approach march to the front, C Company's commander, Major Warren H. Belyea of Newcastle, New Brunswick, administered Field Punishment No. 1 to three men for stealing jam from the rations. They were tied to a tree for two hours a day for the duration of their sentence.

Charles Lawson, perhaps feeling the excitement of finally reaching the front, wrote on the twenty-fifth that "we are due to go into the trenches at almost any time and it will be a relief from the monotony of the billets." The next day and again the following day, a party of junior officers went forward to the trenches to familiarize themselves with conditions before taking the men up. Among them was Captain Frederick F. May, of Charlottetown, who recounted his experiences a year later after returning to New Brunswick. As they went forward it was raining "dogs and cats."

> Captain [Percy] McAvity was ahead of me as we crept along toward our goal. The country is of a rolling character and the Germans occupied the ridge of the hill while our trenches were in the valley beneath. To get to the communication trenches we had to cross over the brow of a hill and when we were on our way the Germans sent up star shells and opened fire on us with rifles. Three times we had to throw ourselves down on the ground in mud and water, when the rifles were trained upon us. It's a peculiar sensation, and unless you've been there you cannot realize it, when you hear the bullets swishing through the grass on either side of you as you lay flat on your face trying to hide yourself.

On September 28, the battalion moved into the front line east of Kemmel, relieving the 22nd Battalion. After almost a year of fighting the battlefield now consisted mainly of farmers' fields filled with shell holes, ditches, blasted hedges and trees, ruined buildings, and the trenches. The rainy season had set in "with a vengeance," Ferguson observed, making the "remarkably substantial" trench lines very muddy. One of the battalion machine-gun pits had heavy brick walls, a concrete floor, and a roof covered with corrugated iron and four layers of sandbags. A telephone was installed in the pit. Ferguson also remarked on the continuous nature of German artillery, machine-gun, and rifle fire, especially from snipers. The Germans also made incessant use of flares to light up the whole front at night.

Life in the Trenches

Unlike the well-developed trenches usually associated with the Western Front, these early lines around Ypres consisted of isolated sections instead of continuous works. Soldiers entered them from the rear via communication trenches, but to move between them meant climbing into the open and crossing above ground, a very dangerous task usually undertaken only at night. Some of the "trenches" were built entirely of sandbags from the ground up because of poor drainage. In some places these breastworks were eight feet high. V-shaped traverses built into them prevented enfilading fire from German flanking positions but they often lacked rear walls, making them vulnerable to artillery fire. The Canadian and German lines were about 100 yards apart, although in places it was closer: Private Frederick L. Howard (#69417) from West Quaco, New Brunswick, noted in his diary that one of their machine-gun positions was only thirty yards from the German trench. Listening posts were located in shell holes about twenty-five yards in advance of the front line, and were manned continuously by two-man teams. No man's land lay between the two lines.

Officers lived in dugouts that were more like huts built above ground. According to Lieutenant Lawson, his was "about six foot square and I can almost stand up straight in it, so it is not a bad place at all.... The hut is built of sandbags with a corrugated iron roof and in dry weather is not bad at all. A sort of canvas stretcher set up a foot or two from the ground makes a very comfortable bed. We burn candles altogether." The troops mostly slept in dugouts as well. Some of the specialist troops, like the machine gunners, were somewhat better off, sometimes sleeping on the floor of the dressing station or even on spring beds when they were available. Water added to their burdens. When they first went into the line near Kemmel, it rained hard during the night, soaking the men and making the trenches wet and muddy. The mud was slippery and sticky, and clung to the soldiers' uniforms and boots.

The troops quickly settled into a routine, staying five days in the trenches, with part of the battalion in the front line and the others in support. Generally speaking, a company kept three of its four platoons in the firing line. Things were usually quiet during the day, but it still took getting used to. Walter McIntyre noted on Sunday, October 10, during his platoon's first tour in the firing line, that it "did not seem much like Sunday. On fatigue repairing parapets most of the day."

The men were kept busy, even on quiet days. McIntyre described his front-line routine in late October: they got about five hours' rest during the day, which included two hours' standing sentry; at night they did one hour on sentry duty or listening post, one hour working on the trenches, and one hour of rest. He noted that, as a specialist bomber, he did no trench work at night, but spent much of his time on listening post. New trenches and dugouts needed digging and draining, and gun pits for the battalion machine guns needed repairing, especially after being hit by shellfire. Muddy conditions also meant that the troops spent much time cleaning weapons and equipment. Platoon commanders and their sergeants took turns in the line while the others slept; the platoon commander always took the night shift, being relieved at "stand down" after dawn around 6:30 a.m., when he slept until noon before beginning the routine again.

Trenching was labour intensive, and so the training they received in Britain on digging could now be put to good use. According to Lawson, "it is necessary to keep at work repairing and improving to keep the trenches in proper shape, and I find the men are much more contented if kept busy all the time, not set aside for sleep. It is a great life and very interesting, and it is surprising how quickly the time passes. Here we have been in France more than a month and it seems little more than a week." They also scrounged the lumber they needed for dugouts and the trenches from old buildings in the area, and used sheets of corrugated iron to bombproof the dugouts. Fortunately, the logistical system supporting the troops was well organized. Rations usually arrived on time. Water was brought up to a dump in carts or wagons, and carried forward every night in gasoline tins that held about two and a half gallons. Nevertheless, water was

Canadian breastworks on the Western Front, June 1916.
Mikan no. 3395464, Library and Archives Canada

often in short supply. A narrow gauge railroad that ran along the main communication trench eased some of the burden.

During the first days in the line, it was easy for the troops to get lost in the maze of trenches. Private Howard noted that, on his first night in the line, he did sentry duty for one hour and then "wandered about all night [looking] for [his] machine gun." In the morning, he had breakfast with one of the platoons, then finally found the machine gun at 10 a.m. Lieutenant Ferguson wrote that "the long walk out the communication trench is always a nightmare to the men, with its winding and twisting till one hasn't any more idea of direction than a blindfolded man."

On the night of September 28, Private Moses Gallant (#69344) of Wheatley River, Prince Edward Island, became the battalion's first fatal casualty when he was killed while on listening post. Others had close calls. Private George T. Hamilton (#69399) of Halifax was buried when a shell struck the parapet in front of him, but he got out alright. Overall, the 26th's front was relatively quiet during the late fall, and casualties were comparatively light.

The men of the 26th also began to understand the dangers inherent in trench warfare. Fatigue duty in no man's land was particularly hazardous. Digging trenches at night, McIntyre wrote, was "quite a risky place all in the open and the bullets all stray ones were whizzing past us all the time." Manning listening posts between the lines was also dangerous. On the night of October 11, McIntyre was on duty in a two-man listening post. "This is quite a place.... You crawl out of a hole in the parapet and run along a mud ditch till you come to the post where you stayed in full view of the enemy listening and watching for anything in the shape of danger from the enemy. The only danger is in the state of the lights [flares]. You have to hug the ground pretty close when the lights go up." The threat from friendly fire was also very real: "I nearly got hit once by one of our own men. He pulled the wire to tell me that the relief was coming. I moved to tell Douglas [his comrade] and the crazy article stuck his rifle over the parapet and fired without looking. The bullet just missed me, knocking the dirt into Douglas' face. If I had not moved I would have got it right between the eyes."

They also learned how demanding work in the line could be. The trench routine provided little time for sleep, the work was physically demanding, and men soon became fatigued. Since everything they needed in the front lines had to be brought up from the rear, much time was spent hauling boxes, bags, and cans, mostly at night. "We was shelled on the way out and had to take to the slits but none were hurt only the parapet being broken in several places," McIntyre wrote about a ration party. "Had to carry two cans of water coming in beside my rifle and ammunition. This was very difficult in the narrow communication trenches. The cans were very heavy and the handles blistered my hands quite a bit." The next time he was assigned to carry water, he tied a sack to them and threw them over his shoulders: "It wasn't so bad although when I got in my back was very sore." He added that they were "shelled on way in and out as well as machine gunned."

The routine in the trenches was nonetheless well organized. Among other things they received mail regularly. Lieutenant Lawson even preferred the trenches to billets. The biggest drawbacks for him were the few chances he had to wash and the lack of sleep. "However it is not half so bad as it sounds and it is surprising how soon one gets accustomed to almost anything." Lawson made great use of the portable stove his sister sent him, having hot cocoa or tea every night, "and I can tell you it [is] great." He frequently asked his family to send cans of sterno for the stove, as the locally available fuel did not work as well and was very expensive.

Being at the front also gave the troops a greater sense of purpose, and in fall 1915 morale was high. "It is interesting work now and we feel that at last we are doing a little something," Lawson wrote. "The men so far have behaved splendidly. They put up with discomforts and mighty hard work very cheerfully with no grumbling at all. We certainly have a splendid body of men." But the nature of trench warfare left Lawson feeling conflicted: "The only thing that strikes one is the uselessness and childishness of the whole business. It does not seem worthwhile. It is almost wholly a game of machinery, it seems so silly to be down behind a bank with someone waiting for a chance to pot you if you give them a chance. And probably in the end both sides will get tired and give it up."

The Crater Fight: "Bloody Initiation"

Fighting on the 26th's section of the Ypres front was then intermittent. Occasionally, the Germans detonated mines under the front line, but most infantrymen fired at the enemy only infrequently: Private Howard did not fire his first shots at the enemy until December 23, 1915, almost three months after first entering the trenches. Larger-scale offensive operations were exceptional during the battalion's first several months at the front, so when they occurred they stood out. The 26th fought its first major action on October 13, only three weeks after entering the line. The Crater fight, as it was called, was the unit's baptism by fire, and helped to establish its reputation as "the Fighting 26th." It would be commemorated for many years afterwards.

The operation originated on October 8, when the Germans detonated a series of mines on the 5th and 6th Brigade fronts, including one about

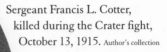

Sergeant Francis L. Cotter,
killed during the Crater fight,
October 13, 1915. Author's collection

fifty yards in front of "Trench K1 New." Divisional and battalion headquarters became anxious about the purpose of the crater, worrying that it was to be used as a base for bombing the Canadian line, digging another mine, or even for discharging liquid fire from German flame-throwers. As Lieutenant Ferguson saw it, it was clear "those ingenious fiends are surely up to some devilry." On the ninth, the 26th returned to the trenches in front of the crater and began preparing for offensive action. On the tenth and eleventh, the men dug a sap to within forty yards of the crater. Both Brigadier-General David Watson, 5th Brigade commander, and Lieutenant-Colonel H.D. De Pree, the divisional general staff officer (GSO) 1, inspected the trenches on the eleventh and twelfth, respectively. On the twelfth, an artillery bombardment was fired in a failed attempt to destroy the crater, which, in hindsight, likely put the Germans on alert. A section of the 25th Trench Mortar Battery was also placed near the lines to command the crater. When divisional headquarters ordered a smoke demonstration along their front for the thirteenth to support a British attack at Loos to the south, the battalion decided to use it as an opportunity to make a reconnaissance in force of the crater in daylight to find out what the Germans were doing and destroy any works.

The 26th planned to attack with men from two platoons from A Company, supported by a portion of B Company and a detachment of the battalion's bombers, all led by Major Walter R. Brown, A Company's commanding officer. Spearheading the assault was a ten-man advance party under Lieutenant C.E. Fairweather, No. 3 Platoon commander. They would attack from the sap, capture the crater, and clear the way for succeeding support sections, while Lieutenant T.M. McPhee of the 5th Field Engineering Company and four sappers inspected the works and wired any defences for demolition. The follow-on force consisted of two twenty-man parties made up of sections of bombers and bayonet men who would advance from opposite ends of the crater and cover the advance party, the forward sections being led by Sergeants Frank L. Cotter (#69157) of Saint John and William C. Ryer (#69805). The entire force numbered about fifty men. Additional support was provided by the trench mortar section and three machine guns under the battalion machine-gun officer Lieutenant Albert D. Carter, placed on either side of the attackers so they could keep up a constant enfilading fire from the flanks. The hazardous nature of the attack was clearly understood. Major Brown warned the troops beforehand about the risks they faced, telling them that it was "not likely that any us would come back alive and if there was any man who was not keen on going that he had an opportunity to drop out. Not a single man dropped out."

The attack began at 2:00 p.m. with a two-hour artillery and trench mortar bombardment. At 3:20, troops threw smoke bombs over the parapets. At 4:00, Brown and the main force exited the left side of the sap, and a few moments later the advance party leapt out of the right side and raced across no man's land to the crater under cover of the smoke. It soon became apparent, however, that the Germans were alert, and they met the attackers with a hail of rifle and machine-gun fire. RSM Roy Edwards described what he called "the desperate rush": "Then came the word to 'go' and with a rush we broke cover and headed for that crater that was pouring a storm of bullets across the open ground. Suffice it to say now of the encounter we drove the charge home and captured the crater, but at a heavy cost, our losses in the few minutes it took to reach the crater and drive out the Germans being 25 killed outright and 30 more or less wounded."

The crater allowed the attackers to be enfiladed from both flanks, something Lieutenant Fairweather encountered as he led his advance party forward: "We advanced under a cross fire of rifle and machine guns with bombs added when we got close, and although the distance to be travelled was only about 40 yards that little trip was warm." An unidentified soldier who was on the left of A Company described the advance as it was seen from the trenches: "No words can describe the scene. The men rushed forward cheering and shouting; around them the shells burst with an awful roar and red flashes of flame, dense white clouds of smoke 100 feet high rolled towards the Germans and all around sounded the sharp crack of rifles and the rattle of machine guns." From the front line, 26th men "poured in all the rifle fire we could to support A Company till our rifles were too hot to hold."

The first Canadians quickly drove off the enemy, and entered what turned out to be a series of unconnected holes. Private Roy Brady (#69060) from Cape Tormentine, New Brunswick, who was shot in the arm within ten feet of the crater, wrote: "I did not mind it a bit, and went on putting the bombs to them. I could throw two to their one." He and his mate, Private William E. Reid (#69809), also from Cape Tormentine, were fighting side by side when a big shell explosion buried Brady. When Reid dug him out, Brady "was all covered in mud, but not otherwise hurt, and when I got my eyes cleaned I got at them again."

The Germans fell back through a communication trench to their front line on higher ground, where they continued bombing the crater below them. Unable to reply to the German bombers, Canadian casualties quickly mounted. Lieutenants Fairweather and McPhee made a quick inspection of the position, found no sign of work having been done, and, deciding nothing could be gained by staying in this "death-trap," McPhee ordered the men back to their own lines. By then, the smoke had begun to clear, so when the men began returning across no man's land, they came under heavy rifle fire. Shortly afterward, the Germans fired another mine, which went up with a roar. Although the official report stated it did no damage, eyewitnesses suggest otherwise. According to Lieutenant Carter, the mine blew up the first party of bombers quite close to the crater: "they were blown into the air and practically everyone was killed or wounded." Of the twelve men from Sergeant Cotter's section, only three made it back to their own trenches. The intense German fire during the retreat inflicted more casualties. In a letter to his brother Will, Lieutenant Ferguson described what he saw from inside the front line: "The smoke and din was awful. The crack of machine guns and rifles a continuous roar, with the thudding, earth shaking booms of the bombs both sides were hurling at each other and the wind whirling the dense smoke about, through which darting forms and flashes were visible intermittently as it thinned a little here and there. It was war, Will, war alright enough."

The Canadians deployed more smoke, and under its protection they began bringing in the wounded. C Company called for volunteers, and together with the attackers and stretcher bearers, they helped whom they could back into the trenches. Many acts of heroism took place. Sergeant Ryer, from Middle Clyde in Shelburne County, Nova Scotia, took up a position to watch the Germans advancing to reoccupy the trenches as his men retired. He shot eleven of the enemy "as cool as if he were on the range." On his way back he picked up Cotter, who was mortally wounded. When Cotter died, Ryer placed him on the ground and returned to retrieve another wounded man, Private Dawson Winchester (#70032) of Dalhousie, New Brunswick. With the help of Private Frank L. Daley (#69211) of Saint John, Ryer hoisted Winchester on his back, and securing him with the wounded man's puttees, carried him back to the trenches. Unfortunately, Winchester died of his wounds the next day. Ryer received the Distinguished Conduct Medal (DCM) for his actions, the first to be awarded to a soldier from 2nd Canadian Division. The fight was the stretcher bearers' first experience under fire in the open, and, according to the after-action report, "they all came out like heroes."

The battle, however, was not yet over. About 5:00 p.m., the Germans opened a heavy counter-bombardment all across the battalion front. Some of the troops had close calls. Corporal Fred Breau (#69039) from Tabusintac, New Brunswick, a battalion bomber, described a near miss by a shell: "It is as bad as I want to see it...one fellow got hit with a bomb, and was thrown up in the air fifteen feet from where he was and fell right alongside me. I was standing alongside him two minutes before he got hit, and I thought to myself I better move away from there, so I got up and walked away some fifteen feet, and about two minutes after I saw a German bomb fall right between a bunch of fellows and it killed two of our men and wounded a few more. I tell you it was God's blessing I moved away from there, as I suppose my time had not yet come." A little later, he got hit in the side of the head by a piece of a German bullet, but it did no damage: "After all the fight was over and I saw I had pulled through alright, I said to myself, lucky Frenchman."

Private Hugh Wright from No. 1 Platoon later wrote to his father, telling him they had "had a little scrap. No doubt you will see it in the paper long before this reaches you. We lost quite a few men. I knew most of them well and most were in our [company]. I was right in the thickest of it and came off without a scratch so I have something to be thankful for." Lieutenant Carter was not so lucky: he was hit late in the action around 8:15 by a shell fragment that pierced his kidney and lodged in his thigh. The lower part of his body was paralyzed, but he felt very little pain, possibly because the fragment was red hot when it entered his body and cauterized the wound. After the fighting died down, he was brought in by stretcher bearers and evacuated to hospital. Carter never rejoined the battalion.

That night, they brought in what they thought were all of the wounded. Private Richard T. Moore (#69551) of Waterford, in Kings County, re-counted how, on the following night, he went into no man's land to recover the bodies of the dead when he heard a soldier give a moan. "He'd been lying out there in the open for 30 hours. When he was brought in there was no signs of any wounds, but he died soon after," likely from shock and exposure. Moore described how "dragging in dead bodies isn't at all pleasant, but the job I did hate was to stay out there with two men and guard the 'dead ones' till daylight [on the first night]. Lying there in the half-light with twisted bodies and mud covered clothes, their faces upturned, but hardly recognizable though they were all well known to us." Sergeant Cotter's was the only body that was never recovered. Men from the unit believed the Germans had stripped his corpse. His name appears on the Menin Gate Memorial for Commonwealth soldiers missing in Belgium.

The fight took a heavy toll on the unit: twenty-one killed or died of wounds, and three officers, including Major Brown and Lieutenant Fairweather, and thirty-one other ranks wounded. A Company suffered the majority of the casualties (thirty-nine all ranks), especially No. 4 Platoon, which lost 20 percent of its strength. Lieutenant Ferguson wrote that the "string of wounded was the heartrending portion, but gamer men never lived or died than those fellows." Some of the wounded accepted their injuries stoically. Toward the end of the fight a German bomb killed one man and wounded two others, among them Private James McDavid (#69660) of Matapédia, Quebec, whose arm and left shoulder were badly injured. When fellow soldiers readied a stretcher to carry him to the rear, he refused, saying, "let someone else have the stretcher. I'll walk," which he did for about one and a half kilometres to the dressing station. Among the dead was Private G. Almon Savidant (#69878), whom Ferguson knew from Campbellton. Ferguson wrote: "A big piece of shell that got a couple of others hit him about waist high, killing him instantly. He probably never knew what hit him for he was dead before the stretcher bearer had time to open his coat."

The Crater fight was the battalion's first experience of high-intensity combat — what Ferguson called "the day of days ... [when] the 26th were tested by fire good and solid." Captain George Keefe, from Saint John, noted that they had a number of South African War veterans in their company, and "everyone said ... they had never heard or saw anything to equal the fight we put up." According to Charles Lawson, the battalion had its "first real dose of shell fire of all kinds and descriptions.... It was quite an engagement, entirely artillery in our section, but the right of the battalion were at close quarters. The battalion is considered to have made a very good showing indeed." He wrote later that "the men all stood up to it mighty well." He also acknowledged that the heavy casualties made a strong impression on the troops, since so many of them knew each other. Among the dead was Lance Corporal Reginald F. Peacock (#69743) of Saint John, one of three brothers with the battalion, including Hubert, who became Lawson's platoon sergeant after his predecessor was wounded during the fight. Lawson wrote: "It was altogether too bad about Reg

Peacock for he was a very fine fellow and a mighty good soldier. Everyone in the battalion who knew him spoke mighty well of him....I was going to write to young Peacock's people but a third brother is with the machine gun section here and I told him to tell his mother and father how much I thought of the boy. I had him in school for a while when I was teaching Grade X." Clearly, the men of the battalion still knew each other well, so the effects of the losses were deeply felt.

The fight on October 13 instilled pride in the battalion among its troops. Despite the heavy cost, the men felt the unit had done well, destroying the German position and inflicting many more casualties on the Germans, with estimates ranging between four and five hundred. As Captain Keefe wrote, "we have just finished our first big scrap. We took no big towns, but played our little part, and it was done very creditably." Some saw its importance in the wider strategic context. An unnamed soldier from C Company wrote: "I'm proud to belong to the 26th. Through the attack we drew the Germans to us, and the British have captured three lines of trenches one day and two the next."

The Crater fight helped to establish the 26th's reputation as a fighting unit. Lieutenant Fairweather commented that "the men behaved splendidly and in fact were complimented by brigade as well as divisional headquarters and now the 26th battalion is the envy of the whole division." It became known as the first attack across no man's land by a 2nd Canadian Division unit. The fight was widely reported in newspapers in Britain, where the attack was highly commended. Max Aitken, Canada's eyewitness at the front, included a description in one of his newspaper articles, as well as in volume two of his *Canada in Flanders*, published in 1917. Reinforcing a recurring theme in his writing about the inherent fighting skills of Canadians, Sir Max prefaced his account of the Crater fight with a stirring tribute to his fellow New Brunswickers: "The fibre of the race that province breeds has become indurated by generations of contest with the elements, and has taken on something of the unbending hardness of the North. They were now to test these ingrained qualities against a new antagonist, for immediately on their front the enemy one day blew up a great mine."

At home, local newspapers featured articles on the fight for several months, and the exploits of the battalion became known in intimate detail. On October 18, the *St. John Standard* reported: "Last week's operation formed practically their baptism of fire and a thrill of pride will go through the province this morning at the intelligence that, when the opportunity came, they did their duty in the manner expected of men of New Brunswick." Many people back home took pride in the accomplishments of their provincial battalion at the front. On October 17, New Brunswick-born J. Douglas Hazen, minister of marine and fisheries and of the naval service in the cabinet of Robert Borden, received a telegram from Sam Hughes informing him that the 26th had greatly distinguished itself. Hazen thanked him and replied that "New Brunswickers can be depended upon to do their duty like men under the most adverse circumstances." The unit's provincial identity would continue to grow throughout the war.

The Crater fight became a red-letter event in the battalion's history. A year later, the anniversary of the fight was observed in provincial newspapers, among them the *Daily Telegraph*, which featured an interview with Colonel McAvity, who by then had returned to Saint John. McAvity recounted how he had watched the attack with General Watson: "All we could see was a cloud of smoke out in 'No Man's Land,' and I knew that out there my men were wrestling with the Germans, bleeding and dying, killing and being killed." The article ended by asserting that, "on the first anniversary of the Crater fight their memory is still fresh in the hearts of all New Brunswickers. Their imperishable gallantry will always be remembered." As late as October 1939, the Crater fight was still being observed on its twenty-fourth anniversary by the 26th Battalion Overseas Club.

Winter in the Line
From late October 1915 to March 1916, the 26th held the line in the Kemmel area before moving to the St. Eloi sector, south of Ypres. During that long, wet, raw winter of 1915/16, the weather was the enemy, and the troops endured hardships that exacted a heavy toll on them, both physically and psychologically. In early October, cold and damp weather arrived, "most uncomfortable in the extreme," according to Lieutenant

Ferguson. After a brief fine spell later in the month, the heavy rain returned, it became colder, and sometimes hailed. The rains caused streams to overflow and turned low ground into swamps. The local clay soil could not support its own weight when drenched, so the walls, traverses, and parapets of flooded trenches fell in, dugouts flooded and collapsed, and communication trenches filled with four or five feet of water, making them impassable. Walter McIntyre described how, in one trench, he had "to wade to the waste [sic] in water and mud and then I fell so when I was back I was soaked through all over."

It was difficult for the troops to adapt to these harsh, unfamiliar conditions so unlike the winters they were used to. In early December, Private Fred Harvey (#69418) of Fredericton wrote to his mother: "I don't think much of the winter weather here and would rather have the deep snow. The night before last the mud froze quite bad." Major McKenzie wrote that "wet weather is our bad time. The trenches then are rotten. Imagine living for six days in one of the ditches the town digs when putting in water or a sewerage. It is just like that when it rains." Earlier in October, Corporal Frank Wallace (#70219), originally from London, England, wrote home complaining of how it had rained for nearly a whole week, sometimes quite hard: "We had only our great coats and blankets, and we never had our wet socks and boots off for a week or washed either. The food was insufficient and not enough drinking water. I am not grumbling as things could not be altered, except for the food."

The troops coped with these conditions as best they could. It was not until late October and early November, however, that they received rain and cold weather equipment, including heavier underwear, rain capes, rubber boots that reached to the hips, and fur- or sheepskin-lined short greatcoats ("British Warms"), although the coats were still too long for the trenches. Socks were in great demand, and proper boots were much sought after. Lieutenant Lawson was able to buy a pair of Corrigan boots from Palmer-McLellan's shoe company in Fredericton from another officer who found his too small: "They are considered to be the only absolutely waterproof boots obtainable, and cover the leg to the knee. I was very fortunate to be able to get them." A short time later, however, he reported that his batman had put the boots too close to the fire, "with the result that I need a new pair. I am sending an order to Palmer's Fredericton.... The price is something like eleven dollars."

Fortunately, some of the support-line billets, like Sand Bag Villa, located several hundred yards behind the firing line, were fairly comfortable. Rest and comfort in the cold, wet weather was important for the troops, and they sometimes described their arrangements in detail. Walter McIntyre slept in a large room with three men to a bed: "We have a bed of straw, two rubber sheets, and a fur coat under us and so we are pretty warm. Slept all night and had a good rest." The troops used their ingenuity to improve their comfort: Lieutenant Ferguson, for example, constructed a small stove out of a chloride-of-lime can and, for a chimney, a tube used to transport ammonal explosives.

Nevertheless, winter conditions had serious consequences for the troops. In late October, Ferguson observed that the cold, driving rain "penetrates to the marrow of one's bones. We will likely have as many casualties from now on due to exposure as we will from bullets. A man hit in the trenches now will be in a bad way unless he can be taken out quickly." As he had predicted, by early November, the men lost to exposure increased, among them Lieutenant Charles D. Knowlton of Saint John, who, on November 5, "gave up the ghost, going out with the ration party tonight." Men were also buried and injured by collapsing trench walls, and wounds were made more dangerous by the effects of exposure. Flooded communication trenches forced troops to move around above ground in the open, making them more vulnerable to enemy fire, especially from snipers, and confining most movement to nighttime. It also cut off communication between the platoons during daytime. The urgent need to repair the trenches meant that the troops spent most of their time trying to keep ahead of their deteriorating positions, "which seems almost a hopeless task." Ferguson commented that he now understood why the British and French troops who formerly occupied the area had built their parapets of sandbags beginning at ground level and kept digging to a minimum. To limit the effects of fatigue on the men, front line tours were reduced to four days in early December. Relief from that duty brought little rest, however, because those in the rear were

Lieutenant Charles Lawson, former Saint John High School teacher.

Lawson, JI-F37-56, New Brunswick Museum

constantly called on to supply fatigue parties to continue the trenching work. As Ferguson wrote at the end of October, "six days fatigue under the name rest is what billets actually mean." The fatigue work made "life miserable and almost unlivable for our poor chaps by utterly playing them out."

The only good news was that the wintry conditions slowed down the pace of operations as both sides struggled to endure. Different forms of contact with the enemy under these conditions became more noticeable. When the 26th first arrived at the front, it took over one of the quietest sectors of the line. According to Major Brown, the Germans did not fight if the opposing troops did not bother them: "However, it was different when the 26th got into the trenches. They did not believe in sleeping on the job; they wanted to be fighting and get a run for their money. They were no sooner there than they began throwing bombs and assaulting the troops opposite, until now it is known as one of the hottest parts of the front."

During the winter, however, the situation became more complex. In April 1916, a member of the 26th, Private Vaughan Henshaw (#69384) of Perth, New Brunswick, wrote that he found a great difference between different kinds of Germans: "Saxons were our good 'friends.' It got so that they would not fire a shot unless we did. 'You no shoot, Canadians, we no shoot,' they said. They learned some of our songs and used to sing them. It was a different matter with the Prussians. As soon as they came on they started a rapid fire right off and kept it up. We did likewise — and then some. But we and the Germans used to yell back and forth what we would do to each other though we could always shut them up when we told them that we'd give them a bayonet charge."

There are indications that the Canadians encountered this "live and let live" mentality early on. At the beginning of October 1915, Lieutenant Ferguson reported the Germans yelling across no man's land "Cut it out you blank blank Canadian blanks. Don't you know this is Sunday?" In another instance, an unnamed soldier from Saint John described in detail how a few soldiers from the 26th fraternized with the Germans. He wrote that when things got quiet the men talked with the Germans across no man's land and threw tins of bully beef to them. He recorded how, early one morning, a German hailed one of the 26th's trenches and struck up a conversation in good English. One word led to another, and then the German said, "Come over and have a drink."

> Well that sounded good to the boys, so one of them answered back: "Stick your head up over the parapet and we won't fire." The German did so, and so did the chap of the 26th. The latter said "Stand up" and the German obeyed. The German was requested to throw down his rifle. He did so and similar action was taken by the Canadian. The German walked half way between the trenches, and the 26th man did likewise. They shook hands and exchanged souvenirs. Then the 26th chap walked back to the German trenches and went in and had a drink. After he had the drink he called out to some of his mates and six of them went over and got a drink. The Germans told them that at twelve o'clock they were going to start bombarding and to lie low then. Sure enough they did. It just goes to show you that some of the Germans are not bad fellows after all.

More conclusive evidence suggests that fraternization occurred on Christmas Day 1915 that was reminiscent of the famous Christmas truce of 1914. 5th Brigade's war diary states that the battalions in the front lines were instructed "that there must be no fraternisation between our own and the enemy's troops. Any attempt on the part of the enemy to bring about a temporary cessation of hostilities must be met by rifle fire and, if necessary, the artillery to be called upon." When the battalion re-entered the line on Christmas Eve, it prepared for a German attack, "taking along a good supply of bombs and a good watch was kept all night but nothing happened," according to Walter McIntyre. He reflected on Christmas Day in the trenches, writing, "did not think last Xmas that I would be here this year." Firing along the front slackened during the morning. Dinner consisted of cold Maconochie's stew, hardtack, and tea. "Not much of a Christmas Dinner," McIntyre wrote. During the afternoon, the firing practically stopped, and the troops began to interact. Although official records, including the battalion's war diary, indicate that no fraternization took place on the unit's frontage, soldiers' accounts tell a different story. According to McIntyre, "both sides rose above the parapets and called over greetings to each other. We waved anything at hand at them and no doubt we would soon have had them over in No Man's Land to see and meet us if the artillery had not opened up with some shrapnel ordered to do so by the 24th [Battalion] major. The shells were sent to explode high so no one was hurt but it scared the Germans and spoiled the fun for the day. At night things went on as usual." Ferguson's detailed diary entry offers a similar description of the day's events:

> In the early morning, the Bosches were firing a bit with machine guns and rifles, but when day broke, they quieted down and, all through daylight, not a single shell came over at us and the lone crack of a rifle occurred only a couple of times throughout the day. The Bosches seemed inclined to be exceedingly friendly and all kinds of white flags floated over their parapets. They got up on top of their parapets and waved their hands and shouted with great éclat. We could have "cornholed" a bunch of them and I was right against a machine gun that was trained on a large group of the "blue-grays," but I hadn't the heart to fire. War is war and I like everybody to have a fighting chance. I want that myself if ever I get in a similar position. Our fellows answered the Bosch yells with several "Matapédia war hoops" and the Bosch and Canadian alike wandered about as freely behind their respective lines as though strolling along the Strand.

Private Fred Howard indicated that things went even further, recording that "we were all up on the parapet all afternoon talking with the Germans who were also up. Some of the fellows went over to the German trenches and exchanged cigarettes and badges."

By New Year's Eve, the troops were back in billets at Locre. Although soldiers such as Walter McIntyre had no money to spend, they still found

Water-filled crater at St. Eloi. Mikan no. 3329064, Library and Archives Canada

ways to celebrate. Two sections from his platoon were comfortably billeted in the attic of a house: "We had a concert to send the old year out and the new one in on. There were speeches, songs, readings, and recitations. We had got some of our parcels so had a good feed too. Everything came off fine and we went to bed happy and with our minds made up to do our best to win this war during 1916."

In early April 1916, the battalion moved northwards to the St. Eloi front, where it remained until May. Before leaving, on the morning of March 27, the British blew a series of mines in marshy ground at St Eloi, located at a main crossroads about four kilometres south of Ypres, and then captured many of the resulting craters. During the German retaliation for the attack, the 26th faced a heavy pounding that killed seven men and wounded another eighteen. York House, in the rear, was a particular target, taking ten direct hits that killed one and wounded three others. A 26th soldier from the Miramichi using the initials "F.B.W." — likely Frederick B. Wathen (#70022), whose family lived in Doaktown — described the attack: "[T]he Germans bombarded us with artillery, the heaviest we have yet been against. It was pretty hard to keep clear from getting hit, blowing up dugouts all around us and emplacements, and blowing in the

parapets on top of the boys in lots of places." The next day, the bombardment continued and another four were killed. Private Benjamin Gaskill
(#69356), a stretcher bearer from North Head, Grand Manan, was in a
fatigue party that brought out the dead. The heavy losses had an effect
on him. On March 28, he noted in his diary that eleven of his comrades
were buried in the 26th Battalion's cemetery.

The Battle of St. Eloi
On April 4, 2nd Canadian Division was ordered to relieve the British
around St. Eloi. When they arrived, the Canadians found difficult conditions: the defensive line was located among a series of craters and muddy,
disconnected trenches under German observation. The Germans also had
a preponderance of artillery that continuously pounded the Canadian
positions. To bolster their defences, each of the division's infantry units
sent forward their Lewis machine-gun teams — the 26th's consisted of
five men and the machine-gun officer, Lieutenant Frank Lockhart from
Petitcodiac, New Brunswick. When the 26th arrived, it went into billets at
the divisional rest area at Reninghelst, about eight kilometres behind the
front lines. Meantime, on April 6, the Germans launched a major counterattack to recover their lost ground, overrunning many of the Canadian
troops holding their narrow salient — among them Lockhart's team,
from which only one member survived; none of the bodies of the others
was recovered, and their deaths are commemorated on the Menin Gate
Memorial.

Over the next several days, the Canadians tried, mostly unsuccessfully,
to recover the lost ground. By the time 5th Brigade, including the 26th,
entered the line on April 12, however, offensive operations were beginning
to slow down. The 26th occupied trenches to the north of St. Eloi, near
the south bank of the Ypres-Comines Canal. The platoons were scattered
among detached posts that were mostly wet and muddy and frequently
under heavy German artillery fire. The battalion spent much of its first
tour organizing large working parties to improve the lines. By the time the
men were relieved, active operations had ended, but the working parties
kept at it during their time at rest.

During the latter stages of the battle around St. Eloi, the 26th experienced occasional German bombing attacks and almost constant heavy artillery fire. On April 17, Lieutenant "Goog" Mowat from Campbellton, a recently arrived platoon commander, was leading a party of four men to their position when they ran into a twelve-man German patrol in a disused trench in front of the 26th's line. A German bomb tore away one of the feet of Private J.F. Bamsey (#412677) of Devon, England, who subsequently died of wounds, while Mowat was hit in both feet. The next man, Private Kennedy, was struck in the chest by a bomb that failed to explode. The final man, Private Richard Chatteron (#413002) of Fort Stewart, Ontario, ran for help. Once reinforcements arrived, the Germans retired, and the wounded were brought in.

Many of the troops remarked on the intensity of German artillery fire in their letters home. Major McKenzie, acting commanding officer in Colonel McAvity's absence, described St. Eloi as "some warm spot....We had 1,000 shells, heavy ones too, in a small area in a few hours one day." An article in the *Daily Telegraph* reported that military observers estimated that German shells fell at the rate of twenty-five rounds per minute, "still further churning the soaking earth and adding to the difficulties of movement." "F.B.W." wrote that holding the crater front "was living hell.... The Germans were changing batteries and opened up with both full force of a ten mile frontage on a 600 yard frontage, so you can have a slight idea of what it would be like from a 5.9 up to 12 inch. It was fierce. We held them back, but suffered quite heavily." He added that they expected it would be more or less like this "all summer now, but for my part I don't want to see the like of it again, with a lot of the boys coming out of it maimed for life."

Change of Command
In mid-April 1916, Colonel McAvity was hospitalized, suffering from chronic gastritis brought on by the stress of service, and Major McKenzie assumed temporary command of the battalion. The forty-eight-year-old McAvity had been ill for some time: Harry Ferguson had written in early December 1915 that McAvity had serious stomach trouble, and it was believed he would be sent back to England on sick leave. Then, in July,

McAvity relinquished command and returned home on sick leave for three months. In early August, McKenzie was promoted to temporary lieutenant-colonel and officially took charge of the 26th.

McAvity had been extremely popular with his officers and other ranks alike. When Lieutenant Arthur Legere returned to New Brunswick in February 1916, he said he could not "say too much in praise of Col. McAvity. He is certainly a wonder and is well liked by every man in the battalion." After returning home in November 1916, Captain George Keefe stated that McAvity and the other officers were "to a large extent responsible for the high esteem in which the battalion is held by the people of New Brunswick. No man ever had men into battle better fitted for the task than Col. McAvity. He was a soldier and a gentleman and for the part he played in immortalizing the '26th' he was altogether too modest when he arrived home," giving all the credit to his officers, whereas "he himself was responsible in no small measure for that success. He had a splendid control of the men, they would do anything for him and he was always ready to go anywhere with his men and never asked a man to perform a duty he was not willing to do himself." Private Vaughan Henshaw observed that McAvity was like a father to his men, going to hospitals to talk to the wounded and looking after everyone in the same way. On a few occasions, Henshaw said, McAvity brought his rifle to the trenches and, using a sniper's position, "picked off a few [Germans]." McAvity did have a reputation for strictness, however, especially about attending church parade: even officers who missed were reported for not attending, and were obliged to submit written explanations explaining their absence. McKenzie stayed in close touch with him, writing frequent letters about the battalion's later exploits.

On July 14, McAvity arrived back in Saint John to a huge welcome that rivalled the battalion's send-off more than a year earlier. An estimated twenty thousand people gathered at the train station, including troops from the 140th Battalion, 62nd Regiment "St. John Fusiliers," and 3rd Regiment, Garrison Artillery. Also present were about fifty returned soldiers, some from the 26th and others from the Convalescent Home, as well as representatives from the European War Veterans organization. As the *St. John*

Standard colourfully described, McAvity's exit from the station "was the signal for cheering and for fully five minutes the crowd voiced its welcome, the strident notes of automobile horns lent their unmusical sound to the noise, the street car bells clanged, the whole combination a veritable din to the roaring of the big guns to which the colonel's ears have been so long attuned could scarce outrival." After a stirring official welcome by the acting mayor, a large procession moved off along streets decorated with bunting and the flags of the Allies and lined by hundreds of people, many in windows and on housetops. The procession headed to the colonel's home on Hazen Street, where a large reception took place.

McAvity talked about returning to France to resume command of the 26th, but remained in New Brunswick, working as a strong advocate on behalf of the unit, raising funds and organizing comforts to send overseas. He also became involved in the European War Veterans organization, soon to become the Great War Veterans Association. In October 1916, after he had recovered, McAvity became the province's chief recruiting officer, and in 1917, when the New Brunswick Regiment was formed, he took command of the 1st Depot Battalion at Camp Sussex.

The Battle of Mount Sorrel: "The hardest test"
On June 2, while 2nd Canadian Division still occupied the front line in the St. Eloi sector, the Germans attacked to the northeast at Mount Sorrel, overrunning 3rd Canadian Division's trenches. Heavy enemy shelling spread south, engulfing the 26th, which stood to all day and night. Signaller William J. Swetka (#69913), from Saint John, was wounded when a whiz bang — a 77-millimetre German artillery shell that travelled at a higher velocity than other shells — exploded on the parapet next to where he was sitting and shrapnel wounded his forearm. After the stretcher bearers bandaged him, he went to the dressing station at battalion headquarters, but had to wait until dark before he could move to the rear. By then, the bombardment had become very heavy, "the worst I've heard, shells exploding everywhere, all kinds."

The bombardment continued until the battalion was relieved on the night of June 5 and moved into corps reserve. On the seventh, 2nd Canadian

German dead at Mount Sorrel, June 1916.

Division was drawn into the battle, replacing 3rd Canadian Division near Mount Sorrel. The next day, the 26th moved into support lines near Maple Copse and Square Wood, to the rear of Hill 60, and furnished carrying parties for the units holding the front lines. During the tenth and eleventh, German artillery fire was again very heavy. On the eleventh, the battalion was relieved and moved into reserve for three days, during which 1st Canadian Division carried out a successful counterattack, recapturing most of the ground lost on June 2.

On June 14, the 26th returned to the line, taking over the front trenches to the left of Hill 62, and remained in position for six days. This was the most difficult part of the battle for the battalion. Much of the area had been devastated by the fighting. While moving up to the front line the troops passed Sanctuary Wood. Private Cecil M. Bennett (#69075) of Saint John described the scene: "It was a wood once, but lately it has been the scene of some awful fighting, and all that is left of it is some leafless and broken stumps and about every yard a hole big enough to set a house in." Much of their time was spent rebuilding the trenches destroyed during the earlier fighting and then flooded. The soldiers lived under terrible conditions: as Bennett wrote, "Well, I thought I had seen war, but after what I saw that night [June 14] and the following days made me think war was truly h___. Along the roads dead bodies in all conditions, mostly Germans, were strewn everywhere. We got to our place and found there was no cover to be had, everything had been blown to pieces." Corporal Fred Breau, the battalion bomber who had had a close call during the Crater fight, encountered similar conditions, writing that "it was awful where we were; the dead were lying all around, Canadians and Germans, but about five dead Germans to one Canadian." They soon learned that few dugouts were still intact, and not nearly enough to shelter all of the troops. Bennett remarked that "standing in an open trench with shells flying as thick as hailstones was not a pleasant outlook."

During most of their stay, they were again subjected to heavy bombardment. On June 16, Lance Corporal Walter McIntyre died while sitting on a sandbag in the reserve trench when a German shell struck, killing him and seven others. Among them was a soldier in the line for the first time, whom McIntyre was consoling "when Fritz got both," wrote a friend, who closed by writing, "War is hell and the infantrymen are the men of the hour." The same day, Corporal Breau was hit in the hip by shrapnel. He had to remain in the trenches all day until dark, but with no place to shelter: "all the trenches about us were knocked in with shell fire and there were no dug outs. It was a terrible place to be, I tell you, but we had to stand it, as it was up to us." On the eighteenth, Private Bennett was hit. After finding a German dugout, he and another man sheltered there for two days, but on the third night an enemy shell entered, coming within a foot of him and "completely wrecking our home. I was in a kneeling position and was buried completely. My chum's both feet and legs were buried, two of his toes being crushed; it was a miraculous escape, and it's a wonder we were not both killed." Bennett was dug out and placed on a stretcher, his hand and arm were bandaged, and a broken leg placed in a splint using a German rifle. Like Breau, he had to wait until dark before he could be taken to the rear.

The 26th spent much time patrolling its front to locate the enemy's positions and intent, resulting in numerous contacts with German patrols and working parties, which were driven off using bombs and artillery fire. On June 19 the battalion was finally relieved, and moved back to Camp Alberta at Reninghelst to begin ten days' rest. Even though the battalion had not been engaged directly during the initial German attack or later Canadian counterattack at Mount Sorrel, casualties over three weeks at the front were still heavy, with the unit losing about a quarter of its strength. On June 28 it moved back to the St. Eloi front, where it remained until the middle of August.

Minor Operations

Near the end of their time on the St. Eloi front, the men of the 26th carried out two minor operations that featured the type of fierce fighting in no man's land that characterized nighttime encounters at this point in the war. The "stunts," as the soldiers called them, gave the unit valuable experience planning and executing offensive operations, both by using its expanding specialist troops and weapons and by cooperating with other arms at the brigade and divisional levels.

The battalion's first trench raid took place on the night of June 30/July 1 when it successfully raided the German lines on the left sector of the St. Eloi trenches known as Spoilbank. The attackers aimed to capture prisoners for identification or, failing that, equipment that might reveal the enemy's unit. They were also to ascertain if any gas cylinders or mine shafts were located in these lines. Their thorough planning and organization shows how far minor operations had advanced in the eight months since the Crater fight. The raiding force consisted of Lieutenant Francis B. Winter, the officer in charge, Lieutenant Arthur G. Fleming, and CSM Alexander G. Gunn (#69352), along with about twenty-five riflemen, bombers, stretcher bearers, signallers, and scouts. The force was divided into four sections: the assault party of bombers and riflemen led by Winter; a party of wire cutters, bombers, and snipers; two small flanking parties; and the rear party of stretcher bearers, telephonists, and scouts under Fleming. Every man would carry six bombs and fifty rounds of small arms ammunition in addition to what the bombers carried in their haversacks. The troops would leave behind all means of identification, blacken their faces, and, instead of helmets, wear fatigue caps or balaclavas.

Beginning at 11:00 p.m., the infantry would be supported by sixty-pound trench mortars followed by artillery fire at Zero Hour on the enemy's flank and support trenches. Stokes guns (light mortars) would conform to the artillery barrage and thicken the fire. The battalion's machine guns would fire from the flanks to sweep the enemy's parapet. The entire party would leave the trench at about 10:30 and advance to an agreed-upon point, where the rear party would take up a position about forty metres from the German parapet. The wiring party would then push forward to cut through the belts of thick concertina wire by hand — a challenging part of the operation — and lay out tape to guide the advance party back to the rear. The assault and flanking parties would then slip through the wire under the cover of the artillery fire and enter the trench. While the flanking parties secured their flanks, the assault party would set about capturing prisoners and carrying out their reconnaissance. When they had completed their tasks, Winter would give a series of short blasts on his whistle, signalling the men in the trench to withdraw, rejoin the rear party, and make their way back to their own lines. The bombers would take up positions at the rear of the force and cover them against bombing attacks by German pursuers. Winter would relay times for these actions using prearranged code words through the advanced telephone station with the rear party to battalion headquarters and the artillery. If the telephone failed, electric lamps and runners would be used for communication. The assault was timed to begin about midnight.

Even though they had only one night to reconnoitre the German lines, the decision was made to carry out the raid on the night of June 30. Winter's group left their trench around 11:00 p.m. Among them were signallers Corporal Daryl Peters (#69776) of Saint John and Private Robert Green (#70125), who crawled out into no man's land equipped with a field telephone to establish communications with the artillery. From their position, they informed the gunners to lift their fire to allow Winter and his party to move forward. While passing through the third belt of German wire, they were spotted and came under rapid fire. They pushed through the concertina regardless, and about 1:34 a.m. entered the German trench, which was about two meters deep and in excellent condition with "bath mats" (floorboards) and wooden fire steps. The trench was very lightly held, the raiders encountering only three Germans, all of whom fled. One kept shooting through a covered loophole until Winter shoved his revolver through and fired, forcing the wounded German to flee without his rifle. Advancing a couple of bays along the trench, Winter found another German firing, whom he shot, but again the enemy soldier escaped. The raiders explored the trench for about forty metres, but saw no dugouts or any sign of gas cylinders or mine shafts. They did, however, find several pieces of equipment, which Winter collected and sent back to the rear party.

By 1:45 the assault party was being bombed quite heavily with rifle grenades and mortars, so Winter gave the order to withdraw. Throughout the fight, Peters and Green remained at their post, sending exact information at regular intervals that allowed the bombers and gunners to support the raid. Once Winter's group reached the rear party, the signallers directed the gunners to adjust their fire to cover the raiders' withdrawal. The gunners, along with the trench mortars and Stokes guns, quickly opened a barrage along the entire length of the enemy's front line. After waiting in no man's land for about fifteen minutes, the party reached their own trenches by 2:30 with all of their wounded. They had nine casualties, one serious, all of which were caused by German shellfire just before or after reaching their own trenches.

The raid was seen as a tactical success. Although they had taken no prisoners, the equipment they collected enabled them to identify the Germans as the 124th Regiment, XIII Corps. According to the after-action report, considering the short time they had to prepare the raid, it was "in our opinion a genuine success under the circumstances and in view of the quality of the wire to be crossed.... Communication was maintained throughout without a hitch," and cooperation with the artillery, trench mortars, and Stokes guns was excellent. For his leadership during the raid, Winter was awarded the Military Cross (MC), the first for an officer from the 26th. Signallers Peters and Green also received the Military Medal for their actions at the advanced signalling station throughout the attack and for carrying a badly wounded man back to their lines. The raid received further attention when Max Aitken included an account in volume three of his *Canada in Flanders*, writing that "Dominion Day (July 1st) was celebrated by the 26th (New Brunswick) Battalion in a manner little appreciated by the grey ranks across the way."

A smaller encounter more typical of these kinds of actions occurred on the night of August 6/7, when the battalion sent a strong contact patrol against the German lines to reconnoitre their wire and possibly raid a listening post to secure a prisoner. The patrol was led by Captain Richard E. Russell, with assistance from Lieutenants Andrew S. Boa and Wilfred H. Carling, the acting bombing officer, and consisted of about twenty bombers, riflemen, and members of a Lewis gun crew. When their advance party reached the German wire about twenty-five metres from the enemy's parapet, they found the defenders alert, with several men inside their wire who soon discovered the attackers. According to the battalion war diary, at that point, "a lively encounter ensued for about 8 minutes in No Man's Land" when the Germans opened up with trench mortars, grenades and machine guns, and the patrol replied with Mills bombs (hand grenades) and Lewis gun and rifle fire. After a few minutes, an enemy searchlight found the Canadians, whereupon Russell decided to pull back. When Boa, who was in charge of the covering party, observed a couple of dozen Germans emerging from their trench, he moved his men forward and bombed them. According to the brigade war diary, "at such short range, bombing and revolver shooting was very effective," and they claimed to have inflicted at least fifteen casualties on the enemy. Shortly afterwards, the patrol withdrew into their trenches under covering fire from their Lewis gun and the unit machine guns. Boa and two bombers were slightly wounded.

Later in August, the battalion withdrew from the line to undergo re-organization and training in preparation for the Canadian Corps' move south to join the British Army's ongoing Somme offensive. There, they would be called upon to put their hard-won battlefield skills to the test in their first experience with high-intensity, semi-open warfare.

Chapter Three

Life at the Front

The Western Front tested the physical and psychological resilience of the men who fought there. They lived and battled in trenches in close proximity to the enemy, and injury or death was close at hand. Learning how to cope with the discomfort and danger became an important step in the troops' transformation from novice soldiers to seasoned fighters. Well-organized infantry battalions such as the 26th were a major source of strength for these troops in their struggle to survive.

Living in the Trenches

Harsh conditions in the trenches, especially during the winter of 1915/16 when the 26th Battalion was still making the transition to front-line service, affected the troops in different ways. Even without enemy fire, the front was an unhealthy place. The dead lay all around until they could be recovered and buried, and human waste from soldiers packed into a narrow space added to the fetid environment. Not surprisingly, sickness rates among the men rose when they spent time in the line. Among the diseases was enteric or typhoid fever caused by drinking contaminated water found either in the trenches or local wells. To reduce its incidence, the unit supplied clean water to the troops from carts and ordered that any man found drinking polluted water be arrested. These measures were effective, and the incidence of typhoid fever remained quite low, afflicting only seven of the battalion's original members.

The more common ailment known as "trench fever" was also linked to the filthy conditions. Shortages of water, except for drinking purposes, made it difficult to wash. On October 2, 1915, Private Fred Howard noted that he had not washed and shaved for five days. On another occasion, he went without performing his ablutions for seven days. Under these conditions, the troops literally became lousy. Early on, steps were taken to eliminate the parasites by spreading NCI powder (made of naphthalene, creosote, and iodoform) at least once a week on both clothing and men, and by working vermijelli, a mixture of mineral oil and soft soap, into the seams of their clothes, where the lice nested. But the battle to control them was never-ending. In late April 1916, Howard described how he had to get up from sleeping at 4 a.m. and hunt for lice, "as they were biting so hard I could not sleep." Some took it in stride, making light of their plight. In a letter written to his mother in early December 1917, Lieutenant Graham McKnight of Douglastown, New Brunswick, joked about receiving lice killer in a parcel from a friend at home: "[B]ut I can sure use it to good advantage. Those animals are the most sure crop in France, but I am well used to them now and don't mind them growing a particle.... Some of them wear long service medals and can run like rabbits. It's a fine feeling when they start forming fours on the middle of your back, carrying out strategical maneuvers, but I will stop their pranks with Onez's compliments." In time, doctors recognized that lice were the source of high fevers that caused many soldiers to be evacuated to the rear for treatment, and the affliction became known as "pyrexia of unknown origin"; at least fifty-seven of the original members of the battalion contracted it (see Table 4).

During the winter months, a more common ailment was "trench foot," caused by restricted blood flow in the lower legs resulting from continuous immersion in icy cold, liquid mud, which produced painful inflammation and swelling in the toes and feet. In more serious cases, sores erupted that often became infected and could result in gangrene and sometimes amputation. Men were often invalided to hospital for up to three months while they recovered from even mild cases. Steps were taken to prevent trench foot. Each man was directed to carry an extra pair of socks in his uniform pocket under his greatcoat, where it was believed wet socks would dry in a few hours. The Army Service Corps supplied whale oil to be applied to the feet before going into the trenches, and in places where the lines were continually wet, each man was directed to change his socks, dry his feet, and apply the grease once daily. Beginning in late October 1915, men's feet were inspected after each tour in the trenches and their condition reported back to headquarters. The British Army kept close watch on trench foot, believing its incidence indicated slack discipline and a failure to follow procedure.

Conditions in the trenches also had psychological consequences for the troops. At first, some soldiers were excited about being at the front. On October 4, Lieutenant Frank Lockhart wrote: "Have had a week in the first line trenches and can tell you I enjoyed it immensely! At times rifle fire was brisk and we were shelled several times, but it was more fun than anything else. At the last of it the field guns were a welcome change from the incessant rifle fire; got showered several times.... One high explosive shell hit my parapet in one place... and blew the whole thing into the trench and completely buried two men.... The men all thought it great—a great joke and laughed uproariously." Later in the letter, he commented: "[T]he men are a perpetual wonder to me. They swing right into the work like veterans and they sure have nerve. I am proud to have command of such a party."

The mood changed, however, especially as routine took hold. In early October 1915, about two weeks after the 26th first entered the line, Lieutenant Charles Lawson wrote that "we are certainly having some experience here and the novelty has not warn off yet, but I imagine it will be monotonous enough before we are through with it." Later, he wrote that, most of the time, trench life was a regular routine: "I dare say we shall be well 'fed up' with it before the winter is over." Toward the end of October, brigade and battalion headquarters began noticing a growing slackness among the troops: NCOs had stopped calling the rolls at Tattoo; drill had lost some of the "snap and precision that was expected of the [battalion] before it went into the trenches"; the men were not saluting properly; and sentries and guards were slack. Battalion orders for October 17 stated: "There is a great deal of danger in slackness creeping in, especially when the men are at the front and when their clothes, etc. becomes badly damaged. It has been found, however, that allowing men to do pretty much as they please in matters of discipline instead of improving their conditions makes it infinitely worse." Officers and NCOs were directed to take this matter more seriously, and over the next few weeks were issued various directives aimed at tightening up discipline, ordering more close-order drill, and warning that NCOs who did not comply would be reduced in rank. As well, when in the trenches, men not required for working parties or sentry duty were to be kept busy with small fatigues, such as picking up cartridges and clips and collecting cans. As Headquarters explained, "the more the men are kept employed the better is their health and less dissatisfaction and grumbling exist. This is all the more important now that the cold weather is at hand." Officers in the unit supported this approach. In a letter written on October 17, Lawson described their ongoing work, which was necessary to keep the trenches in proper shape, adding: "I find the men are much more contented if kept busy all the time not set aside for sleep."

During their early days at the front, the troops received little respite, even during the rest period they took once a month behind the lines, especially once the winter weather set in. The break was often short lived, for as many as four hundred troops from the battalion "at rest" were assigned to fatigue duties in the front lines most nights. According to Private George H. Kempling (#455581) of Toronto, the biggest part of the job was getting to the front lines and back: "A man walks from ten to fourteen miles every night besides his work." They repaired trenches and dug new ones day and night, often in heavy rain and under fire. In mid-October 1915, Walter McIntyre was on fatigue all day at Whiz Bang Corner, near Kemmel. He noted how he could see in the air the whiz bangs (small-calibre German artillery shells) that gave the place its name: "They looked just like baseballs as they passed over us. It was a very dirty place to work." Lieutenant Harry Ferguson summed up the feelings of many troops when he wrote that "'rest' in billets is a joke."

Headquarters soon became concerned that units were not taking these working parties seriously. At the end of October 1915, a battalion order reported that lax conduct had been observed. According to the engineer officers in charge, the parties reporting for duty were often well below strength, and the men frequently reported without haversack rations and had to be sent home without doing any work. It was also reported that the officers in charge of the details appeared to be disinterested and allowed their men to loiter at their work. The order reproved these parties for not working vigorously and cheerfully, especially now that the wet weather was at hand. The divisional GOC warned that in future he would deal promptly with offending parties and the battalion commander would be held responsible for the conduct and strength of their working parties.

Being under Fire

Soldiers in the front line also had to learn how to face the danger and stress of enemy fire. Early combat in the trenches took several forms and affected the troops in different ways. Enemy artillery fire caused many casualties and, as Private Robert Dickie (#69249), an Englishman from Lancashire living in Saint John when he enlisted, wrote, "like the poor, it was always with us." The Germans shelled the Canadians frequently, especially during the daylight hours. On November 8, 1915, Walter McIntyre described his experience coming under shellfire during a carrying fatigue in the reserve line:

> The fellows I was with had to take a truck load from the road to [Trench] K3. We got two loads through all right although we were shelled both times. The third time [was] heavier than before. We had to leave the truck and take cover. One shell burst over us and Corporal Johnston and E. Poirier were wounded, Poirier in the hand and Johnston in the mouth. I had taken cover behind a hedge and after the shell burst I came out to find McLaughlin calling me. I went out to where he was and found Corp. J. lying in a ditch bleeding pretty hard. I lifted him some and 4 of us carried him out. We had to drop him 3 times as shells burst over us but no one was hit. We got him fixed up and sent him out while I stayed behind

to help take the truck farther on. I was covered with blood and looked more like a wounded man than anything else.

The more experienced the troops became, the better able they were to limit casualties. Dickie noted that "it is peculiar about shell fire. Sometimes when it was heaviest the losses would be very small." He recalled that, during a bombardment in April 1916 along the Ypres-Comines Canal in the St. Eloi sector, "the shells fairly rained, [but] the men escaped miraculously...somehow the men—or more probably the officers—could gauge the enemy's objective and seemingly avoid it." Nevertheless, losses caused by artillery fire were unavoidable. Sheltering in dugouts was no guarantee of safety. Some 26th men became victims of collapsed roofs caused by German bombardment. According to Dickie, "when one of their dugouts caved in sometimes three or four men would be crushed to death. Imagine the weight of the corrugated iron, steel girders, brickbats in bags, sod earth, etc. and you can see what a chance a man would have." He added, "to the credit of the 26th...we accounted for every man, no matter how deep the burial. Sometimes life would be extinct but the [officer commanding] was insistent that every man be given his chance."

Artillery fire took a toll on men's nerves. "One [shell] came pretty close," McIntyre wrote. "I heard it coming and ran a few steps and then dropped and waited. The waiting was awful. It seemed to me as if it were going to take me between the shoulders it come so close. I got quite a scare." The loss of friends to shelling was also hard on the troops. On November 17, 1915, McIntyre described how, during a heavy bombardment, a shell hit a telephone position, burying Lance Corporal Hubert M. Meehan (#69607), a Newfoundlander by birth who had served with the 62nd Regiment before the war, and Private Cyril C.P. Vigot (#70014), who was born on Jersey in the Channel Islands: "It was a terrible experience to hear fellows call for help and know that we could not do anything to help them. They called hard for help but the shells were coming too thick to get to them. They died before we got to them."

Soldiers reacted to these kinds of events in different ways. McIntyre reported that, on November 17, he went sick, "partly from the wet. I had to

Canadian soldiers "standing to"; one is looking at no man's land through a trench periscope. C-006984, Library and Archives Canada

wade in mud to my waist and partly I think from the shock of the shells." He came out of the firing line at night and slept in a warm dugout. The next day he went to see the doctor. "I carried my pack all the way and nearly collapsed when I got there." He stayed the morning at the dressing station, then went back to billets, where he spent the next two days lying in and "having a good feed of potatoes and meat." On the twenty-second, he headed back to the trenches apparently none the worse for wear, for he took charge of No. 4 Section of his platoon as an "acting Lance Jack [Corporal]."

Some soldiers saw machine-gun fire as being particularly dangerous. Private Dickie wrote: "Shell fire no matter how terrifying has nothing on the rattling machine guns." German machine-gun fire became more threatening as they learned the location of Canadian roads, lines of communication, and communication trenches. They often swept these areas, "seeking whom they might devour." The closer the men got to the front line, the riskier movement—especially carrying up rations—became.

Even movement at night carried risk.. Dickie described his way of coping with the fire: "It is in man's nature to stand still but we found the best way to do was to go along as if nothing was happening. I have often heard the bullets whizzing in front of my face, over my head and several did go through my kit bag but through it all I was untouched." Farther to the rear, the men were sometimes hit with spent bullets with little effect. But "up in the front line of trenches where the bullets come with greater force they will go right through a man without doing much damage. That is if the devils opposite haven't flattened the noses down, for there were a good number of dum-dums coming our way."[7] George Kempling also took machine-gun fire in stride. In early August 1916, he recounted how, at night, the Germans would fire bursts across no man's land, searching for working parties: "One Hun machine gunner is an artist. He teases us, just firing three or four bullets at a time. Just as we get off our bellies and begin working, he fires another bunch of bouquets at us. He don't seem to care whether we get any time to work or not."

Enemy snipers were another ever-present threat. Sometimes they were so close the Canadians could hear the action of their rifle bolts. They inflicted numerous casualties on the New Brunswickers. Among their victims was Lieutenant Harry Ferguson, killed on March 15, 1916, while walking up a communication trench toward the front line. In time, some Canadian officers wore privates' tunics and carried rifles to conceal themselves from snipers. Canadian troops retaliated by sniping back at the Germans, sometimes with the aid of periscopes, although "it was largely guess work," according to Dickie. As a pioneer, Dickie did not carry a rifle, but he did have a good periscope given to him by an artillery officer, and he "used to amuse myself in directing some other men where to fire.... Looking into the periscope I would see perhaps a piece of board sticking up behind the German trenches, carried presumably by a Boche. I would then call out the direction and the other chap might take a chance for half a second, peek over the parapet and let the Hun have it.... We

---

7   Dum-dums — named after the British arsenal at Dum Dum, India, where they were first developed — were bullets with flattened noses that caused grievous wounds. Canadian soldiers widely believed the Germans engaged in this cruel practice.

never know how many we were getting." The more serious retaliation was left to the battalion's own sniper section.

The troops experienced some parts of the fighting more as spectators than as participants. Early on, they watched the air war overhead with curiosity, especially aerial combat between scouts, or fighter aircraft. Dickie commented: "These air fights were very pretty and it was [the] one time our men exposed themselves for they almost crowded the parapet to look. If the Germans had not also been human enough to watch I am afraid I would not be here to tell this story." Initially, the effects of the air war on 26th men were indirect. The main role of aircraft was spotting for the artillery, which increased the effectiveness of German shellfire. Troops also had to take precautions against observation by reconnaissance aircraft. By the end of October 1915, sentries watching for the approach of planes warned the troops to take cover with three or more blasts on a whistle. When the aircraft had passed out of range, a longer blast signalled the "all clear." Increased German air observation also compelled the Canadians to camouflage their entrenchments. By 1916, communication trenches, seen easily from the air, had to be laid out in irregular patterns. As Kempling wrote, these rear lines "wander all over the field before arriving at the front trench. It is not safe for them to be regular or Fritz would find them by aeroplane and blow them to pieces."

Over time, the air threat became more menacing as troops began suffering casualties directly from enemy bombing, although it was generally inaccurate up to mid-1916. On July 19, 1916, Kempling recorded in his diary how, on the previous day, a German plane persisted in scouting over their lines from a great height. "Our anti-aircraft guns got after them, and it was a pretty sight to see the fast graceful looking machine flying swiftly from one cloud bank to another. On every side of it bright flashes would flare out followed by puffs of downy looking smoke which would hang in the air for half an hour afterwards." Early that morning, another plane, flying low, dropped three bombs on their officers' quarters behind the lines, but they failed to explode. The troops welcomed intervention by the Royal Flying Corps, which drove the German airmen back, preventing accurate observation of their positions and disrupting their bombing attacks.

The Effect of Combat on the Troops

Just living in the trenches was dangerous enough, but it fell to the infantry on occasions to leave the safety of their lines and cross no man's land to engage the Germans or defend their own positions against enemy incursions. Combat affected the soldiers in various ways. Many, especially those recently entering the line, had mixed feelings about the prospect of fighting. Shortly after joining the 26th at the front, George Kempling wrote that he felt "a little sick at the stomach at the prospect of a hand to hand fight; and excited too, but I was really hankering for a mix up. I guess it is the old John Bull in a fellow." The act of killing the enemy at close range was a challenge. In a letter to his parents written in December 1915, Private Athanase Poirier (#70265) of Balmoral, in Restigouche County, described killing a German soldier at close range and the complex feelings he experienced, among them pride, fear, religious conviction, and patriotism:

> I have been face to face with some [Germans], and although they are known as good soldiers, I, poor little Canadian recruit, whom, a few months ago, knew nothing but the forest and the farm, came out vanquisher more than once. The first one I met was like a lion; his eyes were like fire, and his face red with rage. He sprang toward me, murmuring something in his language, which I took for oaths. Really, I thought I had taken my last supper. But summoning all my courage and energy, and thinking of our Blessed Mother, our kind and the country which I had come to defend, I took my gun firmly in my hands, and thrusted my bayonet in the heart of that beastly foe. I could feel the steel deep in the human flesh, which concealed the wicked heart of that d____. It was awful. With a deep roar of pain and rage, he fell heavily on the blood-washed ground.

Poirier continued lunging at other Germans until his officer's whistle signalled the end of the fight. He acknowledged that killing at close range

Lieutenant Harry Ferguson, killed by a German sniper on March 15, 1916.

2009.4.2, Restigouche Regional Museum

did not come easily to all soldiers: "Some poor fellows find bayonetting positively beyond their strength."

The casualties sustained by the unit exacted a toll on many soldiers. The loss of junior officers such as Harry Ferguson was keenly felt by the troops—as Lieutenant-Colonel McAvity acknowledged, Ferguson had been a personal friend of many of them. One soldier wrote: "When Lieut. Ferguson was killed it hit the boys pretty hard. That's the roughest part of fighting and I suppose every business has its drawbacks; that's the drawback of soldiering. Ferguson was a hero and gentleman and he never met a man who wasn't his friend afterward." Ironically, Ferguson had written only ten days before his own death that soldiers often became indifferent to death, "and it is a blessing that he can."

The experience of combat and casualties among comrades also affected how the troops viewed the Germans. During the first several months at the front, the Canadians rarely saw their enemy up close. In early spring 1916, however, the British captured a number of Germans, giving Dickie his first look at the enemy. He described his impressions of this encounter: "Prisoners are all kinds but some are very glad to give information in exchange for a cigarette. In case they tell all they know they beg piteously to be sent to the uttermost ends of the earth, to some British colony where they will never see or hear of Germany again. Some are surly, uncommunicative and cannot be bribed to speak. These are what we called 'real Germans.'"

Canadians had conflicting views about their enemies that occurred on at least two levels: pragmatic and ideological. At the pragmatic level of combat, many 26th soldiers respected their adversary's fighting skills. After returning home in November 1916 to recover from serious wounds received in July, Captain George Keefe told the *St. John Standard* that there was no denying the Germans were "wonderful fighters, and they have a splendid method organizing. Although they are not as aggressive as they were during the first year and a half of the war, yet they fight with that same tenacity which characterized their earlier attacks." McAvity spoke similarly about German troops after returning home in July 1916, and cautioned that "the people of Canada should not discount that fact.... They are well trained and fight with great determination."

Later on, however, the Canadians became more callous toward the Germans. In their letters, many 26th soldiers frequently referred to the Germans as barbaric Huns, or Boches, a derisive French term for Germans. Others elaborated on their attitudes by passing on stories about atrocities committed by the Germans during the opening campaign of the war in 1914. In late 1915, Private George F. Rossborough (#69808) of Prince William, New Brunswick, wrote to his mother relating stories he had heard when they were billeted in barns: "Five or six German soldiers violated the 13-year old daughter of the farmer on whose place we are now stopping. She is partly paralyzed and her mind is affected as a result of their brutality.... Another little girl just above here had her fingers and toes cut off by the Germans." Their own experiences often confirmed this outlook. Shortly after entering the trenches for the first time in September 1915, Dickie received his "first taste of the devilishness of the Huns." He recalled that the troops were resting, eating food received from home, and having a "regular old-fashioned sing song with Stokes — formerly of the Imperial [Theatre] orchestra, playing his faithful old flute as accompaniment. We sang through our repertoire, everything from Tipperary to Home Sweet Home and when we nicely started in some hymns the Germans across the way surprised us by joining in. We thought then they weren't such bad fellows after all, but as soon as Stokes got nicely into the strain of God

Save the King, the Boche opened up with shell fire and rifle bullets. They didn't like that tune, but believe me, we rolled it out to the end."

Many Canadians took on hardened attitudes toward the Germans. On Christmas Day 1915, Lieutenant Lockhart described in a letter home how "some of the Germans got bold and thought as it was Christmas they would visit us, etc. A few rounds of shrapnel soon put them under cover again. Personally, I want nothing to do with them, and as for arranging a temporary Armistice, they can count me out. They are not to be trusted, and I don't give them any chance words." Some soldiers wrote about how they were unwilling to take prisoners in the heat of battle. In early February 1916, Private J. Hanford Tait (#69991) of Smith's Creek, in Kings County, wrote about an attack on a German position that was preceded by a heavy artillery barrage: " We could see the poor Germans running everywhere and when we charged there was few left but wounded, and we left none of them; some of them shot our fellows in the back as they went by, and when we were putting them out of their misery they begged for mercy. We found one of our chaps who had been wounded and a wounded German crept up and stuck his bayonet through him. The bayonet was still sticking in our comrade when we found him. These Germans are dirty and don't receive any quarter." Tait concluded by adding that "they had their trenches in great shape and plenty of food but 'no nerve.'"

Although some, like Kempling, respected the Germans as fighters, writing that they were ingenious fellows and that the Canadians had learned many valuable ideas from them, they still had little sympathy for them. In late July 1916, Kempling related how, when two Germans came out into no man's land to give themselves up, one of the 26th men in a listening post killed them both. "This is the price Fritzie pays for treachery for our men are afraid to trust them," was his comment.

The troops also revealed their attitudes toward the enemy through souvenir hunting. Kempling described how, during the Battle of the Somme, "our lads would walk alongside them hollering 'souvenir' in their ears and grab their hats or cut the buttons from their coats. As a rule, the Germans were like frightened sheep and were very passive under this ordeal." They also got souvenirs from German dead. Dickie noted that, one day, he found a dead German outside the parapet who had been there for months: "I got his knife and a German mark for a souvenir." Sergeant John Hodgson (#69373) from Saint John sent his family some souvenirs from Courcelette, including a map showing the scene of the battle: "It is a German map which I found in a German Sergt.-Major's day book; needless to say, he won't want it anymore, as he has gone west." The troops saw these souvenirs as war trophies, often sending them home to their families. In late 1917, Tait sent his wife a box containing pieces of shells, parts of German uniforms, such as shoulder straps, buttons and belt buckles, and different kinds of money. When Lieutenant Arthur Legere returned to New Brunswick in February 1916 to join the 165th (Acadian) Battalion, he placed a number of hand grenades, German shells, and other souvenirs in the window of the Legere Drug Store on Main Street in Moncton, where they attracted much public attention.

Whatever their personal feelings about the Germans, most Canadian soldiers were convinced victory was only a matter of time. Many believed the Germans were in a state of decline, and few doubted they would prevail, although they soon recognized it would take some time to defeat the enemy. This self-confidence was a sign of the high morale of Canadian troops, and was one of their strongest sources of strength needed to cope with the demands of the front lines.

Enduring

Soldiers found various ways to cope with the demanding conditions they faced in the trenches, especially the ever-present threat of death. Some maintained their resilience by developing a positive attitude toward their circumstances, becoming philosophical about their lives at the front and accepting their lot. Charles Lawson wrote that, although conditions got worse during the winter, "still you can always enjoy life if you make up your mind to put up with things as you find them." Others became fatalistic in their outlook. Sergeant Hodgson wrote: "I had a few narrow shaves, but my number was not on any of the shells that Fritzie sent." In early March 1916, RSM Roy Edwards offered a sobering account of the effect the trenches had on these soldiers and how they coped by becoming hardened to their surroundings: "It is grim work out here. In the five months that I have been at the front I have seen awful things. I have seen sights bad enough to make a strong man weep, but over here men soon become philosophers, fatalists if you will. We quickly harden to our work. These awful things that we see become, as it were, a part of our day's routine, and as we go about our duties never knowing who among us will next be called by the steel messengers of death that are forever searching our trenches for victims, each of us is happy in the knowledge that the bullet bearing his number, has not yet come this way."

Some soldiers became superstitious. Frank Lockhart believed he and his men had luck working in their favour, which increased their odds of surviving. On Christmas Day 1915, he reported to his mother that, "[m]y platoon has been singularly lucky, by long odds, the luckiest in the battalion. Had my first man wounded last trip in. He is all so far. The platoon next least has lost eight so you see I'm lucky. There are sixteen platoons — over two hundred casualties, so you can figure out the average for yourself." In another letter written a few weeks later, he returned to this theme: "We sure have been lucky and my platoon the luckiest of all. So far I have had none killed and only three wounded....I hold the battalion record but am not bragging for we sure have good luck." Other soldiers turned to religion for strength. When Kempling went into the line for the first time, he seemed to be "strangely calm and quiet": "On my winding path up here I tried to think how I would feel if I was mortally wounded, and thank God that in spite of my unfaithfulness to him in many things I felt a sincere surety that all would be well. I found myself pointing confidently and expectantly to my Savior. When I felt sure of this I took heart and no longer felt afraid. Praise be to a patient and merciful God for all his goodness."

Comradeship became one of the central supports the soldiers of the 26th drew on to endure the stresses of the front. Often these connections had been made at home before they joined up. Some were linked by family ties: a number of brothers served in the unit, among them James, John, and Joseph McElhiney (#69670, 69626, 69677) from Saint John. Fathers and sons also served together, including Bertram and Douglas Hooper. Others had known each other in civilian life, having grown up in the same community, gone to the same schools and churches, and played sports together.

The troops were accepting of one another, and new troops were often readily welcomed into the platoons. When Private Kempling joined No. 5 Platoon on July 15, 1916, as a reinforcement from the 59th Battalion, he met "a splendid bunch of fellows, very chummy, like a big family of brothers. If anyone gets anything from home it goes around as far as it will." Still, it took a while to fit into the soldiers' life. Kempling noted that, shortly after arriving, he began reading the Bible daily: "The fellows respect me for it. They are a nice bunch...though so many get drunk every night. But I am out of a lot. If a man don't drink, chew, smoke or gamble, he is out of it all apparently."

Moreover, front-line troops understood that not everyone was cut out for duty in the trenches. Sometimes men were given unit jobs behind the lines. Speaking about one of his fellow soldiers, Robert Dickie stated: "Exposure in the trenches was too much for him, but as the man in charge of the bath house, I can tell you he became one of the most popular men in the battalion. We always depended on him to keep our clothes from walking away." This practice of looking out for each other might explain a noticeable trend among the troops where statistically older men suffered far fewer casualties than younger men. Table 2, based on a sample of 608 "original" soldiers of the 26th, shows how the casualty rate steadily declined as the soldiers' age increased. Dickie's observation that some men were given safer "billets" within the unit in the rear or were sent back to base might have applied to older soldiers, who then spent less time in harm's way than their younger comrades and were less likely to become casualties.

Camaraderie was bolstered by pride in the unit, or esprit de corps. Kempling described himself with pride as a Canadian citizen soldier: Although, as he wrote, they did a "bit of grousing because things are not more comfortable...there is a fine material in the Canadian 2nd Division and one doesn't need to look far below the surface to see the

Table 2: Casualty Rates, 26th Battalion, by Age Group

Age Group	Number in Sample	Number of Casualties	Casualty Rate (%)
18 and under	74	52	70.27
19-21	157	110	70.06
22-24	137	88	64.23
25-27	76	49	64.47
28-30	50	28	56.00
31-33	45	19	42.22
34-36	32	11	34.38
37-39	18	2	11.11
40 and over	19	5	26.32
Total	608	364	59.87 (average)

Survey of a sample of original members of the 26th Battalion

Curtis Mainville.

good fighting quality of the Canadian soldier. He is a resourceful, bright and hardy soldier." Most men identified quite closely with their own unit. Many saw the 26th as the best battalion at the front, among them Arthur Legere, who, in February 1916, wrote: "[I]t looks rather funny to have such a statement from me, but when General Watson openly says that the 26th is the best battalion in his division, then it must be true."

Another factor sustaining these soldiers was ongoing connections with home. They spent a lot of time writing and reading letters. This correspondence helped them to stay in touch with the civilian lives to which they hoped to return. They wrote to their parents, brothers and sisters, wives, friends, and, in some cases, children. In February 1916, while recovering from a wound in hospital, Private Tait wrote to his young son Ora: "Got your letter OK, write again soon and be good to Mum, Nora, and little Hanford. I suppose you are a big man now, and I suppose you will soon be over here to take Dada's place. I expect to get out of hospital soon and return to the trenches we call 'Don't know where.' Be a good boy and kiss Mum, Norah, and little Hanford for me."

Soldiers often asked relatives to write as often as possible, and they

NOTHING is to be written on this side except the date and signature of the sender. Sentences not required may be erased. If anything else is added the post card will be destroyed.

I am quite well.

~~I have been admitted into hospital~~
~~{ sick }~~ ~~and am going on well.~~
~~{ wounded }~~ ~~and hope to be discharged soon~~

~~I am being sent down to the base.~~

~~I have received your~~ ~~{ letter dated _____~~
~~{ telegram ,, _____~~
~~{ parcel ,, _____~~

Letter follows at first opportunity.

~~I have received no letter from you~~
~~{ lately.~~
~~{ for a long time.~~

Signature only. } *C.M. Lawson*

Date *Nov. 15/15*

[Postage must be prepaid on any letter or post card addressed to the sender of this card.]

(B12220)—Wt. W 3497/293—1000m.—9/15. S. & S., Ltd.

Field service postcard sent by Lieutenant Charles Lawson, November 15, 1915.

Lawson JI- F-35-10 (back) New Brunswick Museum

eagerly anticipated letters, packages, and family photographs that looked "like old times." Harry Ferguson recorded that "letters form our only connecting link with home and we like to make the most of them. But at this game, none of us can receive too many letters." Families were just as anxious to receive details about conditions at the front, and the wait could be agonizing. Soldiers asked loved ones to be patient, as it took at least a month from the time a letter was written until they got a reply. The letters tended to become shorter and more matter-of-fact once the troops went over to France. Regulations prevented them from saying where they were or details about what they were doing. Also, soldiers' letters were censored by their platoon commander, which might have deterred them from writing about more intimate details. Even the officers' letters were subject to censorship, much to their exasperation. Later on, in October 1917, Graham McKnight informed his mother that "it makes me mad to think that I have so much to tell you about, could fill several pages, but it's all restricted so might just as well carry on without growling." The increasing pace of operations also prevented soldiers from writing more often. Instead, they sent field service postcards, known to the troops as "whiz bangs," to let their families know they were still alive.

Sometimes the soldiers were not very forthcoming about the realities they faced. Charles Lawson was slow to reply to his younger sister Jessie's request for more details about the trenches. Perhaps hoping to allay her fears, he wrote that it was difficult to explain what things were really like. Instead, he offered that "[i]t is very different from what anyone who has not been actually in it would think. No one who has not been here can have any idea what this war is like, it is so different from any previous wars." He did ask Jessie to keep their mother cheered up, advising her that "things here are not half so bad as they are represented. In fact men who have been in the trenches complain at being brought back to billets, which they claim are not half so comfortable." Before leaving Britain for the front, he once more urged his mother not to worry about him: "I calculate that there is an even chance in this and that is about all there is in ordinary life." And once he reached France, he cautioned: "[N]ow just because we are in France I don't want you to be worrying about me. I am well able to take my chance with the rest of them and shall come through all right. Above all do not listen to all the fool yarns they tell over there about what is going on." He was more forthcoming with his mother about how long the war might last. On August 3, 1915, he wrote: "Don't pay any attention to these stories that the Germans can't hold out very long. The prospects are that this is going to be a long war, and England is going about it on that basis. There is not suggestion over here that [Germany] is near the end of her tether."

The troops received other forms of support from home that kept up their spirits, including "comforts" from both family and the numerous women's comfort associations that organized in communities around the province. Their parcels frequently included cold-weather clothing, such as heavy socks and hooded balaclavas, cake and candy, and local newspapers. Harry Ferguson wrote that these newspapers made "one feel a little bit nearer." The troops also appreciated receiving cigarettes and cigars. McKnight wrote to his mother thanking her for a package of cigarettes: "I don't smoke much. I don't know what we would do if we didn't have something to smoke while in the line; they are a soldier's best friend." Supporters at home found many other ways to show their appreciation. Charles Lawson received a sweater coat from his fellow teachers at Saint John High School, and the school continued to pay his salary while he was overseas. Each year New Brunswickers raised funds to ensure that the troops had special dinners at Christmas. Frequently, the soldiers wrote to their supporters, thanking them for their generosity and expressing how important these acts of kindness were in keeping up their morale.

Maintaining contact with home was aided by different agencies overseas. Among them was New Brunswick's agent general in London, Frederick W. Sumner, a prominent Moncton politician and hardware merchant who was recruiting officer for Westmorland and Albert Counties early in the war. Later, he spent three years overseas assisting local soldiers. Sumner wrote to all wounded soldiers from the province and visited those in hospitals in Britain, bringing them books to read. He also wrote their families back home, notifying them about their loved ones' hospitalization and sometimes forwarding letters from the soldiers. He sent lists of these wounded soldiers to local newspapers for publication. His office on Southampton Road in London also provided a location for soldiers away from the unit to pick up their mail from home. Soldiers from the 26th greatly appreciated Sumner's efforts, writing letters of thanks that were frequently published in the Moncton papers.

The soldiers also kept their connection with home alive by visiting those they had known before the war in nearby units and in the same camps. Lawson wrote about meeting an old friend who dropped by to visit while he was in billets: "We had quite a chat, and I was certainly glad to see him. It reminded me of [Saint John High School] again."

In some cases, family joined the soldiers overseas, especially mothers and wives who travelled to Britain to be with their sons and husbands. Private W. Henry (Harry) Lingley (#69514) was born in Saint John, where he was living with his wife Margaret when war was declared. On November 23, 1915, Lingley was wounded at the front, and returned to Britain for hospitalization. In May 1916, Margaret joined him at Folkestone, where he was performing light duties while recovering from his wounds. On the evening of May 25, 1917, they jointly experienced the direct effects of the war when twenty-one German Gotha bombers attacked the area, including Folkestone, a main embarkation port. The raid lasted about fifteen minutes, during which seventy-one people were killed and ninety-six wounded, making it one of the largest German air raids to date.[8] According to Margaret, the losses were high because it took place on a Friday, payday, and the streets were crowded with shoppers, who were so caught by surprise by the attack that they were unable to take shelter. The Lingleys had a narrow escape when a bomb exploded less than three metres away, the concussion throwing Harry to the ground and covering Margaret with mud. She also reported that some of the victims were literally blown to pieces by the explosion. This was not her last brush with the enemy, however: during her return home a few months later, her ship was chased briefly by a German submarine.

---

8   The Germans also struck nearby Camp Shorncliffe, inflicting over one hundred casualties, mostly to Canadian soldiers.

The army also took steps to bolster the soldiers' morale and resilience when they were in rest billets in the rear. There, life took on a more comfortable routine: about six days' rest, a hot meal, sleep in a tent, barn, or house, and a bath and change of clothes. In late October 1915, Lawson wrote: "I have had the greatest pleasure this morning I have had for a long time — a fine hot bath in a regular good bath tub. We are able to have one for a franc in a convent a short distance from billets and it is a great comfort. It was the first really satisfactory bath I have had since leaving home." Men also got new underwear and a chance to change and wash their clothes. On October 30, 1915, Fred Howard noted that, while in billets, he washed some socks and towels, and that night, while lying on the floor of a barn, he slept with his pants off for the first time since leaving England six weeks earlier.

The troops got paid once a month, receiving forty French francs, about four dollars, which allowed them to buy extras such as chocolate, apples, canned goods, and postcards, or have supper in nearby towns. With money in their pockets, soldiers also enjoyed visiting *estaminets* — small restaurants run by local families in their homes. In early February 1916, Signaller William Swetka described an *estaminet* he frequented in Belgium: "We are sitting in a sort of restaurant or lunch room, just after having some porridge.... The people who keep this place are very nice and sell excellent pastry, put up fine dinners, etc. of pork steak, potatoes, onions, etc. coffee, tea and cocoa. When we are out of the trenches we often drop in here to have some pastry and cocoa." The Belgian owners had lived in a house just behind the lines until it was hit by a German shell; they then moved farther to the rear and set up their room. "They all speak English fairly well, enough to understand practically all they say." Soldiers' clubs were also set up behind the lines, where they could get good suppers. Graham McKnight described one such meal of oysters, hors d'oeuvres, soup, beef, cauliflower, potatoes, peaches and cream fruit, biscuits, and cheese: "Didn't I fill up! Talk about war, this is the best one I was ever in!" he commented.

During these rest periods, troops spent as much time as they could between fatigue duties relaxing and amusing themselves. Gambling was popular, especially pitching pennies, and playing Crown and Anchor and

Gravesite of men of the 26th, La Laiterie Cemetery,
near Kemmel, Belgium. Harold Wright collection

Banker Poker. Soldiers patronized the YMCA tents set up in most rest areas, sometimes attending the nightly ten-minute-long religious services that featured three or four songs, a short Bible reading, and a closing prayer. Troops often went to films shown in camp. Charlie Chaplin's films about "The Little Tramp" were particularly popular among the soldiers. Entertainment troupes also offered diversion with their vaudeville shows. According to George Kempling, "the value of such [entertainment] is incalculable, as it helps to keep the soldiers happy and bright."

Sports were an important part of the Canadian soldiers' life behind the lines. Lieutenant McKnight, who played baseball and competed in track and field events, was impressed by how sports went on no matter where they were. In September 1917, he marvelled at how they laid out a ball diamond to play on in a field filled with shell holes. Baseball was a favourite pastime among Canadian soldiers during the Great War. The 26th Battalion formed a team while still in Saint John, which continued to play in France and Belgium during rest periods, allowing the troops to escape momentarily the rigours of the front lines. Both officers and other ranks fielded teams. The 26th's regimental team was highly successful, winning the 2nd Canadian Divisional championship in June 1918 and awarded the Haldane Cup. Signaller Swetka captured the soldiers' pride in their team. In mid-June, he wrote: "We are still having glorious weather and lots of baseball is going on everywhere there are colonials. Our baseball team play day after tomorrow for the divisional championship. It is sure some team and we are backing it to win.... We were in the front line trenches when our team played last game and we received the score over the phone. What do you know about that? The best of it was as each inning's result came through it put our team in the lead as a rule.... Some excitement, even more than if we had taken Heine's front line." Later, they competed in the Canadian Corps championship, but were narrowly defeated by a team from 1st Canadian Division.

Perhaps the greatest test facing these soldiers was finding ways to cope with the deaths of their comrades. Many dealt with these losses through acts of remembrance. Early on, the focus of their remembrance was a section of La Laiterie Cemetery, located about a kilometre behind the front trenches on the road between Kemmel and Vierstraat. The area surrounding the cemetery had once featured groves of trees and fine residences, but since had been blasted by shellfire. Within the cemetery, a section was set aside for the burial of fallen 26th soldiers, and was marked by a large board bearing the battalion's name. In October 1915, Harry Ferguson described the cemetery to the parents of Private Almon Savidant, who had been buried there a few weeks earlier: "The graves are laid out in even rows, each man buried singly. The graves are all neatly sodded with fresh green sods and at the head of each a uniform cross standing about three feet high, upon which is nailed an aluminum metal plate with the name, number and battalion of the one who has made the last great sacrifice and now lies buried beneath." Within the 26th's section was a double row of small white crosses at the head of each burial mound. Sixty-seven members of the battalion were buried there, beginning with the first 26th soldier to die in action, Private Moses Gallant on September 28. To ensure that the identity of the soldier in the grave was not lost if something happened to the cross, the man's name was inserted into bottles that were placed at the head of the grave and beneath the body. On either side of the rows of graves were neat concrete walkways constructed by members of the unit. Soldiers sometimes placed wreaths and flowers on the graves of their friends. While the 26th continued to serve on this front, every time the men entered and left the trenches they passed the cemetery and remembered their fallen comrades.

Funeral services would be conducted by the chaplain or, if he was unavailable, the colonel. During the first year at the front, the unit covered the bodies of their dead with a Union Jack that originally flew over a store on King Street in Saint John. It was taken by two members from the battalion during their march to the harbour on June 12, 1915, and carried to Britain and then to Belgium, where it was used during Private Gallant's burial. In time, the flag took on great meaning for the unit; in the words of a somewhat overdrawn article that appeared in the *Daily Telegraph* on September 25, 1915, "it became a thing of great worth. Revered by the most thoughtless in the battalion. A mark of honor it was to every man who fell. It represented the dignity and sorrow of a nation and the more intimate mourning of gallant comrades." Colonel McAvity brought it to Saint John in June 1916, where it was used on the coffins of 26th men who died after returning home. The first occasion was the funeral of Private George R. North (#69724) on December 20, 1916, at St. Peters Church.

Some funeral services were large and elaborate. On March 20, 1916, Major W.H. Belyea, the battalion's acting second-in-command, was mortally wounded by a high-explosive shell that detonated in a communication trench he was using to go forward to inspect the troops. The next day, he was buried in the churchyard cemetery at Locre in a funeral that was attended by more than one hundred officers, including the corps, division, and brigade commanders Generals Alderson, Turner, and Watson. According to Robert Dickie, Belyea was buried in full uniform with his army boots, "as a good soldier should rest.... Lieutenant Knowlton made a trip down the line for black cloth to drape the coffin

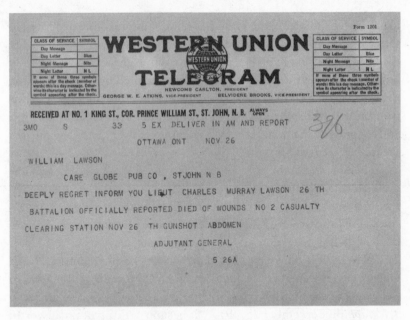

Telegram to William Lawson informing him of the death of his son, Lieutenant Charles Lawson. Lawson, JI- F37-49 New Brunswick Museum

and nothing was left undone to pay honor to the fallen officer." The regimental band led the procession; next came the coffin, carried on a General Service wagon; followed by Kenneth Christie, Belyea's nephew, leading the major's horse; and then the rest of the procession. During the service, the Last Post was sounded, and each officer stepped forward to salute the grave as the band played "Abide With Me."

Troops continued to look out for one another, even in death. Despite official and self-censorship, the soldiers' families could not be completely shielded from the awful effects of the war, especially when a loved one was killed in action or died of wounds. Families learned about the deaths of their loved ones in different ways. The earliest notification likely came through a telegram from the adjutant general in Ottawa. For example, on November 26, 1915, William Lawson, father of Lieutenant Charles Lawson, received a telegram that his son was officially reported as having died of wounds in No. 2 Casualty Clearing Station on November 26 from a gunshot wound to the abdomen. As well, troops often wrote letters to the families of fellow soldiers who had died. Sharing their stories with these loved ones back home had a cathartic effect on the soldiers. When they reached France, some soldiers agreed to write to each other's friends in the event of their death or serious wounds. In the case of Private Gordon Morrell (#69550), who was killed on January 21, 1916, two friends wrote to a woman from Hatfield's Point, in Kings County, in mid-February providing details of Morrell's death from a stray bullet while doing sentry duty near the front line. They informed her that they had distributed the contents of two parcels received after Morrell's death to his closest friends "in the way he would have liked." They also enclosed a ring that he always wore which had her initials on it: "We don't know whether this would be your wish or not but thought we would forward it." They closed by writing, "the whole platoon to a man wish us to send you their deepest sympathy." In one case, the friend relaying the sad news about his fellow-soldier's death was the loved one's brother. On October 15, 1915, Private Charles J. McFee (#69701) was killed in action. A half-finished letter addressed to Miss Etta Stevens of Hartland was found in his pocket. The letter was given to Etta's brother, Private Roy L. Stevens (#69862), one of McFee's comrades, to forward to his sister. McFee might have met Etta through her brother before the war when McFee and Stevens both served in the 67th Regiment "Carleton Light Infantry."

Frequently, commanding officers of deceased soldiers wrote letters of condolence to the family, as did comrades. These letters sometimes contained detailed descriptions of the deaths of loved ones, and offered words to console the families. The Anderson family in St. Stephen received a lengthy letter about the death of Sergeant Angus R. Anderson (#69021), an original member of the battalion who was killed at Hill 70 on August 15, 1917, from a comrade from his platoon, Private Benjamin Gaskill. In a letter addressed to Angus's brother Ross, at home recovering from wounds received in France, and published in the *St. Croix Courier* on August 27, Gaskill extended "the sympathy of those of us who are left" to the family. He related how it seemed hard, after being at the front for nearly two years, enduring hardship, "to meet with death now." He assured the family "that

Angus died a noble, heroic death and the words of the gospel come to us clearly: 'Greater love hath no man than this, that he lay down his life for his friends.'" He went on to describe at length how, during very heavy fighting, Angus was killed when a sniper's bullet struck him just above the heart. "He lived only a short time, but was conscious until the end, but did not suffer. He knew all until the end." He then related how the "boys of No. 1 Platoon buried him and his grave is marked by a wooden cross." Unfortunately, Anderson's grave must have been lost subsequently, as his name appears on the Vimy Memorial among the missing who have no known grave.

Finally, some soldiers of the 26th remembered their fallen comrades in verse. Throughout the war, they wrote numerous poems, many of which were printed in local newspapers. An unnamed member responded to a negative newspaper article about soldiers who enlisted by composing a defiant poem entitled "The Common Boys," inspired by the memory of two friends who died during the Crater fight. Sergeant Orlin A. Reid (#69838) submitted it to the *St. John Standard*, which published it on December 9, 1915:

> They came from farthest East and West,
> Cape Race to Nootka Sound,
> They left their homes at duty call
> To fight on foreign ground.
>
> They're of English, Scotch and Irish blood,
> But all of them were game;
> All were whelps of the Lion
> British in more than name.
>
> Some still do their duty.
> Some died neath a foreign sky;
> And here's to each and all of them
> Come raise your glasses high.

And drink to those boys; those Common Boys,
Those boys you didn't know,
Who answered to the Lion's call
Who face the common foe.
They fight for you, are facing death
On Belgium's grave strewn soil,
When you slight their fallen comrades
Must not their hearts blood boil.

During the first year on the Western Front, the routine of service in the trenches followed by periods of rest continued without much variation. By mid-1916, however, the pattern began to change as the 26th left the trenches behind and began preparing for its first major offensive on the Somme. Here, the men of the 26th would face a new set of challenges.

Chapter Four

Into Battle: The Somme and Vimy Ridge

It was on the 15th of September, Sir,
Yes, I remember it quite well;
When the gallant boys from Canada
Charged the Huns, like very hell.
The sight of that fight was glorious,
And I never shall forget
How Jack Canuck smashed old Fritz
When we captured Courcelette.[9]

In early September 1916, the 26th Battalion moved south to the Somme front in France. The upcoming battle would mark a major change in the men's experience of the war. As Private Robert Dickie reflected, apart from the Crater fight, most soldiers of the 26th had never seen any Germans, alive or dead. Nor had they known what it was to advance, "to charge with the bayonet or repel a sustained attack from the enemy. There we were, month after month, doing our bit holding our ground, seeing our men fall on every side but not knowing what damage we might be doing to the enemy." The Somme offensive, however, would bring the New Brunswickers face to face with the enemy and high-intensity combat.

In early August 1916, the battalion was still in the Ypres sector, manning trenches on the St. Eloi front. After being relieved on the eighth, they were inspected by General R.E.W. Turner, the divisional commander, and by Brigadier-General A.H. Macdonell, commander of 5th Brigade. Then, on the fourteenth, they received a surprise visit from King George V, eleven months after he had reviewed them in Britain. The King was accompanied by the

---

9   First stanza of the poem, "Courcelette," written by Philip S. George Horne (#444380) of the 26th, in hospital on September 19, 1916. The remainder of the poem is in the Appendix.

Prince of Wales and General Sir Herbert Plumer, 2nd Army commander. Having been selected as the Canadians to be inspected by the King, the men of the 26th were directed to carry on with their usual work and do nothing special. But it was hardly an ordinary day. Waiting for the royal entourage at the corner of the training field were Lieutenant-General Sir Julian Byng, the Canadian Corps commander, the three divisional commanders, Generals Currie, Turner, and Lipsett, and their staffs. According to Lieutenant-Colonel McKenzie's lively report, "for many minutes before our Royal Visitor arrived our boys were the object of many expert and critical glances. They were also the object of many comments from this brilliant gathering and some of these remarks were overheard, and they were flattering indeed." Once the royal party reached the battalion's lines, McKenzie accompanied the assemblage through the men's huts and then they watched the men drill on the parade ground. Contrary to orders, the men stopped briefly to cheer the King, and then got back to work. McKenzie wrote: "[W]hat His Majesty saw, was as fine a lot of brawn and brains as ever made up a British Regiment, saw some of them practicing the handling of those great little Lewis Guns, some looking like goblins in their grey masks were doing bayonet fighting, others practiced rapid loading and unloading their rifles and a dozen other things that are all part of the day's work for modern infantry. He saw them put that swing, that snap, and ginger into their drills that they have so consistently put forth against the Bosch, the stuff that has earned for them the name of 'The Fighting 26th.'" The war diary recorded: "Although the visit was short, yet it was a Red Letter Day in the History of the Battalion."

After a brief sojourn in the line that included instructing the 87th Battalion, from the new 4th Canadian Division, the battalion got ready to move to the training area near St. Omer in preparation for the Somme offensive. The war diary noted that "all ranks in the best of spirits and eager to effect all details in the number of days training [for] SOMME OPERATIONS."

Preparing for the Somme
The battalion had changed considerably since it arrived on the Western Front almost a year earlier. Surviving "originals" began noticing how their

numbers were dwindling. As early as the end of February, Lieutenant Arthur Legere noted that they had lost 350 men from all causes since arriving. In a letter published in the *Daily Telegraph* on May 1, 1916, Lieutenant William McFarlane of St. Stephen, an original who commanded No. 9 Platoon in C Company until he underwent surgery for appendicitis and was subsequently transferred to a pioneer battalion, described visiting the 26th, including his old platoon, "or at least what is left of them." He noted that Lieutenant Winter was the only original C Company officer left and that the battalion as a whole had had nearly five hundred casualties. In late June, Private Fred Woodbury noted that only about two hundred originals were left. He commented: "I do not think the citizens will see the old 26th march through the streets, as we are another personnel now." By the beginning of August, Private Albert Ashford (#69006) of Fredericton believed that only 180 members of the original battalion remained.

Reinforcements filled the diminished ranks. Many were from outside of New Brunswick, including drafts from the 35th, 39th, and 59th Battalions from Ontario and Quebec and from the 40th Battalion from Nova Scotia. Battalions raised in New Brunswick, including the 55th and 64th, also sent men in the days before the move south. (The subject of reinforcements is examined in greater depth in Chapter Six.) Fighting on the Somme would complete the demise of the original 26th.

On August 26, 1916, the battalion began marching west to prepare for operations. The war diary recorded that the "physical condition of all ranks found to be exceptional after long Trench Fighting and the morale of the troops excellent." They reached their battalion billets near St. Omer on the twenty-eighth, and the next day began six days of training, although heavy rain made it difficult. Private George Kempling described their experience on the twenty-ninth:

> Well, we practiced open order work, going ahead in short spurts and flopping quickly in the mud, then getting up quickly, running a few yards and dropping again behind any cover you could get. This is all practice for the open fighting we are to have down on the Somme. The British are slowly

pushing forward, and this means a lot of hand to hand fighting and fighting in rushes. We were to have practiced until 4 pm but it rained so hard we left at 3. On the way home it didn't rain, it poured. We were soaked through till our clothes squeaked all over. The bully beef hash we had for supper put some life into us but many of the boys had no sleep because they were cold and wet. This is one of those times that a drink of rum is a God-send.

On August 30, the battalion exchanged its Ross rifles for the British Short Magazine Lee-Enfield. According to Kempling, the Canadians welcomed this change, as the Ross was "an unnecessarily clumsy and heavy rifle," while the Lee-Enfield was shorter, even with its longer bayonet. It also did not jam as easily. Over the next few days, they learned how to load and fire the new rifle and adjust its sights, and then practised on the range wearing both helmets and gas masks.

On September 1, the 26th began three days of training in semi-open warfare under conditions based on reports on operations on the Somme. According to Kempling, the officers warned the troops that "the Somme was likely to be rough and hard. No regular trenches but live for a while in shell holes, ditches, at any place we could find, so we are expecting to have some genuine times." He proved to be a keen observer. This new, open-order fighting meant greater responsibility for junior leaders, so casualties were simulated by having platoon and section commanders fall out of the training and their next-in-command take charge: "This took place simultaneously in several positions both in major and minor positions. We practiced the company formation—two platoons in line, with fixed bayonets, with bombers on both flanks and a couple of Lewis gun crews in front a little. The third platoon supported and besides carried picks, shovels, and sandbags. The fourth platoon was in reserve. Every man in the company is made conversant with the immediate plan of battle and [location of] the battalion and brigade headquarters. This is important for if an attack is broken up, or men separated, a man will be more certain of finding his way back."

On September 4, they began moving to the Somme, initially by rail and then on foot. The long march tested the troops' resilience. The weather turned so hot that, according to Kempling, "our feet were either scalded or badly blistered. Some of the fellows have chafed badly. So some of us went bare foot for the dinner hour." On the seventh, they marched thirteen kilometres, a short distance, Kempling believed, compared with what they had covered in Canada. He was beginning to recognize the increased demands active service conditions placed on them, especially now that they had left the trenches behind: "The life we live, the thin rations, the heavy loads we carry makes the difference. The rations are regular army rations, but they seem inadequate to a citizen soldier. It will not be so bad when we get used to the change." By the time the movement ended on September 10, he admitted that the march had "toughened us up fine."

Some grew thoughtful about what the coming battle would mean for them, especially the numerous reinforcements like Kempling, who had yet to participate in intense combat. On the sixth, he wrote: "I guess we will soon be in the thick of it. Well let it come. I am prepared to meet whatever comes." The next night, as he lay in a field where they had bivouacked listening "to the steady thunder of the British heavies," he grew more

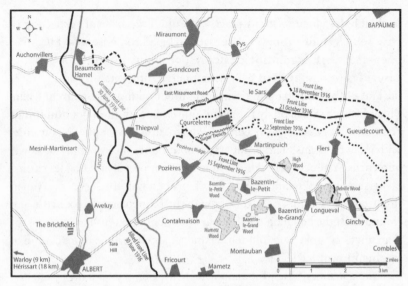

Map 2: The Somme Battlefield. Mike Bechthold

contemplative: "[I]t was but natural that our thoughts sent a silent prayer, formless but urgent [it] rose to God. For we well knew [what] that thunder meant [for] thousands of brave fellows on either side; and well we knew that before many hours we expected to be in some corner of this terrible hell." Then, on September 9, as they neared the end of their approach march, he wrote that "the troops are in very high spirits at the thought of a scrap with Fritzie." They also began hearing stories from men returning from the front about the early success of the Canadians, which further buoyed their confidence. Kempling wrote on the tenth that they said "we are putting over 50 shells to Fritzie's one. Against this the Germans can't possibly hold any position." He also noted on the same day that they were told each division would enter into the fight twice and then be relieved for the winter and sent back to the Ypres front. Of this he was less confident, writing that, "as orders changed overnight, we put no credence in this story." Events soon proved the orders were correct, except in their ultimate destination.

On September 11, the battalion reached billets at the Brickfields, a large, sprawling camp, and entered into corps reserve. Between the eleventh and thirteenth, the 26th provided working parties to lay cable in the front line at Pozières. Then, on the fourteenth, they took part in a brigade manoeuvre practising communicating by signalling between aircraft and troops in forward positions. The next day, they entered the battle.

The Somme offensive had begun on July 1 with a disastrous attack in which fifty-six thousand men had become casualties, the worst single day in the history of the British Army. But the battle continued and by early September the British had pushed forward about five kilometres across the crest of the Pozières Ridge toward the third German line. A major advance was planned for September 15 by the British Fourth and Reserve Armies. The Canadians would mount an attack to protect the left of 4th Army around the village of Courcelette, with 2nd Canadian Division providing the main effort while 3rd Canadian Division protected its flank to the west.

Kempling was detached from the battalion on the twelfth to work with the divisional ammunition column behind the front lines, and had a chance to survey the battlefield where the 26th would begin its attack. On September 13, he wrote in his diary:

> I can by stepping out of any dugout face a living panorama not equalled in reality by moving pictures. I stand with my face to the German line. Behind my right shoulder is the much battered city of Albert.... Pozieres is on my left front, won at such great cost by the gallant Australians and away off on the left and north is the strongly German held town of Thiepval. There is a terrific bombardment taking place. All around me is high rolling country. Our front line at last victoriously straddling the highest ridge, is hidden by another ridge, a few hundred yards in front. These different named towns are all hidden in folds in the ground though all near at hand. There is a regular thunder of British shells screaming overhead, and just in front, the ground is constantly torn up by huge German shells, persistently nosing out our batteries.

Courcelette: "A Wonderful Feat of Arms"

On September 15, one year after arriving on the Western Front, the 26th Battalion fought its first major battle. Starting at 6:20 a.m., 4th and 6th Brigades carried out the initial attack aimed at capturing the German front trenches (named Sugar and Candy) and the Sugar Refinery defending the approaches to the village of Courcelette. 5th Brigade was held in divisional reserve far to the rear, ready to move forward against Courcelette and beyond if the opportunity arose. By 7:30 the walking wounded passing through the rearward areas reported that the initial attack had taken its objectives. During the early morning, 5th Brigade received a warning order that it would likely attack during the day. In the afternoon events began to move quickly. At 1:15 p.m. an attack was ordered for 6:00, later changed to 6:15. The brigade would advance with the 22nd and 25th Battalions in the front wave, followed by the 26th, which would act as the mopping-up party, clearing the village and sending back German prisoners. The 24th was in brigade reserve. The advance would be covered by an artillery barrage established on the southern edge of the village. At zero hour, it would lift at a rate of 50 yards per minute to a final barrage line 300 yards beyond the village. Getting the units into position and the attack organized in such a short period was a major accomplishment for the corps.

The 26th pushed forward to its assembly area about 2.3 kilometres south of Courcelette on the near slope of Pozières Ridge. Here they formed up in two waves, with A and D Companies (from right to left) up front, and about 140 metres back C and B Companies, as well as the Headquarters party, including Colonel McKenzie and his battle staff, and the machine gun, bombing, scout, and signals sections. The two right-hand companies (A and C) would follow the 22nd Battalion forward through the eastern section of the village, while D and B Companies on the left would support the 25th in the western half of Courcelette. A portion of the 26th, including the second-in-command, Major Brown, two of the company commanders (Majors Charles Fairweather and Charles Leonard), and the assistant adjutant (Captain Harold Wood), as well as a percentage of the NCOs, specialists, and men, remained at the wagon lines in the rear to help rebuild the battalion in the event of serious casualties.

At 5:00 p.m. 5th Brigade advanced on a wide front across the crest of the ridge and down the slope to their jumping-off line at Sugar Trench, where the men prepared for the final attack on Courcelette. They quickly learned that the German artillery was still very active. McKenzie later wrote to Colonel McAvity describing how the brigade formed up in the open under shellfire, "the worst we have ever seen.... It was like a parade movement on Manchester's field, only we had no shells there and we had no waving swords here." He noted how a German balloon hovered in front of them, "looking us in the face and no doubt directing the artillery fire." Once the battalion reached Sugar Trench, the companies changed into open formation and at 6:15 p.m. pushed off toward the village under intense enemy artillery fire. The German bombardment inflicted heavy casualties on the lines of troops advancing in the open. In a letter written in September 1917, Private Thomas MacCallum (#69630) of Matapédia, Quebec, described the effects of being blown up by a near miss.

> A big shell landed about eight feet in front of me, and when I was right on top of it, up it went and I went with it, about forty feet in the air. I thought I must be killed, but when I saw that I wasn't I thought I was wounded anyway, but I gave myself a shake and after a little of the daze worked off, I saw that I wasn't hit at all. I looked ahead and my comrades were still going on, so I ran and caught up with them. I lost my rifle when I went up in the air, but as soon as the next man fell, I had another one. Even then, with all the horrors that was going on around me, after I came to my senses a little, I couldn't help but laugh to think what a narrow shave I had.

Major Percy McAvity, commanding B Company in the second line on the left, was wounded as soon as the attack began. A recent arrival from the 55th Battalion, Captain Clarence E. Williams from Centreville, New Brunswick, serving with C Company, was struck by a shell and killed instantly. CSM J. Wallace Corey (#69124) of D Company left a detailed account of his part in the attack. A farmer from Cherryvale, in Queens County, Corey had enlisted

Company Sergeant Major J. Wallace Corey, seriously wounded at Courcelette, September 15, 1916.

Author's collection

in the 26th on November 10, 1914, having served with the 28th "New Brunswick" Dragoons for three years before the war. The twenty-two-year old was a sergeant in April 1915, company sergeant major in March 1916, and warrant officer class II in June. He described the long advance under German artillery fire: "A shell would strike in our ranks and a dozen poor chaps would lay groaning but we could give them no aid as it was against orders to fall out to help the wounded....At last we got within three hundred yards of our objective—the town. Then the enemy opened fire with machine guns and rifles. Our men fell fast but we soon reached the first German trench and then our bayonets ran red in the sunset of that wild September day—for there were many dead comrades to be avenged."

Shortly afterwards, Corey was hit in both legs by bullets and fell head-long into a shell hole, bleeding badly. He passed out, and when he came to, he crawled about 500 metres to the rear, looking for shelter. "With the coming of daylight I became delirious and wandered around feeling the clammy faces of the dead, seeking to find the Red Cross men to bind up my wounds. I believe there were thousands of dead British and Germans at this spot—trenches and shell holes full of them." After lying wounded on the battlefield for three days and nights, he was finally found by French Red Cross stretcher bearers, who carried him to the rear, but not before he was hit again in the back. He was transferred by stages to Boulogne, then to hospital in England.

Private Henry G. Gibson (#69331) also made the long advance. A Scot from Glasgow who moved to Saint John, where he was a labourer, Gibson had already served in the Scottish Rifles for nine years and the 62nd Regiment for another two years. He described the beginning of the attack: "It was a terrible experience standing waiting for the word to go, but we were quite calm and were quite cheery. We had about a mile of open country to get to our objective, but we got there; it was like going through hell's fire but we did not flinch." As the unit reached Courcelette, Gibson was hit in the left leg by a piece of shrapnel, taking "the fight out of me." He got into a trench and "dug myself in with an entrenching tool before my leg got stiff." A stretcher bearer dressed his wound, and he lay there until just before daybreak, when he struggled back to a dressing station where he was "fixed up" and sent to the rear.

Soldiers continued to be wounded by German artillery fire once they reached Courcelette. In a letter written to his sister from hospital after the battle, Corporal Ross Anderson (#369008) of St. Stephen described how shrapnel fractured his jaw and struck his hand and side as he was taking the village:

> I fell into a shell hole and laid there all night. I did up my
> wounds as best I could. The next morning I crawled into an
> old trench. I was so bewildered and weak I didn't know it
> was a German trench. By the way our shells were bursting
> I soon discovered that I had turned about, but about twelve
> o'clock on the 16th the [24th] Battalion charged and took
> the trenches and they found me there. I was just dying for a
> drink and when they saw me I was a fright. They gave me
> water and showed me where our own battalion was. The
> water relieved me and I managed to get down to our machine
> gun section. They got a stretcher bearer who bandaged me
> up and took me to the dressing station

The ruins of Courcelette. PA-000710, Library and Archives Canada

Eventually, he made his way back to a field ambulance outside Albert, and from there back to England.

After the 22nd and 25th Battalions moved through Courcelette and beyond, the 26th entered and began mopping up. The area was a nest of dugouts and concealed machine-gun pits, still full of isolated parties of Germans. In some cases they were men who had surrendered to the first wave of Canadian attackers, hidden, and then resumed the fight. The 26th soldiers began clearing the Germans out from their dugouts, putting their machine guns out of action, and silencing their snipers. Here the skills they had developed in trench warfare, especially minor operations such as raids, were likely more useful to them than the pre-battle training they had received in open warfare. The work took all night to complete.

The troops were impressed by the deep German dugouts. "I was in some of the dugouts forty feet below ground," Sergeant John Hodgson wrote. "They are boarded all around and wall papered, electric lights, chairs, tables, feather beds and everything up to date. They get plenty to eat and drink." They were less impressed by the Germans they captured. Indeed, some Canadian soldiers expressed a robust self-confidence in their military prowess, and remarked on how quickly the German defenders gave up. Hodgson recounted how "Fritz has not got the heart to face the bayonet and they surrendered in dozens. 'Mercy Kamerad' is all you can hear when you get up to them. What makes me laugh is they are big men, and it is amusing to see them surrender to a little man. It is their artillery or machine guns that do the damage to our boys. If they had to meet us in the open the war would soon be over." Colonel McKenzie also noted that "they came out of dugouts like flies to surrender." Some soldiers claimed they did not take many prisoners. Sergeant John D. Giggey (#69320) of Saint John, who took charge of his platoon after his officer was lost during the advance, noted that the Canadians, who were greatly angered by the loss of so many comrades, "didn't spare anyone that trip." The numbers, however, told a different story: according to McKenzie, "we did it in good shape and bagged between 500 and 600 prisoners. (We are officially credited with 600 prisoners: more than our whole strength)."

The capture and consolidation of Courcelette had been a major victory for the corps, albeit a costly one. Afterwards, A and C Companies occupied trenches on the right of the village, while D and B took up positions in the village and to the south. The 26th remained in the line until the eighteenth. On the sixteenth, B Company shifted to the right, and on both the sixteenth and seventeenth the battalion was heavily shelled, especially on the seventeenth, when the 24th Battalion attacked on the right. On both days the 26th also had to repel German counterattacks. Once again casualties were heavy: Kempling, who was still behind the lines, wrote on the seventeenth that the "26th has done itself [proud] but at a terrible cost. The battalion is practically shot to pieces, sections, platoons and companies being practically wiped out. We wonder how they managed to live, for the ration party of the last two days taking food to them has been simply obliterated by shell fire." Losses among officers were especially heavy: Captain Fairweather of A Company and Lieutenants Ward and Brock of D Company were killed, and five lieutenants (Eaton, Shand, McCullagh, Marsh, and Fleming) were wounded. Twenty officers entered the battle; only nine came out still fit for duty.

Private Thomas Madden offers one of the most detailed accounts of a soldier's experience of the battle. Madden, a forty-year old longshoreman from Cork, Ireland, and his wife were living in Saint John when he joined the 26th on November 28, 1914. Before immigrating he had served for seven years in the regular British Army. He was one of the 26th men arrested in April 1915 during the Saint John riot. In a letter to his wife, he described the attack on the evening of the fifteenth: "I will never forget what the poor 26th faced. It was something terrible. Shell after shell landing in front of us or behind us and now and again one landing in between and killing and wounding so many. Some went crazy with shell shock but on we went, those who could get there, until we reached the village where we fought and captured about 600 Germans." He stated that it was a "great capture, as they outnumbered us more than two to one."

The next day, Madden volunteered to help carry Corporal Frederick Ballard (#405182), who was wounded in the stomach, to the rear. "We had some time carrying that poor fellow out." Madden and three other men started off at 8:00 a.m., and it took them four and a half hours to cover the five kilometres to the dressing station. He wrote that Ballard was glad to reach their destination and thanked them for bringing him out safely. What Madden probably didn't know was that Ballard died of his wounds on the sixteenth.

Returning to the unit was just as bad. "I might say that walking over this ground is no easy task as one shell often kills a dozen and there were hundreds of dead on the ground.... [A]s soon as we reached the sugar refinery it was wild. No human being could face it any further, so we decided to turn back and wait in a shell hole until morning," whereupon they rejoined the unit.

Madden's luck ran out the next day. On the evening of the seventeenth, as the 26th was waiting to be relieved, he was hit by shrapnel in the arm and leg. He recounted how a piece the size of an apple went through the muscle on his left arm, missing the bone, and also taking a slice out of his leg. "I had a miraculous escape from death as it cut a book I had in my breast pocket. It was God who saved my life." Because the relief was just beginning, Madden and several others had to be left behind with the promise that the stretcher bearers would return. He waited three days to be evacuated. "We had no food nor water. In that time we were drinking rain water out of a mud hole." A few days later, Captain A.H. McGreer, a chaplain at Canadian Corps Headquarters, led ninety men from the 2nd

Battalion back to the trenches, and they carried Madden and nine other wounded comrades three and a half kilometres to a field ambulance. "This is my experience of taking Courcelette," Madden concluded. In a letter to Mrs. Madden, Chaplain McGreer congratulated her on her husband's splendid courage and patriotism: "He is one of the men who has made Canada's name great." After being brought out, Madden underwent surgery in France, and was then evacuated to Charing Cross Hospital in London, where he needed another operation to remove shrapnel from his leg.

Madden's experience of Courcelette, however, was still not over. On the battlefield, he had found the body of a Canadian who was wearing a valuable solitaire diamond ring. Madden identified him as Captain Maurice Bauset of the 22nd Battalion. He removed the ring and placed it in his pocket. After reaching Charing Cross Hospital, he gave the ring to a nursing sister for safekeeping while he looked for Captain Bauset's next of kin. After contacting R. Bauset, the assistant city clerk of Montreal, the ring was sent on to the captain's relatives. According to an article in the *Daily Telegraph*, Madden was "commended favourably by the authorities of the hospital, but Private Madden told them that he was simply doing his duty as an honest man. Moreover, it was an act of charity which one Canadian was doing for another."

Once the relief on September 18 was completed, the battalion, now numbering about two hundred men, marched to bivouac at Tara Hill. Private MacCallum described the unit as it came out of the line: "Well, what a sad looking sight. I counted ten of us out of the old A Company that left St. John in June 1915. All that was left from the old original Co." Many of them bore the marks of spending time in the enemy's trenches. "We were a tough looking bunch; some of us had German great coats on, some those long spike helmets, some German boots, and some rifles. Well what a gang! Anybody didn't know us would have sworn that we were German prisoners." The march out also took its toll. The war diary recorded that "heavy and continuous rain ... greatly told on men after their previous hard experience in 3 days operation at Courcelette." When they reached the rest area, the men received tea and rum, and 2nd Canadian Division's commander was on hand to compliment the

Names of some of the men memorialized on the cenotaph, St. Andrews, NB.
Author's Photo

battalion on its conduct. From there they marched on to Warloy, where the corps commander, General Byng, "highly congratulated [them] on [their] conduct displayed during the attack and holding of Courcelette." On September 21, General Macdonell also acknowledged their part in capturing Courcelette, writing: "With the short time at our disposal for making a reconnaissance of the country over which the advance took place and the rapidity with which the brigade was thrown into action, the way in which it went forward to its objective and consolidated it, was nothing short of a wonderful feat of arms. NEW BRUNSWICK may justly be thrilled with pride at the deeds done by her lads in this particular fight." He added: "I deeply deplore the fact that many of your comrades have fallen in action but they shall always live in our memory as having bled in a great and just cause."

On September 19, the battalion moved into rest billets at Hérissart, where they remained for six days. A muster parade revealed the grim cost of capturing Courcelette: 5 officers and 75 other ranks killed or died of wounds, 6 officers and 239 men wounded, for 325 lost in two and half days of fighting. These were the highest losses the battalion suffered during a single battle during the entire war. Colonel McKenzie wrote that the parade "would make you feel sick. As the name was called out someone would answer 'killed' or 'wounded' or 'missing' and some New Brunswick or Canadian home would mourn or worry about some loved one who had done his best for our great cause." In early November, Private Fred Woodbury wrote about how these losses on the Somme affected him: "Many...were great friends of mine, some lifelong friends and some since I joined, but I knew them as no one else had ever known them in civilian life." Referring to two close friends from St. Andrews, Privates Frank Purton (#369789) and Percy Markee (#69615), killed at Courcelette, he added: "all were close old friends and good pals of mine for many years and we had been comrades through many dangers and many adventures, but I hope what is left of us will see the day when we can do something else than fight and the memory of the brave boys who are gone will always be sad but also a glorious remembrance to me."

On September 20, the process of reviving the battalion began with the reorganization of the companies, followed by the examination of NCOs for commissioning in the field to fill the junior officer vacancies. Time was also found for church parade and to host a visit at battalion headquarters by Sir Frederick Palmer and Beach Thomas, representatives of the London press.

Courcelette became a hallmark battle for the Canadian Corps, for 5th Brigade, and especially for the 26th Battalion. CSM Corey described the attack on the fifteenth as "a day that will surely live in the history of Canada." Colonel McKenzie explained that "this is the first brigade in the whole army since Mons (so we are told) who attacked absolutely in the open and attained an important objective." Soldiers of the 26th found different ways to memorialize the battle. Private Philip S. George Horne (#444380), a native of Bristol, England, who moved to Saint John, where he became a painter, was wounded at Courcelette with the 26th. By then, he was an experienced soldier. At the time of his enlistment in the 55th Battalion in April 1915, the thirty-three-year-old had seen much military service, having spent three years with the King's Own Yorkshire Light Infantry, three years in the Canadian Army Service Corps, and four months in the Canadian Garrison Artillery. On September 19, 1916, while in hospital, he wrote a lengthy poem about the battle entitled "Courcelette," describing "how Jack Canuck smashed old Fritz, when we captured Courcelette." In December, it was published in the *Daily Telegraph* (see the Appendix).

The anniversary of the battle was commemorated a year later. The *Daily Telegraph* interviewed Thomas Madden, who by then had been discharged and was back in Saint John. He said that, "on this date last year Canada was made great by the splendid work of her sons in taking Courcelette." He vividly recalled crossing those 2,500 yards under heavy German artillery fire: "Men were torn to pieces, some were running mad, shell-shocked, others were going ahead for all they were worth. Just imagine shell after shell falling and exploding among the advancing men! What a sensation when one thinks of it!" He also recalled the men he had fought with during the battle, some by name, many of whom died in the fighting.

Regina Trench

On September 25, the refurbished battalions of 5th Brigade marched from rear billets to the Brickfields, where they rested until returning to the front-lines two days later. What followed was a brief but intense period of confused and frustrating operations. During the day, the 26th was placed under 6th Brigade, and in the afternoon ordered forward into the Courcelette area in support of the 31st Battalion. Owing to mist and darkness and inexperienced guides, however, they did not arrive until 5:10 a.m. on the twenty-eighth. Upon reaching the headquarters of the 31st, the men were told they had been ordered to seize and occupy Hill 130 before daylight. The hill lay about 1,500 metres from the Canadian front line, on the far side of Regina Trench, a strongly fortified German position running east and west on the reverse slope of a ridge north of Courcelette believed to be empty. The battalion's bombers and B Company, supported by C Company, would move north along the East Miraumont Road, bomb Regina Trench if it was occupied, and dig in on Hill 130. D Company would follow on and hold Regina Trench, while A Company remained in close support in Courcelette Trench.

The battalion moved forward as quickly as possible, reaching the East Miraumont Road about 5:25 a.m. Heavy mist hung over the battlefield and, according to a battalion report, "it was hoped that with the aid of this the battalion would move well up to the objective without being observed by the enemy." After they had advanced about 600 metres, however, the mist lifted and, with the day breaking, the Canadians were exposed to the German defenders, who immediately opened fire with three machine guns, instantly inflicting about forty casualties and forcing the attackers to seek cover in the sunken road. Later, B and C Companies attempted to reach Regina Trench, but failed when they again drew heavy machine-gun fire; they remained pinned down for the rest of the day, although mistaken reports claimed they had occupied the trench. About 3:00 p.m. the 26th made a third attempt to enter Regina Trench, this time without any artillery support, but were again forced back. At 8:40 they made yet another "bold attempt" to rush the trench. By then, they were only about two hundred men strong and, despite a strong bombing attack, they were again forced back. Retiring to Courcelette Trench, the 26th tried no further attacks against the Germans, who remained firmly entrenched in their positions.

The war diary succinctly summed up the situation: "Regina Trench proved to be very strongly garrisoned." Losses on the twenty-eighth were again heavy: 3 officers and 43 men killed or died of wounds, 3 officers and 125 men wounded, and 2 prisoners of war, totalling 176. When combined with the losses at Courcelette, casualties totalled 501 all ranks, likely about the same number lost in the year spent in the trenches before coming to the Somme. Among the attackers was George Kempling, who had returned to the unit from detached duty. He wrote that, as the growing daylight gave them away and the Germans opened up on them with machine-gun and rifle fire, "many of us were picked off as we started to scramble down the road again about 1 1/2 miles through the mud.... I just had a scratch thank God. For the most of the day we hid in the dug outs along the road, trying to get away from the persistent snipers. I like to be absolutely fair, but Fritzie is no sport. He sniped off more than one stretcher bearer visiting the wounded fellows in the dugouts. Our boys showed up well, in persisting to rescue wounded men in the open under heavy sniping. I managed to work my way down the road, dodging from dugout to shell hole to a much safer place, and there stayed til dark."

Among the battalion stretcher bearers who worked with the casualties was Private Ben Gaskill from Grand Manan. The thirty-two-year-old bank clerk had joined the 26th in December 1914 and become a stretcher bearer in England. In June 1916, he was briefly hospitalized, suffering from shell shock and myalgia. For his gallantry under fire on the Somme, Gaskill was awarded the Military Medal.

Throughout September 29, the 26th remained in the front lines, often under heavy fire. During the bombardment, a German shell made a direct hit on the roof of a dugout in which Kempling was sheltering with some stretcher cases. "Owing to it being an extra heavily timbered roof the shell did not burst inside. But it bashed the roof in and drove a beam down on my head, forced my front teeth out a bit and splintered all the front ones. After I had recovered myself, I ran out to a near-by dug out with three comrades, all of us dazed." He went back and helped move the stretcher cases about

Lieutenant Fred Foley, killed on September 30, 1916, when his dugout was hit by a German shell. Courtesy of Josh Powers

two and a half kilometres to the doctor's dugout in the rear. While sitting in the dugout trying to eat something, Kempling "collapsed and cried like a baby. I want to stay and help our brave stretcher bearers out with the rest of the gallant fellows who were lying out in the front line, wounded, but a day, a night, and a day with nothing to eat, fighting and working continuously, with no sleep and at last, this crack on the head did me." Later in the day, he was evacuated as a shell-shock casualty. On October 7, as he made his way farther to the rear, his diary entry gives some insight into his plight: "God grant that I may get to England for a while as my nerve is gone for a while. Every time I think of the front line experience I had, I turn violently sick at the stomach." Kempling was hospitalized in France and Britain, where he was diagnosed with neurasthenia and then shell shock. In time, he was discharged and reassigned to the Canadian Forestry Corps in France, but in June 1918 suffered a relapse and returned to hospital. Finally, in early 1919, he was invalided back to Canada, where he was declared medically unfit for service and discharged from the army.

The battalion was relieved the night of the twenty-ninth and moved back to take up a position supporting the 22nd Battalion in Sugar Trench. On September 30, artillery fire was intermittent, but at noon a German shell hit the dugout housing the battalion machine-gun, bombing, and scout officers, killing Lieutenants E.H. Welch and Fred D. Foley. Foley was a twenty-three-year-old civil engineer from Saint John who had served for two years in the 62nd Regiment and in July 1916 joined the 26th as a replacement officer from the 55th Battalion.

That night, a battalion working party moved forward and dug a new trench 200 metres in front of the Canadian line in preparation for a major attack the next day. On October 1, the battalion, its fighting strength now numbering just 160 men, advanced into the front trenches to provide close support during the afternoon attack on Regina Trench by the other three battalions in 5th Brigade. Unfortunately, that attack also failed. The next morning, the 26th was relieved by the 27th Battalion and moved back to Usna Valley, near Albert, in the rain, then to the Brickfields and Bouzincourt. The 26th was finally done on the Somme. By then, the entire battalion numbered fewer than three hundred men.

The End of Somme Operations: "very few of the old bunch"
On October 3 the unit moved by motor bus to a rest area at Berteaucourt, 24 miles west of Albert. The war diary summarized the final stages of its time on the Somme: "Weather again very wet but all ranks most cheery and after a very hard tour as usual with spirits undaunted. The arrangements for good food, etc., through the days 22nd Sept. to Oct 2nd had been very good and on arrival Berteaucourt hot meals were ready for all ranks. The excellence of service by A.S.C. [Army Service Corps] and other units must always be noted and the co-operation throughout the various branches of the services is a mark for continued praise."

The battalion rested at Berteaucourt from October 3 to 9, post-battle recovery the order of the day. The muster parade at 3:00 p.m. on the fourth was a sad occasion. As the war diary noted, "ranks of Battn. had never been so thin but in the minds of all was the thought of very successful work at Courcelette and the excellent name attained by the 5th Cdn. Inf. Bde. for the extent of ground gained and severe losses inflicted on the enemy." Sergeant Peter E. LeBlanc (#69546) from Dalhousie reflected on these losses on a more personal level: "Well we did our little trick down in the [Somme] which was a regular hell for us all, but the boys in the old 26th kept their name up all the same, although our casualties were quite numerous on our first attack, next was not so bad simply because we did not have the men to lose. Believe me, there are very few of the old bunch left with us now, things are somewhat different about this Battalion at present."

Over sixty of the men killed on the Somme were originals, as were a large number of the wounded. These losses all but meant the end of the old battalion. By mid-November, Captain George Keefe reckoned there were only one hundred men and five officers from the original battalion left on the firing line. Although some of the wounded and sick returned once they recovered, the original 26th had passed into history.

The battle also took a heavy toll on the early reinforcements who had joined the battalion before it moved south. At least twenty-one men from the 64th Battalion were killed on the Somme. Among them was Captain Frank R. Fairweather, a forty-year-old husband and father of a nine-year-old daughter; he owned a large insurance business in Saint John and was an acting company commander with the 62nd Regiment when he had joined the 64th. Fairweather had been with the 26th for only a few months, serving as a platoon commander in A Company, when he was killed on September 17.

Once again, examination of NCOs for promotion to replace casualties took place, as did church parade. Some members of the battalion also received a change of scenery: half the officers got leave in Amiens, while one officer and twenty-eight other ranks proceeded to a rest camp near Dieppe for five days. Large numbers of reinforcements also began arriving to replenish the unit's diminished ranks. Many were new faces from the 106th Battalion from Nova Scotia. Then, on October 9, General Turner inspected the unit, congratulated them on their excellent work during the Somme operations, and presented Military Medals to NCOs and men for their good work during the battle. Among them was Corporal Karl Vroom (#70010) of St. Stephen. A twenty-one-year-old labourer who had served for a year with the 71st Regiment before the war, Vroom had enlisted in Saint John on November 11, 1914. In an interview conducted in March 1918 by a *Daily Telegraph* reporter after he returned home, Vroom recalled the events related to his award. During the fighting at Courcelette, the call went out for "someone" to carry a dispatch to the front line: "I happened to be the one who volunteered and I was given the

Corporal Karl Vroom receives the Military Medal from 2nd Canadian Division commander General Richard Turner.
Author's collection

dispatch. It was during heavy shell fire and besides being at a crucial point of the 'show' it was also a very dangerous mission. However, I said I would do it and started off. I made my way almost to the front trench. But I was hit twice before I could make it. However, for the effort I had made to get through I was recommended for the Military Medal and that is the whole story."

On October 8, the battalion received word that 2nd Canadian Division was leaving the Somme, but rather than return to the Ypres Salient, they moved into First Army's area north of Vimy Ridge. They began the march on the tenth, and by the sixteenth they found themselves in the trenches around Bully Grenay, to the north of Lens, where they remained until January 1917.

Once again, the Canadians engaged in the now-familiar routine of holding the front line. The Germans were mostly quiet throughout the winter months, and the Canadians spent much of their time improving the trenches. The war diary noted on October 30 that "the comfort of all ranks is greater here than at any previous sector since the Battn. came to France. Every available man is being used to put the line in best possible condition." On November 8, the war diary further noted that "we found trenches in precarious state and all ranks bent their energies for their upkeep." Their hard work paid off: at the end of their tour, 5th Brigade headquarters complimented their efforts, stating, "a large amount of work carried out by your Battn. and that they left the trenches in a far better state than they had ever been in since we took over the sector." These

Identity disk belonging to
Lieutenant Walter C. Lawson.
72.21.2, New Brunswick Military History Museum

favourable conditions continued
into the next month. The entry for
December 3 stated: "Situation very
quiet. Men cheery. Every available man working on front and support
lines also pushing work wiring the front. Transport as usual on time
every evening and rations appreciably good." Casualties were also light.
On December 20, the war diary noted that, during the trench tour that
had just ended, "no casualties occurred, this being the first time since
arrival in the firing line in which the battn. was immune."

Most enemy activity was confined to low-level operations in no man's
land. On November 2, for example, German scouts tried to reconnoitre
the 26th's wire, but they were "bombed off" and forced to retreat. From
the German dead, the Canadians were able to identify the troops opposing
them. Occasionally, the Germans mounted larger operations. On October
17, the day after the 26th arrived, they exploded a large mine in this sector.
Lieutenant Walter C. Lawson of St. Stephen, D Company's second-in-
command, crossed no man's land in daylight to reconnoitre the crater,
then organized a work party that quickly dug a sap forward from their
trenches and incorporated the near lip of the crater into the 26th's line. For
his swift action, Lawson, a nephew of New Brunswick premier George J.
Clarke, received the MC and the crater was named after him. In a letter
to a fellow officer at the end of the year, Colonel McKenzie stated that
Lawson's consolidation of the crater was "favourably spoken about in the
corps schools."

The Canadians also conducted their own offensive operations, with
the 26th carrying out trench raids on November 23 and January 16. The

latter was a large-scale affair practised behind the lines over a taped course. Aimed at entering the German's lines, it consisted of three parties, each numbering one officer and forty-five men. At Zero Hour (4:30 p.m.), a mine was blown under the enemy's front and a heavy artillery, machine-gun, and smoke barrage was laid down. The attackers successfully cleared a stretch of the German front line, bombing many of their dugouts and leaving an estimated forty-five enemy dead behind. The 26th's raiders lost twenty-two casualties during the operation. Among the dead was Lieutenant R.W. Otty Barnes (#69061) of Hampton, New Brunswick. An original who was commissioned from the ranks in November 1916, Barnes commanded the assault party on the right. According to a letter written by Major Walter Brown to Barnes's father,

[t]he line [of attackers] continued to move forward, gained the enemy's parapet and at several points entered the trench, killed a number of the enemy and bombed and wrecked several dug-outs. At one section of the trench where very strong opposition was encountered resulting in a number of casualties, our men were prevented from getting into the German trench, and it was here that Lieut. Barnes was last seen. He was standing on the parapet waving his men forward with his left arm. In his right hand he was holding a revolver and was shooting into the trench. He was not seen again, and it is supposed that he was wounded, dragged into the trench and made a prisoner. A careful search for his body was kept up through the night of January 17 and 18, but it was not found.

Barnes's name is inscribed on the Vimy Memorial to the missing.

When out of the line, the battalion was in brigade reserve at Fosse 10, near Hersin. The war diary noted: "all ranks very comfortable in these billets and concerts were arranged in Church Army Hut for recreation and amusement of the men." On January 20, the battalion was withdrawn from the line, and began three weeks of intensive training that focused on learning how to carry out attacks at the section, platoon, company, and battalion levels, using the Canadian Corps' new platoon organization. Based on the experiences of Canadian unit commanders and French troops on the Somme, platoons were re-equipped with a wider array of weapons (bombs, rifle grenades, and Lewis light machine guns); reorganized into rifle, bombing, rifle grenade, and Lewis gun sections; and taught new tactics for attacking and defending positions by manoeuvring the platoons across the battlefield, using mutually supporting fire. This new approach would be used with great success in the coming attack on Vimy Ridge.

On February 13, the battalion returned to the front farther south, opposite Vimy Ridge, entering divisional reserve at Bois des Alleux. On the nineteenth, they took over the front line in the La Folie sector, where they remained until the twenty-fourth, when they moved into brigade reserve at Neuville-St. Vaast. On March 1, the unit returned to the trenches. Although the front was mostly quiet, the 26th actively engaged in sniping and patrolling no man's land. On March 3, they encountered a German post numbering between eight and ten men and, in a "bombing encounter," D Company drove off the "Huns" and occupied the post. In his diary, stretcher bearer Ben Gaskill noted a three-hour truce "between us & Huns to bring in dead." The weather remained wintery; on the fourth, they had two inches of snow. When they were relieved on the sixth, they returned to divisional reserve at Bois des Alleux. After the usual round of bathing and pay parades, another period of training began for specialist troops, including Lewis gunners, bombers, grenadiers, stretcher bearers, and signallers. Other signs of an approaching offensive included officers' conferences on the "Offensive" and a lecture on "Cavalry." Sunday, March 11, was set aside for a church service in a company hut and band concerts in the afternoon.

On March 13, they returned to trenches in the sector where they would soon attack. The next day, despite steady rain and very wet trenches, the divisional commander viewed their jumping-off trenches to be used in "the Push." The front became more active over the next week. Aircraft from both sides flew overhead; as well, the Germans observed the Canadian lines from three observation balloons. Both Canadian and German artillery and mortars were also busy. On the fourteenth, German trench mortars hit and destroyed a 26th dugout, burying three men, later found unhurt; on the eighteenth, fire from Canadian sixty-pound trench mortars could be seen smashing the enemy's wire along the offensive front.

Training for the Battle

The coming Canadian operation would be part of a wider British offensive to the east of Arras, and, not unlike the Somme attack at Courcelette, the Canadians were given the job of protecting the left flank, this time by seizing the high ground to the north formed by Vimy Ridge. The operation would be a thoroughly planned, systematic, corps-wide advance based on a series of forward "bounds" aimed at capturing and consolidating well-defined objectives that cumulatively would lead to the capture of the ridge.

5th Brigade would attack on the left of 2nd Canadian Division's front, near the centre of the Canadian line to the east of Neuville-St-Vaast. In the brigade's first wave would be the 24th and 26th Battalions on the right and left, respectively, followed by the 25th Battalion in the second wave, and by 6th Canadian and 13th British Brigades in the final wave. Collectively, they were to push through the Germans' defensive system and take the entire ridge in their sector. The 26th were to capture a series of intermediate trenches and then push on to a section of the Black Line, their main objective, where they would establish and consolidate part of the new main line of resistance.

On March 18, with just three weeks remaining before the offensive, the 26th was relieved and moved into brigade support at Neuville-St-Vaast. For the next five days, the whole battalion provided working parties; then, moving to the rear, the men began intensive training at Grand Servins. On the afternoon of the twenty-fifth, officers went over the "tape course" for the first time and then attended a conference. The next day, the rest of the unit, starting with the specialists, began almost two weeks of work on the tape course. They then moved on to company level training and, beginning on the thirtieth, a few days of battalion and brigade training. "Tactical Exercise" training for platoons closed out the month. Then, despite snow and rain, more battalion and company training took place "over the tapes" until April 7. On April 2, groups of officers and NCOs from the companies went to divisional headquarters at Lillers to view a large-scale plaster-of-paris model of the battle zone. On the sixth, company and platoon commanders gave lectures to their men. In the meantime, Colonel McKenzie went forward with the unit scout officer to view the condition of the German wire in their sector.

Many practical aspects of the coming battle were identified and practised during training. It was recognized that getting into the assembly trenches before the battle often took longer than expected, so companies and platoons practised doing so. Where necessary, units would receive ladders with which to climb out of the trenches. They would also take some ladders forward to help get out of deep, flooded shell craters. They also practised rallying small units of men on the battlefield, taking precautions to prevent straggling: some men going forward with working and carrying parties would fall out to join other parties returning to the rear, especially when troops from their own battalion were in the passing unit. Officers commanding both advancing and returning parties were warned against letting this happen. Straggler posts would be established at various places, and the men collected there would be rearmed if necessary and marched back to their units. Troops were also told not to fall out to attend to the wounded: that was the stretcher bearers' duty.

Preparations

The 26th Battalion's disposition for the attack shows in detail how combat infantry battalions were organized for battle at this point in the war. The battalion's planned attack formation was 335 yards wide and 400 yards deep, and deployed in four waves. The first consisted of two platoons from C Company on the right and two from A Company on the left, each formed up in two lines. The platoon sergeant would lead the first line, while the platoon commander followed with the second line. Each platoon numbered around forty-four, all ranks, dispersed in a space 85 yards wide by 20 yards deep. Following ten yards behind would be two lines of moppers-up, consisting of three platoons from C Company, 22nd Battalion — the first destined for the enemy's front-line trench, while the second would make for the support trench. Eighty yards back, the second wave would consist of the two company commanders, C Company's Captain Winter and A Company's Major McMillan and their headquarters party, followed by another platoon from each company, again advancing in two lines. The third wave would consist of three platoons and company headquarters from B Company (Lieutenant Shand commanding); the two flanking platoons would advance in lines, while the centre platoon would array in artillery formation, marching in single file. Finally, the fourth wave would be made up of three platoons from D Company, commanded by Major Charles Leonard, moving forward in artillery formation. Battalion headquarters, consisting of Colonel McKenzie and Captain Wood, the adjutant, and the officers commanding the machine-gun, signals, and scout sections (Lieutenants Campbell, Stayner, and Harrison), and the aid post would be located to the rear near Denis-la-Rocque.

The four companies of the 26th would commit more than half of their strength to the initial attack. In the case of A Company, the headquarters would consist of one officer (Major A. McMillan, the company commander) and seven other ranks, while the three attacking platoons would total three officers (Lieutenants Herman S. Murray, R. McLaren Keswick, and N.E. Sharpe), 130 other ranks, and two signallers, for a total of 140 soldiers out of the company's overall strength of 253, all ranks. The remainder of the company's strength (113, all ranks) would be distributed in a variety of ways: forty-one would be assigned to the reserve platoon, while reserve officers Captain Russell and Lieutenant March would be held at the transport lines in the rear. Riflemen from each of the company's reserve platoons would be detailed to the brigade's supporting specialist units for the attack, which would include 5th and 14th Canadian Machine Gun Companies; 5th Field Company, Canadian Engineers; and 5th Canadian Trench Mortar Battery. The machine guns and trench mortars would join the barrage, while the engineers would strengthen the 26th's position by building a strongpoint, Z, which would be garrisoned by a platoon from C Company and two machine guns from the 5th Machine Gun Company. The company quartermaster sergeant and storeman would also remain in the rear, and two men would be allotted to the battalion trench police. Another large group (sixty-seven, all ranks) would be occupied elsewhere: twenty-six employed away from the unit, twenty-four in hospital, ten on battalion duties, three away on courses, and four in detention. In other words, almost a quarter of the company's complement was unavailable for the assault.

The plan of attack called for the first two waves to push a thousand metres through a series of intermediate trenches to the main objective, a German trench called the Zwischen Stellung—the Black Line, to the attackers —which they were to reach by Zero plus thirty-two minutes. The mopping-up parties from the 22nd Battalion would deal with the intermediate trenches. At Zero plus thirty-six minutes, the support company in the third wave would push through the Black Line objective and dig a new line a hundred yards beyond. The fourth wave would act as the battalion reserve, mopping up positions east of the new trench and then occupying it. Communications between the front and rear would be maintained by telephone and runners. During the next phase of the attack, the 25th Battalion would pass through the 26th's position and establish a new forward line. A and C Companies were to be held in readiness to support 25th Battalion if needed, as well as to cooperate with 24th Battalion on the right.

The infantry attack would be preceded by a dense barrage provided by artillery, Stokes mortars, and heavy machine guns, carefully timed to lead the assault troops through the German front, support, and main lines. Maintaining the momentum of the advance would be the key to success, and various measures were undertaken to ensure continuous forward movement. Assaulting troops were ordered to advance over the surface of the battleground to their objectives; only battalion headquarters, signallers, and the wounded would be allowed to use the trenches. Also, the first wave was directed to follow the barrage as closely as possible, since their safety and success largely depended on this covering fire. The barrage would advance 100 yards every three minutes, but would pause at certain points to give the troops time to cross enemy trench lines. If companies and platoons were held up by the German defenders, neighbouring forces on the flanks would "on no account" check their advance; instead, they would form defensive flanks facing the stalled units and press on in a way that would envelope the centre of resistance. Finally, reserve units moving forward would reinforce successful advances, rather than those forces that were being held up. After capturing the Black Line, the 26th would consolidate its new position, and form a main line of resistance in the rear of the crest of Hill 135, the key terrain feature in this sector.

There was a tendency to overload troops with things to carry during attacks, so the battle planners, given the distant objectives they were setting, took steps to lighten the soldiers' loads. For one thing, the men going into action would leave their personal packs and other equipment behind. Some rolled their Cardigan jackets in their greatcoat or waterproof sheet, instead of in a haversack. Also, given the increased firepower provided by the greater number of Lewis guns throughout the battalion and the small arms ammunition that could be taken from those who became casualties, the troops were directed not to increase the ammunition they carried. Finally, some troops attacking in the leading waves did not carry entrenching tools.

After training was halted on April 7, the 26th men went forward to Bois des Alleux on the eighth (Y Day), and made final preparations for the attack. The troops were issued with one day's rations in addition to their iron rations, as well as two filled water bottles. In the evening they moved off to the front line and took up positions in the jumping-off trenches. Arrangements were made for every man to have a hot meal as close to Zero Hour as possible.

The Battle of Vimy Ridge
On April 9, the 26th was in 5th Brigade's leading wave spearheading the corps-wide attack. Private Thomas MacCallum, the soldier blown into the air during the attack on Courcelette, briefly described waiting for his next battle to begin: "[F]ive minutes before the show, you wouldn't think there was any war at all. Everything was silent. Just at the minute 20 past five o'clock am.,[10] the whole earth began to rock with artillery fire." When the barrage came down on the German front line, the battalion jumped off.

At the outset the attackers encountered awful weather and ground conditions. On the third anniversary of the battle, an unnamed officer from the 26th recalled in a newspaper interview that "it was very dark and a heavy snow storm was raging accompanied by a driving wind. The

---

10   The bombardment actually began at 5:30 a.m.

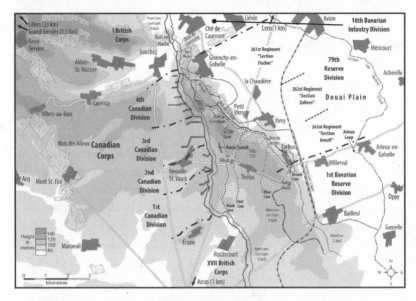

Map 3: The Battle of Vimy Ridge. Mike Bechthold

ground over which we had to advance was a sea of mud and shell holes and very heavy going." Nevertheless, they made rapid progress through the enemy's lines. In a letter written on May 5, 1917, to Colonel McAvity, Colonel McKenzie described how "our chaps went over as on parade. Our training was so complete over the 'tapes' that we knew the German trenches as well as our own. We were very fortunate indeed and we managed to keep behind the barrage and lost quite few men.... I do not know how we ever found the trenches first, second, third and fourth lines which was our objective as the artillery had practically obliterated them."

In the six months since the Somme, the composition of the battalion going over the top had changed considerably with the arrival of numerous reinforcements, including over four hundred men from the 140th battalion, which was raised throughout New Brunswick in late 1915 and early 1916. Among them was Private Stephen J. Pike (#817694) from Grafton, New Brunswick, in Carleton County. An eighteen-year-old mill hand, Pike had enlisted in the 140th in December 1915, proceeded to Britain in September 1916, and joined the 26th in France in October. On April 9, Pike went forward with his friends from the 140th from Carleton County. In a letter to his father written on April 28, he recorded:

> My chum was killed in the fight, a fellow by the name of McDougall [Private Lucius A. McDougall (#817680)], from Bath. He was an excellent fellow and he and I were the only ones from Carleton County together all winter until Wilfred Ralston [Private Wilfred G. Ralston (#817700), also from Grafton] joined the battalion. See Mrs. Ralston and find out if she had heard any word as to what became of Wilfred. He went over about twenty yards from me and when the fight was over he was missing and was still missing up till the time I got wounded [April 15]. I don't know whether he is dead or alive. I went back over the field and looked at all the dead, but could not find him anywhere. I think that he has got wounded and gone to some hospital.

Pike was correct: Ralston was wounded on the ninth, then evacuated to hospital in England.

Another reinforcement from the 140th going over the top on April 9 was Private James L. Kennedy (#817281), a twenty-year-old tinsmith from Saint John. After arriving in Britain, he was sent to The Royal Canadian Regiment, then transferred to the 26th in late February 1917. During the assault on Vimy Ridge, Kennedy was struck in the left leg by shell fragments that shattered his knee joint and required the amputation of his leg at mid-thigh two days later. In mid-September, he sailed home aboard the hospital ship H.M.H.S. *Llandovery Castle*, and arrived in Saint John in early October. Later, he was sent to the orthopedic hospital in Toronto, where he was fitted with an artificial leg and discharged in June 1918.

By Zero plus thirty-two minutes, the battalion had occupied its objective, which the men signalled by firing three white Very lights. 5th Brigade's summary of operations noted that "the enemy was found in considerable force in [the Black] Line. The effect of our artillery fire however was such that with the exception of a few isolated pockets of the enemy, who offered

Canadian troops advance on Vimy Ridge under German artillery fire,
April 26, 1917. Mikan no. 3192389, Library and Archives Canada

stubborn resistance, they appeared to be thoroughly demoralized and readily surrendered." According to the 26th's war diary, "the casualties in the attack were slight [on April 9, the battalion lost 51 killed and 110 wounded], and… the companies spent [the rest of the] day clearing the trench and making shelter for the men." In the evening A, B, and C Companies began digging the main line of resistance; during the night, they occupied the Zwischen Stellung, except for one of C Company's platoons, which garrisoned the new strongpoint Z. Meanwhile, D Company set up in Furze Trench.

On the tenth and over the next three days, the battalion remained at the Black Line, providing working parties during the day and night digging and strengthening the position and providing large working parties for work on the roads. About half of the approximately 465 men at the front sheltered in dugouts in the old German positions in the Zwischen Stellung, some of which could accommodate thirty men each; the rest were dispersed among the support lines.

Throughout this period, the troops endured harsh, wintery weather, especially during the night of the 11th/12th when heavy snow fell. As McKenzie wrote, obtaining their objectives on the ninth "was the easy part.... To hang on under the weather conditions as we did was most trying on everyone. Snow, rain, hail, sleet and our men had no overcoats or blankets." Various efforts were made to keep the troops well supplied. According to field messages, on April 10 the men's greatcoats went forward with the rations, and the next day they received whale oil for their feet and all available socks. Socks were in short supply, however, and on April 12 the company commanders were instructed to collect wet socks and send them to the rear: "We have no more available and the greatest care must be taken that these are collected." On a brighter note, Headquarters informed the COs that a thousand cigarettes and chocolate were being sent up for each company.

Follow-up Operations

Following the main attack, 2nd Canadian Division advanced toward the next German defensive line several miles east of the ridge, on the Douai Plain, and soon reached the Arras-Lens railway embankment east of the town of Vimy. On April 13, the 26th Battalion was ordered to move forward to the new front line early the next day, and from there advance about two and a half kilometres across the plain, where they would dig a new trench facing the main German positions. Colonel McKenzie, Captain H.G. Wood, the adjutant, and the four company commanders climbed to the top of the ridge to view the ground and plan the advance. In an account written in April 1932 for an issue of the *Telegraph Journal* commemorating the fifteenth anniversary of Vimy Ridge, Wood, now a lieutenant-colonel commanding The Carleton Light Infantry, recalled the scene: "The first glimpse of the country beyond was probably, to all who viewed it, one of the most striking sights of the war. The sun was sinking beyond and looking backward nothing could be seen but the greatest desolation brought about by gun fire—ruined villages as flat as the proverbial pancake, and mud and more mud. Forward beyond the railway line [the] Douai plain spread as a green carpet, and beyond, the smoke was rising from the chimneys in apparently happy and contented villages. Little sign of war was visible—veritably the promised land as Moses must have seen another area in days gone by."

The unnamed officer recalled that they were to move forward by companies and rendezvous on the railway embankment. From there they would be supported on the right by 1st Brigade and on the left by 3rd Brigade, and were to be preceded forward by a screen of cavalry and covered by machine gunners: "When we reached the railway we found that our supports had not materialized and we were in a quandary but made up our minds that they only thing to do was to see the thing through and at 5:30...we set off on our advance in the direction of Acheville." As Captain Wood put it, the plan "had miscarried so the 26th was alone in its glory." He went on to describe the advance: "This attack was not a trench warfare show with a heavy barrage pounding down all resistance in front but an attack such as had been taught the budding officer and soldier when in training in Canada—open warfare—companies and platoons advancing in file with interval and distance later breaking out into sections in file in the same formation....As dawn broke and the blanket of darkness was lifted, there was New Brunswick's battalion spread over a front of half to three-quarters of a mile about 500 yards deep following out the old recruiting slogan and trying for the 'free trip to Berlin.'" According to the unnamed officer, "our advance covered about 2,500 yards and in due time we reached our objective where we proceeded to dig in in the front line and support trenches. This trench was named 'New Brunswick' and carried the name throughout the war. This spot represented the farther most point of penetration attained by the British advance at that time."

Also taking part in the long advance was Private Pike. He wrote how "we advanced about two miles and a half and captured field artillery as large as eight inch guns. The Germans did not even have time to destroy them. Our artillery men came up and fired their own ammunition right back at them for they left thousands of shells behind; it was certainly a great victory." Two days later, Pike was wounded in the left hand and evacuated to the rear.

As digging began, patrols were sent forward to reconnoitre the German positions, some of which were held in strength. A patrol that entered Méricourt was cut off and four men were captured, the largest single loss of prisoners by the battalion to date.[11] After eight days of continuous operations, the battalion was relieved during the night of the sixteenth and moved back to the Zwischen Stellung; the next day it came into reserve in the Aux Rietz area, southwest of Neuville-St-Vaast. During the next several days the reserve platoons rejoined the battalion, and the troops rested in their tents, reorganized, and prepared for their return to the line. On April 21, they began another long stretch at the front, occupying their old lines near Neuville-St-Vaast, where they remained in divisional support, providing large-scale working parties until the twenty-sixth, when they moved forward to the Acheville area to participate in the Canadian Corps' attack against the German defences at the Arleux Loop. During the night of April 27/28, the battalion dug new trenches from which units of 1st Canadian Division would mount the main assault on the twenty-eighth.

By the end of the month, the Germans had become more active around the 26th's positions as shelling increased, sometimes becoming intense, although casualties were relatively light. The 26th remained in place until May 2, when it was withdrawn to close support. The unit's part in active Vimy operations ended on May 4 when it was moved back to divisional reserve at the rest camp at Aux Rietz, having been in the line for fourteen days. The war diary summed up the men's latest tour at the front: "A very trying time as trenches heavily shelled and had only been recently dug, consequently little cover, but weather being fine throughout helped considerably and considering the amount of shelling, casualties were amazingly light."

The troops were proud of their part in this latest battle. Colonel McKenzie wrote: "[I]t was some inspiration to us all to look back on

---

11   The soldiers were Private Angus A. Campbell (#716137), Private Paul Caissy (#445223), Lance Corporal James G. Kinch (#69495), and Sergeant Edmund McManus (#445342).

Vimy Ridge from the German side. Our men went over the open in the early morning and dug in in splendid style, all of them realizing they were making history." With great prescience, he further commented that "the situation has developed down to semi-open warfare and we must expect heavy casualties in the future." During May they continued to hold the line to the east of the ridge, by which time operations around Arras had ended and preparations begun for a new British offensive in the Ypres Salient. In June, the battalion entered into Army Reserve, and on July 1 left the Vimy front and took over the line near Lens. There they would join the Canadian Corps' next major battle, the attack on Hill 70, launched in support of British operations in the Ypres Salient. Hill 70 would be almost as costly as the Somme.

Chapter Five

The Struggle Continues:
Hill 70 and Passchendaele

The 26th Battalion's experience of major combat operations in 1917 that began in April with Vimy Ridge continued with the battles of Hill 70 in August and Passchendaele in early November. In both actions, the Canadians secured their objectives in the face of strong German opposition, but casualties were again heavy. Each time, reinforcements who replenished the thinned ranks quickly blended in and took their turn at the front. In 1917, the 26th learned the real cost of front-line infantry service in the Canadian Corps in the Great War.

In the aftermath of the Battle of Vimy Ridge, the 26th resumed routine trench duty on the Vimy and Lens fronts, with periodic tours in the front and support lines, and in brigade and divisional reserve. Casualties were light overall during June and early July. Among those killed during this period was Private David Gibbons, the underage soldier who had stowed away twice to reach the Western Front with the unit. Gibbons finally made it into the front lines, and in mid-April 1917 was wounded in the neck by a gunshot wound. After recovering he rejoined the unit, but on July 4 was killed by a German shell near Lens. He was buried in Loos British Cemetery. In late August, a memorial service was held at the Smith's Creek United Church, where his foster parents, Will and Elspeth Venning, unveiled a marble tablet bearing the inscription "David Gibbons. July 4, 1917, Somewhere in France."

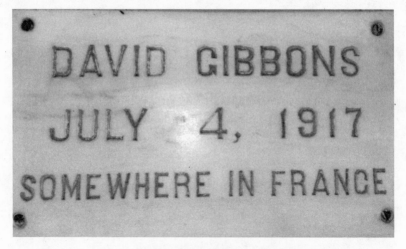

Tablet memorializing Private David Gibbons,
Smith's Creek United Church. Author's photo

The Attack on Hill 70: "A game of this kind"

In early July the Canadian Corps was once again ordered into action, this time to capture the city of Lens. General Arthur Currie, the newly appointed corps commander, rejected the idea of a frontal assault on the city, which the Germans overlooked from two directions. Instead, he favoured capturing the high ground around Hill 70, which would make the German hold on the city untenable. That would force them to counterattack the Canadians, exposing themselves to heavy defensive fire, or retreat from Lens.

Much of the area where the Canadians attacked was covered by coal mines, "fosses" or mine entrances, slag heaps, and brickworks. Local villages and towns, such as Cité St. Auguste, now lay in ruins, providing the Germans strong defensive positions and assembly points for reinforcements. Older trenches sheltered the German defenders, who would mostly fight from machine-gun posts and shell holes.

The battle was thoroughly planned. 1st Canadian Division on the left would attack Hill 70, while 2nd Canadian Division on the right would advance through the mining area closer to Lens. 5th Brigade would lead on 2nd Division's left, next to the divisional boundary line. In the first wave, the 22nd and 25th Battalions would secure the initial objective, the Blue Line, while the 24th and 26th Battalions would push on to the Green Line, the final objective. The 26th Battalion on the far left would take Norman and Nun's Alley trenches. The 26th would attack from the Blue Line in three waves, with two companies in the first wave—D Company on the right, C Company on the left—each sending two platoons. Following these troops would be the moppers, provided by A Company, organized into three platoons. The second wave would consist of two platoons, one from each of D and C Companies, which would provide immediate support for the first-line attackers. B Company in the third wave would act as the supporting company.

The attack was broken down into several phases. Troops of the 26th would assemble in a series of trenches by 2:00 a.m. At Zero Hour, 4:20, when the 22nd and 25th Battalions commenced the attack, waves from the 26th would move forward to the jumping-off positions, where they would reassemble in their attack formations and follow the 22nd Battalion forward to the first objective, the Blue Line. At Zero plus forty-six minutes, the troops would advance through the 22nd's position, conforming to the creeping artillery barrage. C Company on the left would attack Nun's Alley and occupy it by Zero plus seventy-one (twenty-five minutes later). A short time later, its right platoon would bomb their way up Norman Trench (the Green Line) for a hundred metres, then hold their positions. Fifteen minutes later, the other two platoons would rush forward to occupy the rest of Norman Trench in their sector. On the right, D Company would then take a section of Nun's Trench. A Company's moppers would clear the captured trenches, then reform and act as support for D Company. As soon as the battalion's objectives were cleared, B Company's platoons would occupy the neighbouring trenches and support C Company on the left. Once their objectives were occupied, all companies would immediately begin consolidation in preparation for the inevitable German counterattacks, including pushing out forward posts from the new front line. The 26th would be led by Major Walter Brown, who assumed command in early July when Lieutenant-Colonel McKenzie left for England to attend a course.

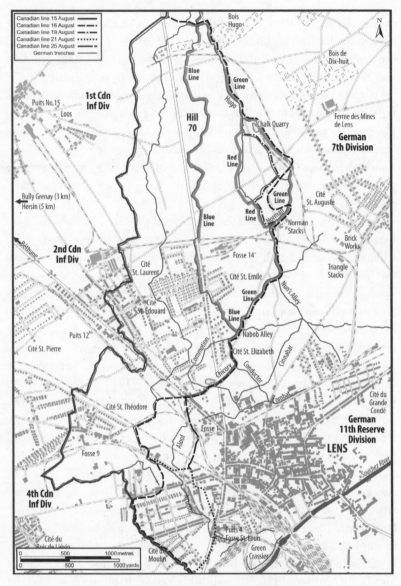

Map 4: The Battle of Hill 70. Mike Bechthold

During the night of July 22/23, the battalion was relieved and marched back to Bois de Bouvigny to begin intensive training in preparation for "the coming show." For the next three weeks, the troops carried out battalion and brigade training on a taped course during mostly fine weather. Preparations for the attack on Hill 70 showed the evolving nature of battle procedure for the Canadian Corps and its attention to logistical support. Personal equipment for each soldier was limited to two filled water bottles, two hand grenades, three empty sandbags, and two flares, plus their own ammunition. In addition, the grenadiers each would carry eight rifle grenades, bombers eight hand grenades, and the moppers fifty smoke bombs, presumably to clear dugouts. The moppers would wear identity markers in the form of white crosses on their backs and white arm bands to distinguish them from German stragglers left behind as the attacking waves moved on. The companies would also be liberally supplied with wire cutters, shovels, and picks. Additional supplies would be moved forward from rear supply dumps to the battle area, and from there fed to company dumps.

For communications on the battlefield, the troops would rely on a variety of methods, including light signals. They had red rockets and Very pistol flares to fire in rapid succession to call for immediate artillery support, while three white Very lights would signal the capture of the Green Line. They would also use flares to communicate their positions to aircraft flying overhead. At Zero Hour, No. 16 Squadron, RFC, would begin to fly contact patrols; two hours later, pilots would sound their Klaxon horns to call on troops to light flares on the ground to identify their position.

On August 14, the battalion moved forward from Bouvigny Huts to Bully Grenay, where the troops drew supplies and rested. At 9:30 p.m. they moved to the assembly area, and by 2:00 a.m. on the fifteenth all companies were in place. Some of the companies moved off a few minutes before Zero Hour to get past the area where the German counterbarrage would fall. The soldiers were also warned about staying behind to attend to the wounded or returning to the rear with minor casualties: the job of assault infantry was to keep moving forward. According to orders, the slightly wounded "should endeavor to remain on duty till objective is gained and well in hand."

At Zero Hour the 22nd Battalion attacked, with the 26th right behind. Advancing in a diamond-shaped artillery formation, then changing into extended order, the unit reached the second assembly area with few casualties. Once the men moved beyond the Blue Line, however, they ran into heavy machine-gun and rifle fire, and here took most of their casualties. D Company on the right encountered a range of hazards, including loose wire in the long grass in no man's land, which made keeping direction difficult. Two of its platoons reached the second assembly area behind Catapult Trench without much difficulty, but the third strayed to the right and lost touch, only connecting up when it passed a point called Fosse 14. There, a German machine gun enfilading them from the right gave them "quite a bit of trouble." Progress was also somewhat hampered by a Canadian eighteen-pounder field gun that kept firing about fifty metres short all the way across the battlefield. Despite these difficulties, the company reached Nun's Alley at Zero plus seventy-seven and had no trouble finding their proper positions. Entering the German lines, they encountered few enemy soldiers, but took eleven prisoners in one dugout and captured another twenty at two nearby brick piles. In his after-action report, Major Leonard, D Company's commander, noted that the "enemy could be seen running back and our men did some good shooting." Later, the badly wounded were carried to the rear by the prisoners, with the slightly wounded men acting as guards.

Once the Canadians halted their advance, the fighting intensified. The Germans began sniping at them, at which point Lieutenant Arthur G. Fleming was killed. A Lewis gun section detailed to occupy a brick pile and establish an advanced post was "all wiped out with the exception of the leader, Private [Harry] Frisbee [#405665] who came in and reported this." Frisbee twice crawled back to the position to retrieve the gun and all of its ammunition, actions that earned him the Military Medal.

On the left, C Company reported the barrage was "very good," with few shorts falling, but it encountered very active sniping and suffered a number of casualties. The objective was hardly recognizable, and "we kept our direction by the wire in front of it." When the men reached Nun's Alley and Norman Trench, they began bombing their way forward. Like

D Company, they secured their position only with difficulty. There was no sign of 1st Canadian Division troops on the left, so they pushed forward a patrol of four men to make contact. When they were held up by machine-gun fire, the sergeant in charge rushed and took the gun, dismounted it, and was returning when he was shot by a sniper. Only one man from the patrol came back, whereupon the C Company men on the left withdrew to avoid being cut off.

At 5:05 p.m. C Company received orders to withdraw from Norman Trench to allow 1st Canadian Division's barrage on its left to advance. The Germans promptly retook the evacuated trench, forcing the Canadians to clear them out again in a sharp bombing and rifle grenade "set to": "We had very few bombs or rifle grenades and were driven back. A bombing and rifle grenade section was at once hurried up by [D] Company on our right and we got about half way up Norman and established a block as we could see no friends on [our] left." Highly accurate German sniper fire from different directions added to the intensity of the fighting, compelling the Canadians "to man both sides of the parapets." To secure their positions, they used their entrenching tools to dig a proper trench connecting the bottoms of shell holes, which "during the tour [we] managed to make fairly passable."

Without any contact with 1st Canadian Division, the 26th's left flank was the air. Troops in the area, however, soon learned the true situation: as an officer noted laconically, "Having been advised that 1st Div. had taken Green Line came to the conclusion that they had donned Hun clothing and helmets as nothing else could be seen on our immediate half left front we having good observation. Knowing importance of linking up we tried again to get up but Hun sticks [grenades] and MG fire put us back to our block." They could also see much movement to their front around the new German line along the railway. Sentries reported seeing "several of our men being taken back by Huns…into houses." If true, they must have been from nearby Canadian units because the 26th had no men captured at this time.

The moppers from A Company jumped off from Marble Trench in sections, and followed the artillery fire forward. The shelling had the desired psychological effect: "Our own barrage was splendid and encouraged the men a great deal." They reached the German front line close behind the D and C Companies. Casualties during the initial advance were "practically nil this due mostly to men watching the enemy barrage." At Zero plus forty-six they continued the advance and began mopping up captured German positions. Soldiers were cautioned to exercise the greatest care when entering dugouts and cellars until they had been examined for "Bosch traps." A party of one officer and ten other ranks from the 170th Tunnelling Company, Royal Engineers, was attached to the 26th to inspect these positions in the battalion area and mark them with signboards reading "Mined," "Dangerous," and "Considered Safe." Moppers from A Company encountered a trap in a dugout consisting of a bomb in a stove with a wire attached underneath it. The wire ran to the foot of the stairs, where it was loosely coiled, no doubt with the intention of catching a foot, jerking the wire, and detonating the bomb.

No. 3 Platoon, A Company, made for Fosse 14. When its commander, Lieutenant Douglas R. Murdoch of Saint John, was mortally wounded, Sergeant McPherson took over and cleared German snipers from the position. The company commander's report noted: "[B]y this time Huns could be seen clear across our area running to the rear." Later in the morning, enemy machine guns located their trenches and inflicted heavy casualties, although it did not hold up the advance. With the exception of one machine-gun crew in Nestor Trench, the enemy showed little fight. "Considerable numbers were in dugouts and were very willing to get out when ordered. 35 prisoners were sent back."

Meanwhile, B Company moved forward behind C and D Company's support platoons, and crossed Martyrs Alley before the German barrage came down. Consequently, all three platoons reached the assembly area with few casualties. The next phase would be much more difficult, however, even though the first two waves had already passed through the area. The right-hand platoon encountered some Germans at Fosse 14 and took them prisoner, but the platoon on the left, like the preceding troops, met considerable opposition and was held up by German machine guns for some time. The centre platoon, moving up Nestor Trench, also met heavy opposition and had to fight every step of the way, encountering a concrete machine-gun emplacement that was still "being worked to good effect causing many casualties." Lieutenant Roland Smith, No. 5 Platoon commander, had his men work up close, "and the gunner was finally put out of business by Cpl. [William] Oakley [#405371] who rushed and killed him, tho he got badly wounded himself." A native of Worcester, England, Oakley was awarded the Distinguished Conduct Medal for his actions. Although receiving much sniper fire, the platoon bombed dugouts as it moved up, securing prisoners from each of them. At one point, the men were held up by about twenty Germans, whom they worked around with rifle grenades and machine guns "until they beat it back only to be cornered in another part of the trench by No. 6 Platoon. They were all taken prisoner." B Company reported taking a total of seventy-seven Germans during the battle.

When the 26th reached its final objective at Norman Trench, the companies lined themselves up exactly according to orders. They began consolidating their positions and sending out patrols to locate the units on their flanks, especially on the left, where there was still no sign of 1st Canadian Division. German snipers located in houses in Cité St. Auguste and the brick piles became very active. To make matters worse, the Canadians discovered that their objective, although a well-defined trench on their maps, was "nothing but a succession of shell holes. The men in this trench had to lie on their stomachs and use their entrenching tool and hands to make cover for themselves." Eventually, they made the trench workable and began using Stokes mortars and rifle grenades to good advantage against the snipers.

The expected German counterattacks soon began. The first, between 6:00 and 7:00 a.m., ran into a Canadian barrage and did not reach the Canadian lines. Another took place around 11:00 a.m., but it too failed to develop into a serious threat. At 5:00 p.m. the Germans made a more determined attack using their 9th Guards Division, brought up from the rear. As luck would have it, the nearby 1st Canadian Division launched an attack at the same time, and the German attackers again got hit by a Canadian barrage and suffered heavy losses. On the evening of the sixteenth, the Germans attacked in force again, but were driven off. In between these

Officers of the 26th, including Lieutenant Reginald A. Major (right) and Captain F.B. Winter (second from left). Author's collection

major assaults, minor counterattacks, often taking the form of bombing attacks, were almost continuous over the span of some sixty hours, some coming from the brick piles.

The Canadians turned back these German attacks, using a wide variety of weapons that were now available to infantry battalions. Around 4:00 p.m. on August 16, the Germans were seen extending out from both sides of the farthest brick pile, where they had a dugout and a post, and the nearby railway cutting. Anticipating another assault, A Company immediately sent up SOS flares calling for artillery fire, and opened up on the Germans with Lewis gun and rapid rifle fire. "They immediately broke for the cover of the brick pile and cutting." C Company also drove them off: "[W]e fed him hand and rifle grenades and after see-sawing up and down the trench managed to hold our position." At 6:00 p.m. the Germans tried to relieve their post at the brick pile. According to Major Leonard's report, "I had the Stokes guns turned on and 10 Huns ran out towards the railway. Our Lewis guns accounted for most of these."

Among the officers participating in these attacks was Lieutenant George B. Hallett. Born in Saint John in either 1866 or 1873—he seems to have lied about his age (perhaps to get in)—Hallett worked as a commercial traveller before the war and served in the 74th Regiment. In April 1916, he enlisted in the 104th Battalion, reached Britain in July, and in May 1917, three months before Hill 70, was taken on strength with C Company. In a letter written on October 20, Hallett described the challenges the troops faced during the battle: "Our last really hot action was on August 15-18, when we won every objective we were after. Believe me, I will never forget those three days and nights. We lost very heavily in men, but we got what we started over the top for, and you know we must expect to lose men in a game of this kind." Hallett played an important part in driving off the German counterattacks. According to C Company's report, "had it not been for the grit and determination of Lieuts. Hallett and [Parker] Fulton in repelling Hun attacks we would have been driven out of Norman." Hallett and Private George DeBow (#709761) of Forest Glen, Kings County, also went out in the face of German grenade attacks to bring back a casualty. For their actions during the battle, Hallett was awarded the Military Cross and DeBow the Distinguished Conduct Medal.

Casualties at Hill 70 were once again high. Between August 15 and 17, the battalion lost 5 officers and 83 other ranks killed, and 5 officers and 175 other ranks wounded. Among them were a number of junior officers, including Captain Francis B. Winter, who was killed, and Lieutenants Reginald A. Major and Roland J.H. Smith (#69920), who were wounded. Winter had been awarded the Military Cross for leading the battalion's trench raid in June 1916 and subsequently was promoted to captain and given command of C Company. He was killed leading his company on the opening day of the attack. Lieutenant Major, from Halifax, went overseas with the 55th Battalion, later joined the 26th, and commanded B Company at Hill 70. Major was awarded the Military Cross for handling his company with great courage and skill, and even though wounded in the leg during the advance, he crawled after his company to their objective, and remained with them through the whole operation, "setting a splendid example for his men." He would not leave until ordered to do so by the commanding

Memorial for Private John H. Cook, killed in action at Hill 70,
Carsonville Cemetery. Author's photo

officer. Lieutenant Roland Smith, from Saint John, enlisted in the battalion
as a private at the outset, became a lance sergeant, fought at Vimy Ridge,
and was later commissioned from the ranks. During the attack on Hill 70,
he commanded a platoon in B Company and was wounded in the right
leg. Smith offered some insightful comparisons between Vimy Ridge and
Hill 70. He believed Hill 70 was "the stiffest fight the 26th ever took part
in. There was much more fighting at Lens [than Vimy], the difficulties to
be overthrown were greater and the position harder to take." The weather
conditions were better at Lens, "which offset to a great extent the obstacles
encountered. Vimy Ridge was a great fight but it did not have the same
terribleness about it as evident in the struggle for Lens."

Among the many casualties from the other ranks was Private Herbert
J. Warren (#817551) of Harcourt, in Kent County. When he enlisted in
the 140th Battalion in October 1915, he was a labourer living in South
Nelson, on the Miramichi. The twenty-three-year-old had served with
the 73rd Regiment before joining up. During the attack on the fifteenth,

Warren was seriously wounded in the head by shrapnel. He was evacuated to the Liverpool Hospital in Étaples, south of Boulogne, where he was able to converse with the nursing sister in charge of his ward, Sister Molly Ward. In a letter she wrote to Warren's sister on August 23, she recounted how the wound had worsened, and he had contracted acute meningitis and died within twenty-four hours. She added that "he was unconscious for the last sixteen hours so his sufferings were unknown to him." He was buried "in a dear little cemetery and a small cross with his name, etc. on it will mark the resting place of another of Canada's brave boys." Today, Private Warren is buried in the Étaples Military Cemetery.

Private John H. Cook (#709139) from Carsonville, King's County, was also among the battalion's fatal casualties. In October 1915, the nineteen-year-old farmer enlisted in the 104th Battalion. He sailed for England in September 1916, and joined the 26th in November in the aftermath of the Somme offensive. Over the next several months, he spent much time in hospital suffering from bronchitis and pleurisy. He rejoined the battalion in mid-July 1917, took part in the Hill 70 attack, and died of his wounds on the sixteenth. He is buried in the Barlin Communal Cemetery Extension, several kilometres west of Lens. On September 16, 1917, a memorial service for Private Cook was held at the Methodist Church in Carsonville, where he attended Sunday school and church. A memorial headstone commemorating his service was also placed in the Carsonville Cemetery.

Among the wounded who survived was Private John Oakes (#817135) from Gagetown. Oakes had joined the 140th Battalion, was drafted into the 26th, and fought at Vimy Ridge. During the Hill 70 battle, he was struck in the eyes with shrapnel and blinded for over a month. The same shell killed six of his comrades and wounded nine others. He underwent extensive treatment in various hospitals in England, and eventually recovered his sight in one eye. In March 1918, he returned home to Gagetown.

During the night of August 17/18, the battalion was relieved and retraced its steps to the old front line. There it was held in support until the twenty-first, when it moved back to the rest area to refit. On August 27, 5th Canadian Infantry Brigade was inspected by the commander-in-chief, Field Marshal

Sir Douglas Haig. Reinforcements also arrived, from the 132nd (North Shore) Battalion, among them Newcastle's Lieutenant Arthur L. Barry, who was born in Oromocto and raised in Fredericton, and Lieutenants J. Graham McKnight of Douglastown, J.E. (Ned) White of Bathurst, and H.W.S. (Winnie) Allingham from Gagetown. They replaced the junior officers lost at Hill 70 and would soon take their turn at the front during the upcoming attack at Passchendaele. Soon afterwards, the battalion moved to the front east of Vimy, where it remained until October. During that time, Colonel McKenzie returned from England and resumed command, while Major Brown went to England to take charge of the 13th Reserve Battalion.

The Battle of Passchendaele

In late October, the 26th Battalion returned to the Ypres Salient to take part in the final stages of the Third Battle of Ypres. The offensive had begun on July 31, when the British tried unsuccessfully to break through the German defences and drive to the Belgian coast. In August, they had launched a series of more limited, "bite and hold" assaults. Initially, these met with success, but the longer the attacks went on, the less ground they gained and the greater the cost. By October, British, Australian, and New Zealand troops had pushed their way forward toward the high ground of the Passchendaele Ridge, and the Canadian Corps would now be called on to capture the ridge before the onset of winter.

The initial attacks on October 26 and 30 had secured the Canadians a foothold on the high ground, and they were now poised to take the rest of the ridge and the town of Passchendaele. During the attack scheduled for November 6 by 1st and 2nd Canadian Divisions, the 26th would be the only battalion from 5th Brigade to take part. The men were located on the far right of the attack, to the east of the road running from Zonnebeke to Passchendaele. Their advance would take them through the outskirts of the remains of the town and beyond to their objective, the Green Line, on the reverse slope of the ridge.

The battalion began preparing for the attack in mid-October, while still on the Lens front. A lecture presented by Lieutenant-Colonel Webber of 2nd Canadian Division described the nature of the fighting and gave

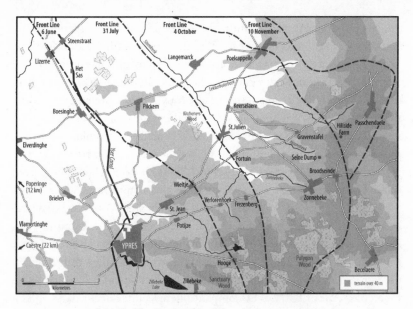

Map 5: The Battle of Passchendaele. Mike Bechthold

pointers on how to deal with certain situations. On the twenty-fourth, the battalion left for the Salient, arriving near Caëstre, several miles west of Ypres, where they would remain for the next ten days undergoing training and preparation. They practised their fighting tactics on a taped course, both as a battalion and as part of 5th Brigade. At Poperinghe, the troops also viewed a large-scale model of the ridge, based on aerial photographs and maps.

On November 3, the battalion arrived at Ypres by train, and the next day passed through the town to Potijze, one and a half kilometres to the east, where they spent the night. By then, conditions below the ridge had seriously deteriorated—as at Vimy Ridge, ground conditions and the weather would be among the greatest challenges facing the troops. Heavy artillery bombardment had littered the battlefield with deep, water-filled shell holes and obliterated many of the landmarks, including the town of Passchendaele, which could be identified "only by its ruins in ash and brick piles." The fighting also destroyed the local drainage system, leaving the battlefield a morass of mud. By November, the only recognizable features were the German concrete pillboxes holding machine guns, headquarters, and dressing stations. According to an unidentified officer from the battalion, they were "the only signs of human habitation in that vast expanse of mud and water, the only places where there was any covering."

At 11:00 p.m. on November 4, about 525 men from the four companies plus the headquarters element of the 26th moved up to an intermediate position at Seine Dump, about two and a half kilometres behind the front lines. There they remained for the next twenty-four hours. According to the battalion summary of operations, the Seine area "could be likened to an island in the midst of a sea of mud." The troops dug small funk holes in the sandy soil, then lay in them throughout the day covered by their rubber sheet, a stretcher, or piece of iron sheeting. The unidentified officer noted that there was no distinction of rank with regard to their comfort. Lieutenant Arthur Barry of D Company offered a more detailed description of the scene on the eve of battle: "There were no buildings of any kind, just mud, with some kind of slit trenches on higher ground to protect against shellfire. [A] Roman Catholic chaplain was hearing confessions standing under what had been a tree. About 50 yards away a poker game was in progress. Occasionally a soldier would fall in, hat in hand, at the end of the line for confession, move on to say his penance and then rejoin the poker game." Battalion headquarters was located farther forward in a pillbox on a commanding knoll at Hillside Farm, about three hundred metres northeast of the present-day location of Tyne Cot Cemetery. From there, they had a "splendid view" of the near slope of the ridge and the town of Passchendaele.

Around 11:30 p.m. on the fifth, the 26th moved up along the road leading to Passchendaele––known to the troops as McKenzie Road—to the jumping-off trenches, which lay to the rear of the 24th Battalion's front-line position on the high ground east of Crest Farm, less than five hundred metres from the centre of Passchendaele. By 3:00 a.m. they were deployed in and around the attack trench. For Corporal Clarence Gillies (#742442) of D Company, this was his first experience of "real warfare," as

Clarence Gillies (centre) in the 8th Hussars before the war.

Clarence Gillies Collection

he described it in a letter to his mother written on the seventeenth. Gillies was born in March 1891 in Bellisle Creek, in Kings County, a cousin to Milton Gregg, the future Victoria Cross recipient from nearby Mountain Dale. In June 1916, Gillies enlisted in the 115th Battalion, having already served in the 8th Hussars for five years. In August, he sailed for Britain, and a year later was sent to France to join the 26th in the field. He recorded that, around four a.m. on the sixth, they got orders to crawl over the parapet into no man's land and stay in shell holes about thirty yards in front of their line: "Fritz had snipers & machine guns not a hundred yards from the front line so we had to lay low as he was shooting all the time. Also putting the big shells around us & almost burying us with dirt."

An artillery duel between the Canadians and Germans began around 4:00 and ended by 5:30. The front then grew quiet in the minutes before the attack. The troops, numb from cold and inactivity, gratefully received a tot of rum. The moments before Zero Hour were a tense time. Private William D. Berry (#709220) was going over the top for the first time. A twenty-six-year-old mill hand from Prosser Brook, Kings County, he had enlisted in the 104th Battalion in October 1915, arrived in England in early July 1916, and finally joined the 26th in the field at the end of May 1917. As he waited for Zero Hour, Berry noticed he was trembling as he fixed his bayonet, "but noticed to his satisfaction that all his comrades were trembling too."

The 26th would attack with A, B, and D Companies in the front and C Company in support. Each company numbered about 130, all ranks, and would have various distances to cover to their final Green Line objectives: D Company on the left would have the farthest to go at about 600 metres. Unlike in previous battles, the men of the 26th would face dispersed German defences mainly located in and around concrete pillboxes, rather than dense lines of trenches. At 6:00 a.m. the Canadian artillery and machine guns began a barrage, and the infantry advanced under its protection. Gillies wrote that "you could see nothing but a blaze of fire & could hear nothing & we sure had a roof over our heads that would not let rain through." The German counterbarrage was slow to develop and was scattered for much of the day; instead, during the advance, the greatest opposition came from machine-gun fire. In the first minutes, D Company was hit by a heavy machine-gun barrage that Gillies described as "thick as rain." It caused about thirty casualties, including five of the ten men from his machine-gun team. As they advanced, casualties declined until they approached their objective, where they lost another fifteen men to enemy machine guns, but the Canadians pressed on, eager, as one source observed, "to settle with the Germans for the loss of a pal." Germans sheltering in their concrete pillboxes "were caught like rats in a trap by our chaps following as closely as possible behind our creeping barrage." B Company took about thirty-five prisoners during their advance.

It was bad enough with the enemy shooting at them, but friendly fire was a problem, too. Major Leonard, commanding D Company, was wounded by a Canadian shell. Years later, Barry described how an eight-inch shell entered the ground behind him, passed underneath, then exploded just yards to his front. The effect was unnerving. "I slid down about five feet to the bottom of the hole, dropped my buckets [of Lewis gun ammunition] and

Canadian pioneers lay duckboards or trench mats across
the Passchendaele battlefield, 1917. PA-002140, Library and Archives Canada

started back towards Ypres. I am not ashamed to tell this. I must have gone
50 yards mowing men out of my way—it was a natural reaction....I regret
that that 50-yard dash was not clocked. I am sure I established a record for
a heavy track. I never saw the ammunition buckets after."

German aircraft also became active during the day, especially once the
Canadians lit ground flares to mark their positions for friendly contact
observers. With aerial superiority, the Germans machine-gunned and
bombed the Canadian positions, although casualties were light. The
Canadians fired back using Lewis guns.

The ground conditions made advancing across the battlefield difficult.
According to an unidentified officer, "[u]ntil they got to the ridge where the
soil was sandy our fellows had to wallow through the mud which seemed

26TH BN. CANADIAN INF.

CAPTAIN
RUSSELL R. E.

LIEUTENANT
ARMSTRONG R. McL.
LOCKHART F. E.

REG. SGT. MAJOR
VASS J. A., D.C.M.

SERGEANT
COTTER F. L.

LANCE SERGEANT
MONTROY O.

CORPORAL
CAMPBELL J. P.
FRISBY H., M.M.
JOHNSTON J.
STATHAM W. P.

LANCE CORPORAL
CHARLTON H. R.
GORMAN H. M.

LANCE CORPORAL
HINKLEY A. J.
McINTYRE J. W.
MACKEY R. B.
MADDIGAN M.
SCOTT D. E.
STRATFORD J.
SERVED AS
RANSOM J.
WEAGLE F. G.

PRIVATE
ALLEN J. A.
ALWARD D. H.
ARCHIBALD E. F.
ATKINSON A. W.
BESONDAY H.
BLAMPIED T. J.
BOUCHER F. C.
BOUDREAU C. H.
BOWSER G. W.
BREEN L. P.
BROWN G.
BUGDON W. E.
BURKE R.

First tablet for the 26th's missing, Menin Gate Memorial, Ypres, Belgium; among the names is that of Lieutenant Robert Armstrong, who went missing at Passchendaele. Author's photo to try to engulf them, to drag them down like quicksand, and if one were not particularly careful of his steps he sank almost to his waist. And it was not an easy job to extricate him. There were no communication trenches, for it would have been useless labor to dig them out, but duck-boards were laid over top of the countless shell holes." The swampy ground became a death trap for many of the wounded and contributed to the large number of men from the battalion who went missing during the battle. Among them was Private William D. Wells (#742849), who had been born in Wellington, New Zealand, moved to Saint John, and enlisted in the 115th Battalion in March 1916, then joined the 26th in the field. According to a letter written a month later by Sergeant Roy V. Powell (#69763), after being wounded, Wells tried to crawl to safety, but fell into a shell hole and drowned. His body was never recovered. One of Lieutenant Barry's men likely met a similar fate. Brothers Fred and Robert Owen Carter, from St. Stephen, had enlisted in the 104th Battalion in November 1915, and by mid-1917 both were members of Barry's platoon. According to Barry, Fred was killed on the sixth, while Robert was wounded, but was able to walk and headed back to the rear. Barry wrote to their next-of-kin expressing his hope that Robert would be home by Christmas. A few weeks later, Barry received a reply saying that Robert had been reported missing. Barry surmised that Robert had "probably received another wound on the way back and was either killed or drowned in a shell hole." Lieutenant Robert M. Armstrong of B Company also went missing. Armstrong was a twenty-two-year old student at Mount Allison University when he enlisted in the 64th Battalion in November 1915; in late October 1916, he joined the 26th as a reinforcement officer. Letters written by Captain Harold Wood, the battalion adjutant, and Captain Gerald Anglin, Armstrong's company commander, stated that Armstrong was wounded and had set out for the dressing station in the rear but never made it. His body was never recovered. Yet another of the missing was Lance Corporal D. Everett Scott (#469950). Born in Jardineville, in Kent County, Scott was educated in Jardineville and Rexton schools and established a local reputation as an athlete. He became a newspaper man, working for the *Review* in Richibucto and later the *Sackville Tribune* as the editor. In September 1915, he enlisted in the 55th Battalion, becoming an acting sergeant by the time the unit went overseas in April 1916. In June 1917, he gave up his stripes to join a draft crossing to France to join the 26th. In what turned out to be his last letter home, Scott wrote: "Mother, I am going into the danger zone. Should I not come out, don't worry but rejoice. Before every engagement I commend myself to God's keeping and all is well." Scott's body was never recovered. The names of Wells, Armstrong, Scott, and both Carters are on the Menin Gate Memorial to the missing. Frank and Martha Carter also memorialized the loss of two sons on the same day by placing their names on the family gravestone in the St. Stephen Rural Cemetery.

Nonetheless, the mud had its advantages, absorbing much of the blast from German shells. According to an unidentified officer, "in the avalanche of shells which the enemy poured on our lines and upon our men advancing, it is not to be wondered that so many were hit but rather that so many got through. Certainly this would not have been the case had it not been for the softness of the ground. The shells sank deep into the mire and exploding throw up less shrapnel but great quantities of mud and water." Lieutenant Winnie Allingham of C Company had a different experience: he was buried alive by a shell explosion, and after being exhumed he continued leading his troops until he was wounded in the thigh by a sniper's bullet.

During the attack, casualties among company officers were again heavy: according to Captain Gerald Anglin, fourteen went into the battle and only four emerged unscathed. In addition to Leonard, two other company commanders, Captains Walter Lawson and Anglin (of C and B Companies, respectively), were also wounded—Lawson by a direct hit on company headquarters by a German shell before Zero Hour and Anglin by a machine-gun bullet—while Captain R.E. Russell, commanding A Company, was killed. As a result, it was up to junior officers to take command of the companies and carry on. Lieutenant Graham McKnight, a platoon commander who had been with the battalion for only two and a half months, took over D Company when Leonard was wounded. As an unidentified officer pointed out, "it speaks much for the material of the battalion that they were found to be of the 'right stuff.'" He also noted that "they could have done nothing had it not been for the wonderful

The Passchendaele battlefield, 1917. Mikan no. 3194756, Library and Archives Canada

support they met with from the N.C.O.'s and men, brave fellow that they are." The RSM, John Vass (#171229), who was left out of battle at the outset, was killed in the rear area along with the 25th Battalion's RSM. His name also appears on the Menin Gate Memorial.

A Company, which had the shortest distance to go, reached the Green Line in twenty minutes, and by 6:58 a.m.. the 26th had secured all of its objectives. 5th Brigade's summary of operations reported that "the men were in high spirits." The troops began consolidating their positions under a protective barrage. The new forward line consisted of advanced posts dispersed in shell holes on the forward slope so as not to present good targets to enemy artillery, while the main line was formed by connecting shell holes behind the crest of the ridge. It was sited to escape direct observation while denying the Germans the crest, should they break through the advanced posts.

Conditions facing the troops during this phase of the battle were not unlike those encountered at Vimy Ridge, although this time their stay in the open was shorter. German snipers and machine gunners inflicted considerable casualties on the 26th. According to the unidentified officer, "during the process of consolidation an enemy machine gun was playing from a shell hole not far away in such a way as to hinder the work and cause loss of life to those engaged. Snipers were also busy and were getting their men." Despite the German retaliation, "our chaps held out in those cheerless, muddy shell holes and hastily dug its trench. Now and then there came a shower of rain making the place still more uncomfortable—it was cold and wet with only a few hours of sunshine." Remarkably, the writer added, "few thought of that—the only thing that mattered was that they had gotten the objective, and that Fritz must never again get a footing on the ridge." On A Company's new front, a sergeant silenced one of these machine guns using a rifle grenade, his men then retrieved the gun, set it up, and used it against its previous owners. By about 11:00 a.m. reinforcements arrived from C Company, including about forty men from No. 11 Platoon under Lieutenant Allingham, although he and ten men were wounded coming forward. A German counterattack failed to materialize, which brigade saw as a sign of how far German morale had declined by the final days of the campaign. Gillies recorded that, once they had dug in on their objective, "a bunch of us had to look for souvenirs & we each would go & get an arm full of water bottles, canned goods, belts, watches, match boxes & I don't know what else & it did not put me out a particle to go through a Fritz."

The awful ground conditions greatly hampered the evacuation of the wounded during and after the battle. Two platoons from C Company spent most of the day carrying out the wounded to a dressing station, often under heavy fire. According to the unidentified officer, "[t]he stretcher bearers worked heroically and to their noble efforts many a man owes his life. They seemed not to know that the air was alive with shells, that bullets were 'dimming their songs o-er the field'—their only thought was to answer the pitiful groans of a wounded man lying helpless in that sea of mud. And after his injuries had been dressed came the difficult task of getting him out to the dressing station. Often a team of four men started out with their load only to be casualties themselves before they reached the place. But there were always other gallant chaps to take their places, and so the

Canadian stretcher bearers evacuating the wounded, Passchendaele, 1917.
PA-002140, Library and Archives Canada

work went on." The battalion summary of operations concluded that the evacuation of the wounded was "very badly arranged" overall and, despite their best efforts, they were unable to quickly clear the battlefield. As a result, a number of men lay out in the open for as long as forty-eight hours without being attended to, with the result that many died of their wounds.

During the night of November 6/7, the 26th sent out patrols to watch for enemy movement. One detected a party of about a hundred Germans forming up for a counterattack and sent up SOS flares. The artillery immediately opened up, inflicting heavy casualties on the enemy and dispersing them. The next day, when the artillery fired a protective barrage, the German artillery response was weak, but shells still found men in their shallow trenches. In the afternoon, several scored direct hits on 26th troops, one causing nine casualties, buried and wounded by shrapnel; as the battalion reported, "it was with great difficulty that these men were

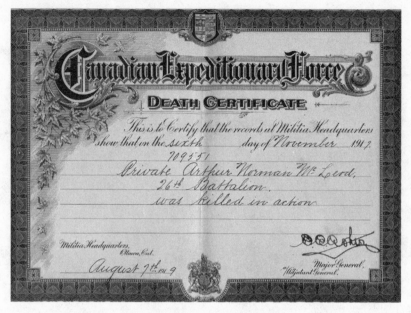

Canadian Expeditionary Force

DEATH CERTIFICATE

This is to Certify that the records at Militia Headquarters show that on the *sixth* day of *November* 191*7*.

709551

Private Arthur Norman McLeod,
26th Battalion,
was killed in action

Militia Headquarters,
Ottawa, Ont.

August 7th 191 9

Major General
Adjutant General

Death certificate of Private Arthur N. McLeod, killed at Passchendaele, November 6, 1917. Harold Wright Collection

gotten out alive." Once again, there was considerable sniping by both sides, and early in the day thirty-five German aircraft came over and bombed the Canadians' lines. According to Gillies, the troops received no extra rations or drinking water during the day, so they caught rainwater in their rubber sheets and drank it.

On the night of the seventh, the troops were relieved and returned to the Seine Dump area. In the morning of the eighth, they moved back to Potijze. Unfortunately, two platoons from B Company were hit hard by German artillery fire while resting in the rear trenches, losing between thirty-five and forty men. The battalion remained at Potijze until November 11, when it moved back to Brandhoek, to the west of Ypres. On November 12, the officers and men were given leave in the surrounding towns. Many took the opportunity to revisit old friends and the numerous graves of fallen comrades; Lieutenant McKnight saw the grave of Major Belyea, a friend and militia comrade from before the war, at Locre.

The cost of success at Passchendaele was once again high, with the unit suffering 284 casualties. A and B companies were hit particularly hard, losing 77 and 98 men, respectively. Among them was Private Arthur N. McLeod (#709661), a thirty-two-year-old farmer from Studholm, in Kings County, who was living in Penobsquis when he enlisted in the 104th Battalion in October 1915. In November 1916, he joined the 26th, and in August 1917 attended a bomb-throwing course. He was killed in action on November 6 and is buried in Tyne Cot Cemetery, close to where he fell.

The men of the 26th were proud of their part in the battle, especially having participated in the capture of Passchendaele itself. Gillies wrote that "the Colonel says it was the worst battle the 26th ever was in & we have got great praise from all sides." In a letter to his mother, written on December 18, Lieutenant McKnight observed that "western battalions were all mentioned in the fighting in the north, and not a word of ours but you'll hear more latter. The truth of the matter is that our battalion went right through that town of [Passchendaele] and I was one of it and well remember it and won't forget it for a long while at any rate."

On November 13, the much-battered battalion departed again for the Vimy front, reaching Neuville-St-Vaast on the sixteenth, where reinforcements began arriving to replace once again the battalion's many losses. The troops soon resumed trench warfare operations, and began settling in for their third winter at the front. It had been a gruelling year.

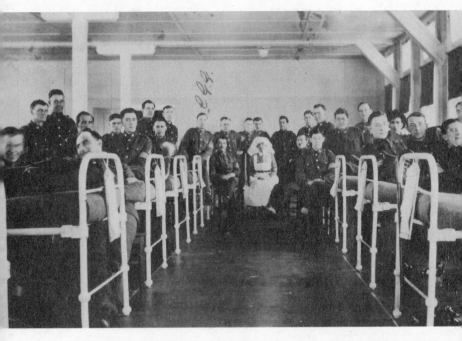

Soldiers' Ward, New Brunswick Military Hospital, Fredericton;
the man beneath the written initials is the 26th Battalion's Sergeant
Clarence Gillies, convalescing from his knee wound. Clarence Gillies Collection

Chapter Six

Goings and Comings:
Casualties, Transfers, Punishment,
and Reinforcements

The 26th Battalion underwent constant changes in personnel throughout the course of the war. Troops were killed, wounded, or left the unit in myriad other ways, and were replaced by men from across eastern Canada. In the process, as the "originals" dwindled, the character of the unit began to change, but over time new ways were found through the reinforcement system to ensure not only that the unit was kept up to strength and efficient, but also that it retained its provincial identity.

Great War infantry battalions suffered extraordinarily high rates of attrition. By the time the war ended, the 26th — with a War Establishment strength of 1,114 all ranks (48 officers, 1,066 other ranks) — had the names of more than five times as many soldiers on its rolls; nearly 4,000 were casualties. When the battalion arrived home in May 1919, only four of its original officers and 113 men were still with the unit. Of the returning officers, only Major James Pringle of Fredericton, the quarter-master, had served continuously with the unit, and many of the returning other ranks had been in England convalescing from wounds and had been permitted to rejoin the unit for the return to Canada. The rest of the originals had been killed, wounded and invalided home, or transferred to other units.

Casualties

Between fall 1914 and spring 1919, 5,719 troops passed through the ranks of the 26th Battalion. Casualties accounted for most of the unit's transformation: from combat deaths, wounds, and missing to prisoners of war and sickness. The largest single factor in this fierce attrition rate was battle. The casualties in some of these battles were staggering. As Table 3 illustrates, the worst campaign was the Somme, where the 26th lost 501 men in two actions: Courcelette (325 casualties) and the attack on Regina Trench on September 28 (176 casualties). Losses at Hill 70 were also heavy, and in the wake of the battle the battalion had to reduce each of its companies by a platoon to keep the order of battle in place until it could be brought up to strength with reinforcements. In that respect, Hill 70 was the first major test of the new reinforcement system put in place in early 1917. During the battles of the Hundred Days Offensive in the second half of 1918, the battalion again lost more than five hundred men. Table 5 shows that, of the sample compiled by Curtis Mainville of 1,026 originals from the battalion, 203, or almost 20 percent, were killed in action, died of wounds, or went missing.

Casualties were rarely spread evenly among the companies. For example, at Passchendaele, A Company suffered by far the most heavily, going into the line with 136, all ranks, and returning with just 34 men. The company's losses represented over a third of the battalion's 284 casualties. Nor did casualties occur uniformly among the ranks. Junior officers serving as platoon commanders, often leading by example from the front during combat, received disproportionately higher losses. During the war, thirty-three lieutenants from the 26th were killed and ninety wounded. Stretcher bearers, who had to move around no man's land in the open, also incurred high casualties. Ben Gaskill, an original from Grand Manan, calculated that during 1917 the battalion lost sixty-five stretcher bearers: twenty-eight killed and thirty-seven wounded. Private James Gaulton (#69332) of Saint John described the stressful nature of the regimental stretcher bearers' work:

> Their's is a constant vigil during the time that the unit
> is in the line. They never know when they will be called.
> Perhaps they will be trying to get a few minute's well-earned

Table 3: Casualties, 26th Battalion, by Battle

Battle	Casualties
Somme, 1916	501
Vimy, 1917	178
Hill 70, 1917	268
Passchendaele, 1917	284
Amiens, 1918	237
Scarpe, 1918	322

sleep when the call comes along "S.B. on the double" and then those boys rush to the wounded and do all in their power with first aid work. It gives the wounded men great relief after the S.B. men has the poor fellows wounds dressed.... Imagine yourself in a trench, whether good or bad, or out with a working party and you are expecting any minute to have to rush to render first aid to some poor soldier who has been wounded. I can assure you that it is very trying on the nerves.... It is very trying work to dress a wound when it is pitch dark night and a light cannot be shown.

Approximately two thousand seven hundred soldiers from the battalion were wounded. Those with light injuries often remained on duty with the battalion; the more seriously wounded were sent to the rear, whereupon they were struck off strength and transferred to the New Brunswick Regimental Depot in Shoreham, England. There, they either recovered after hospitalization and rejoined the battalion at the front, or they were sent home to be discharged. The nature of their wounds varied considerably. Gunshot wounds from rifles and machine guns could be serious, sometimes causing traumatic amputations. On May 1, 1916, Private Herbert Wagg (#70062), a fisherman from New River, in Charlotte County, and battalion

Grave of Private Leon
C. Vincent, Brookwood
Military Cemetery,
Surrey, England.
Author's photo

original, was on patrol in no man's land when a German sniper's bullet
passed through his left hand, carrying away his second finger. By early
August he had been invalided back to New Brunswick. Remarkably, Wagg
re-enlisted in April 1918.

Shell explosions inflicted serious, multiple wounds that had long-term
consequences for the invalided soldier. On August 5, 1916, Private Howard
Ginder (#69315), a twenty-three-year-old clerk from Birmingham, England,
who was living in Fredericton with his wife Gladys when he enlisted in
November 1914, was wounded at St. Eloi in August 1916 while serving as
a stretcher bearer when a shell exploded a few metres away from him. The
same shell killed three of his fellow soldiers, who were lying across him
when he was found. Ginder had four shell fragments in his legs, a badly
damaged left foot, and a fractured skull. After evacuation to hospital, he
remained unconscious for four days in critical condition. After he showed
some improvement, it was found necessary to amputate his foot about fifteen

centimetres above his ankle. His right leg was also impaired by a fractured fibula. Compounding his injuries were a ruptured macula in his right eye, which left him with limited vision, and a ruptured ear drum in his right ear, which caused partial deafness—the latter two injuries the result of the concussion of the exploding shell. After lengthy hospitalization in Britain, Grinder was discharged in late December 1916, returned to Canada the next month, and underwent months of rehabilitation at the Military Orthopedic Hospital in Toronto. He was fitted with an artificial limb on his left leg and a brace for his right leg, but his right leg was reduced to two-thirds its normal size by the loss of muscle tissue. In mid-1917 he was finally released from hospital and discharged.

Some wounds occurred accidentally, especially early on when the troops were relatively inexperienced. Shortly after arriving at the front, accidental discharges from rifles became frequent, several proving fatal. Division headquarters issued instructions through the battalion that only rifles being used in the front and support lines should have loaded magazines, but with the chamber kept empty. Commanders were directed to "take stringent measures" to ensure that these orders were carried out.

A major part of these soldiers' experience was the hospitalization needed for their recovery. Those with light wounds were mainly treated in hospitals located in France. More serious cases were evacuated to England, where some died of their wounds. Private Leon C. Vincent (#742559) from Rothesay was wounded on November 6, 1917, at Passchendaele, evacuated to Britain, and died on November 26. He is buried in Brookwood Military Cemetery in Surrey, the largest military cemetery in Britain created for Commonwealth troops who died in the London area. Those requiring long-term convalescence were returned to Canada, where most were discharged. Some recovered and returned to duty following treatment.

Members of the battalion began returning home in late 1915, and during the second half of the war hospital facilities were set up within the province to treat them. These included the New Brunswick Military Hospital, established in Old Government House in Fredericton, which until then had been used as barracks for troops raised for service with the CEF. Among the many 26th men who spent time in the military hospital was Sergeant

Convalescing soldiers embroidering in the New Brunswick Military Hospital, Fredericton. Sergeant Clarence Gillies is third from left.

Clarence Gillies Collection

Clarence Gillies, who, on April 7, 1918, was seriously wounded in the right knee by a shell near Arras. After undergoing surgery, he spent the next several months recovering in hospitals in France and Britain, receiving both electrical and massage therapy for his stiff knee. Finally, in October, he was invalided back to New Brunswick, where he was taken on strength at No. 7 District Depot and sent to the military hospital in Fredericton to convalesce. There, he continued to receive massage treatment, although by then he did not think it was very useful. The soldiers in the Fredericton hospital also received occupational therapy designed to keep them busy using their hands, including learning how to embroider or knit. For entertainment, the patients wrote and read letters, and attended concerts and dances. Church services were also held in the hospital. Gillies was reasonably ambulatory, and obtained passes either to go into town in the evenings, especially to watch movies at the Gaiety Theatre, or to visit family in the Norton/Sussex area. He was at home when the war ended on November 11. The next day he went to Sussex to watch the celebrations. According to his diary: "A Holiday in the city & one perfect day. Stella [his future wife] and Mabel [his sister] & I spent the afternoon looking at the fine parade of soldiers and automobiles, and it sure was grand." And so his war ended.

Some soldiers of the 26th were shell shocked, a little-understood psychological wound caused by trauma to the brain suffered through exposure to combat. Among the shell-shock casualties was Private William Berry, the mill hand from Prosser Brook, who went over the top on November 6, 1917, at Passchendaele. Berry had been with the unit for a short time, and had only limited front line experience before entering his first major battle. Hospital records describe the onset of his troubles even before the battle. In September, he had worked with ration parties at the front, where they were shelled steadily and lost about half their strength in a few days. Although he hadn't noticed any tremors at the time and had slept well, he had a "hollow nauseated feeling in his stomach & was conscious of fears." On November 6, Berry recalled, he advanced about 400 yards and then dug in as best he could. While sheltering in his position, he noticed he was trembling badly until about 8:00 p.m., when his company was relieved. After lying out on the battlefield for the day, he had trouble getting to the rear, having to turn all of his equipment over to others and be supported as he walked. He spent the night in a safe but crowded dugout, but could not sleep, was jumpy, and continued trembling badly. Following the battle, he returned to the Lens front with the unit. He was still shaky, though not as bad as before, and he began having dreams about the fighting, often jumping out of bed. His feet also became badly swollen, his legs painful and weak, and his head felt heavy. Finally, on November 23, he was sent to hospital diagnosed with "pyrexia of unknown origin."

In early February 1918, after spending a month in hospital at Étaples, Berry was admitted to the 4th London General Hospital with "nervous debility," suffering from tremors in the arms and legs and feeling "mentally sad." As part of his treatment, he worked in the garden. After thirty-five days, he was transferred to Granville Canadian Special Hospital in Buxton, Derbyshire, where he was diagnosed with neurasthenia, the pre-war term for nervous disorders that resembled shell shock. Initially, Berry still had a slight tremor, but "complained of sleepless nights and dreadful dreams," and was unable "to control himself when excited or where there is noise."

He was unable to attend concerts, which made him tremble. His records indicate nothing about the treatment he received other than to say that he walked about half a mile each day. Toward the end of May, Berry was examined by a medical board. His tremor was gone, he was sleeping better, and had fewer dreams and less pain, but the board found that Berry would not "stand the strain of general service" and categorized him as B2: able to stand service on the lines of communication in France. In June, he left the 26th when he was transferred to Bramshott training camp in Hampshire, where he underwent periodic training and was promoted to lance corporal. He remained in camp until returning to Canada in March 1919. By the time Berry was discharged, he had made a sound recovery, being in good health and physical condition with no impairments.

Great War soldiers afflicted with shell shock exhibited other symptoms, including mutism. Among them was Private Roy V. McAulay (#70095), an original from West Saint John. The twenty-three-year-old brakeman with the Canadian Pacific Railway had served for three years with the 3rd Regiment, Canadian Garrison Artillery, before enlisting in the 26th on March 1, 1915. During his first seven months of service at the front, McAulay spent nearly every trench tour on outpost duty. He described his experience in a letter to his mother dated June 21, 1916: "[W]ith a comrade, one goes out over the parapet into No Man's Land as far as the barbed wire. Of course this is at night time. After listening and trying to find out all we can for an hour lying on our stomachs, we return to the trench for two hours rest and go out again. The chief danger is in going and coming, for if they detect us by the light caused by flares, a machine gun is turned on us and possibly bombs, mortars or rifle grenades chase after us. The last time out chaps in the next post were killed by a grenade." He had also participated in the Crater fight, and was one of the few men from A Company to emerge unscathed.

In early April 1916, McAulay was knocked unconscious by the explosion of a ten-inch shell, and the next day lost his speech. He was diagnosed with aphonia brought on by shell shock. Eleven weeks later, he was able to speak after receiving treatment at the King George Hospital in London. The treatment took the form of electrical shocks applied by Dr. Stewart, a civilian specialist. McAulay described the technique in his letter: "Whilst a Sister regulated the batteries, the doctor applied the electrical instrument to my neck, while showing me how to hold my mouth to pronounce 'B' and 'K.' I tried for ten minutes, but could not until finally he got me coughing and at the same time trying to articulate 'K' and 'B.' Then I found I could say it faintly and then plainer until I found myself stuttering and talking with effort." The following morning the doctor was scheduled to give McAulay a lesson in talking in order to ease the effort and eliminate the stuttering. As harsh as the treatment sounds by modern standards, McAulay considered it wonderful, having already been to four other hospitals in France and attended by nine doctors, one of whom used chloroform "to bring me to a high state of excitement and yet I found I could not speak." Afterwards, McAulay rejoined the 26th, was awarded the Good Conduct Badge, and was promoted to lance corporal. In early 1919, he returned to Canada, where he was discharged.

Some soldiers were pushed to the brink by their experiences. CSM James F. Gilbert (#69319) was a twenty-year-old labourer from Saint John with no previous military service when he enlisted in the 26th in November 1914. Once he reached the front, Gilbert achieved an impressive record of service, steadily rising through the ranks and appointed company sergeant major in January 1918. In November 1915, he was wounded in the right hand and hospitalized in England until June 1916, when he rejoined the unit at the front. In November 1917, he was awarded the MM and later the DCM for his actions during the Battle of Amiens, when he took charge of a platoon after its commander and senior NCOs became casualties. He was slightly wounded on August 8 and again on August 27, but remained on duty both times. When he rejoined the unit on August 31, however, he was in a seriously depressive state, with nightmares about the fighting and seeing the Germans he had killed in what doctors later described as hallucinations. Subsequently, Gilbert shot and wounded two of his own men from the 26th who were trying to take down his tent. Gilbert was quickly evacuated to the rear, where he underwent physical and psychological assessments and was variously diagnosed as suffering from melancholia, neurasthenia, and finally exhaustion psychosis.

The doctors' detailed case notes show the steady decline in Gilbert's mental state brought on by prolonged exposure to the stress of his front line experiences, his responsibilities with little respite, and his wounds. Between his return to the unit in July 1916 and the incident in August 1918, he had had only ten days' leave. During July and August 1918, he began to lose weight, was unable to sleep, and became depressed, but was determined to "stick it out." According to the doctors' interviews, by August he had begun to lose faith in his men, believing the new men were not as good in battle as the older ones and that they "hung back on the last 2 occasions of their going over top." The death of his company commander in battle might have been the final blow. The adjutant general's branch of Second Army decided not to proceed with a field general court martial for shooting his comrades, however, believing they would find that Gilbert was "not responsible for his actions at the time he fired the shots that caused the casualties." In January 1919, Gilbert was invalided to Canada to convalesce at the Cobourg Military Hospital in Ontario. There, his mental health improved, and he became active in hospital duties. Finally, in March 1919, he was discharged from the army, being found medically unfit for further service.

Soldiers were also "struck off strength" from the unit when they were captured by the enemy. Approximately twenty-three men from the 26th became prisoners of war — about average for a 2nd Canadian Division infantry battalion. These men were taken under various circumstances, but most were groups of wounded soldiers overrun during battle. On September 28, 1916, three 26th men were lost during the attack on Regina Trench. Another four were captured in Méricourt on April 15, 1917, during the later Vimy operations. Among the latter was Private Paul Caissy (#445232) of St. Omer, Quebec, who was wounded in the left leg and spent the next seven and a half months in a German hospital. The largest single loss came on September 25/26, 1918, during the battalion's advance to the Canal du Nord, when eight men were captured. Fortunately, their captivity was brief. Among them was Private Fred J. Hamilton (#1030091) of Saint John, who went overseas with the 236th Battalion (New Brunswick Kilties) in 1917 and was transferred to the 26th. After being captured, he and his comrades were put to work behind the German lines. At the time of the Armistice, he was part of a 144-man working party scheduled to be sent to an internment camp in Germany. According to a newspaper interview Hamilton gave after his return to Canada, they refused to go, and "taking the law into their own hands, made their way to Liege, five kilometres away," where Hamilton was "nicely cared for at the home of a Belgian gentleman." Later, they went to Namur, where they came under orders of the military authorities and were sent to Dover and then home, where he arrived on March 2, 1919.

Most Canadians were incarcerated in prisoner-of-war camps in Germany, including those at Giessen, in central Germany, and Wahn, near Cologne. In time, their families received letters, but the prisoners were constrained in what they could say. Writing to his mother in West St. John in March 1918 from a hospital in Münster, Private Holly Turner (#66987), captured at Regina Trench sixteen months earlier, related that he was "getting better fast" from an illness and expected to be released from hospital soon. He continued: "I will not be sorry when this affair is over and I will be able to get home. I cannot complain of the treatment I received while a patient in this hospital. The staff did all they possibly could for me during my illness." Wounds generally reduced their chances of surviving captivity. On July 10, Turner died at a camp *Lazarett*, or military hospital, from a brain abscess caused by a bullet wound to the head, presumably received when he was captured. According to a letter written to his mother by the president of the British Help Committee, Turner was buried in a prisoner-of-war cemetery near Münster. "The body was attended by his comrades and the burial service of the Church of England was read over his grave."

Other prisoners also did not survive their captivity. Private William T. Sutthery (#709197) of Red Rapids, in Victoria County, captured on August 16, 1918, died of his wounds on September 23, and was buried in the Maubeuge-Centre Cemetery in German-occupied France. Another was Private James T. Covey (#469902), who was born at New Cumberland, Nova Scotia, near Lunenburg. On September 5, 1915, the nineteen-year-old lumberman enlisted in the 64th Battalion in Sussex, New Brunswick, sailed for Britain at the end of March 1916, and joined the 26th in France on July 7. A few months later, he was reported missing at the Somme, and then listed as a prisoner of war suffering from a gunshot wound to the left leg. By early March 1917, Covey was incarcerated in the prisoner-of-war camp at Giessen. In early December 1918, he was repatriated to France and admitted to 42nd Stationary Hospital near Charmes, in the Vosges Mountains, suffering from a serious case of bronchial pneumonia. He died a few days later on December 7, and was buried in the Charmes Military Cemetery.

Some seriously wounded captives were repatriated to Britain before the cessation of hostilities. Private Andrew Stackable (#70329) from Minto was captured at Vimy. He had his leg amputated, and was released by the Germans on January 7, 1918. The rest of the prisoners were returned in the months after the Armistice was signed and eventually returned home.

Hundreds of soldiers contracted illnesses, and many had to be evacuated, which meant being struck off strength and replaced. According to Mainville's sample of sickness among 1,206 original members of the battalion (Table 4), the most frequent ailments were: viral and bacterial diseases such as influenza (110 cases); soft tissue injuries, such as rheumatism (95); various forms of skin disorders ranging from trench foot to eczema and psoriasis (96); a range of digestive disorders, including dyspepsia (32 cases); ear, nose, and throat infections, including tonsillitis (37); respiratory conditions, including bronchitis (42); and various heart conditions (35).

Venereal disease (VD) was a special case. As Mainville's sample shows, VD was the most common sickness in the 26th (189 cases, or almost 22 percent of the 862 men in the sample who served in England and Belgium/France). The incidence among married men prior to embarkation was lower than among single men, but once overseas, married men were more likely to contract VD. Since it was considered a preventable affliction, it was subject to minor punishment, including forfeiture of the soldier's field allowance and stoppage of pay in the amount of 50 cents for every day in hospital. Hospitalization could last as long as two months before treatment was complete.

Some of these sick men never returned to the 26th. Early on, sickness led to men being declared medically unfit for service and sent home.

Table 4: Incidence of Sickness among a Sample of Original Members of the 26th Battalion

Medical Condition				
Category			**Individually**	**While Serving in Unit**
Cardiovascular system			49	46
	Heart	DAH, tachycardia, endocarditis, syncope, angina, aneurism	38	35
	Blood poisoning	septicemia, anemia	11	11
Respiratory system			86	81
	Bronchitis		45	42
	Tuberculosis	haemoptysis	20	19
	Pleurisy		15	14
	Asthma	dyspnea, emphysema	6	6
Urinary system			16	13
	Nephritis	Bright's disease, kidneys	10	8
	Albuminuria	protein in urine	3	2
	Alcoholism		2	2
	Stones		1	1
Digestive system			100	90
	Dyspepsia	gastritis, colitis, indigestion	32·	32
	Appendicitis		18	16
	Hernia		18	18
	Diarrhoea	dysentery, ptomaine poisoning	11	9
	Bladder	cystitis, enuresis, incontinence	8	7
	Stomach/intestines	enteritis, inflammation of small intestines, myoma	7	5
	Constipation		6	3
Eyes, ears, nose, and throat			92	84
	Throat	pharynx, tonsillitis, laryngitis, tracheitis	43	37
	Eyes	myopia, ametropia, anophthalmos, conjunctivitis, ulcers, diplopia, iritis, keratitis	29	28
	Ears	otitis	16	15
	Nose		4	4

Fractures		11	10
Soft tissue injury		174	156
Arthritis	rheumatism, deformity, synovitis, ICT (inflammation connecting tissue), kyphosis, neuralgia, sciatica, ankylosis	110	95
Sprains	swelling, back pain	26	25
Contusions	lacerations, dislocations, hammer toe	24	23
Feet	fallen arches, metatarsalgia, flat feet	14	13
Neurological		54	50
Neurasthenia	insanity, psychosis, nervousness, colic	25	23
Debility		15	13
Convulsion	epilepsy	7	7
Self-inflicted wound		5	5
Concussion		1	1
Senility		1	1
Viral and bacterial diseases		499	460
STD	VDG, VDS, chancroid, herpes	190	189
Influenza		128	110
Trench fever	pyrexia of unknown origin	66	57
Myalgia		46	38
Measles	rubella	24	24
Diphtheria		11	11
Mumps		10	10
Typhoid fever	enteric fever	8	7
Other	gangrene, infections	7	5
Rheumatic fever		3	3
Scarlet fever		2	2
Smallpox		1	1
Trench mouth		1	1
Chicken pox	varicella	1	1

Other		159	148
Skin disorders	boils, furunculosis, carbuncles, abscess, cysts, blisters, cellulitis, dermatitis, eczema, scabies, erysipelas, impetigo, jaundice, keloid, necrosis, neuritis, papilloma, psoriasis, pyodermia, seborrhoea, trench foot, urticari	106	96
Genitals	balanitis, orchitis, epididymitis, hydrocele, sacrum, paraphimosis, phimosis, urethritis, varicocele	26	23
Hemorrhoids	piles	10	10
Varicose veins		10	12
Glands	adenitis, paratiditis	6	6
Lice	pediculosis	1	1
Accidental	burns, fractures, lacerations, scalding	0	46

Source: Survey of a sample of 1,251 original members
of the 26th Battalion Curtis Mainville.

In mid-1915, Lance Corporal Leonard H. Webber (#70070), a former bank clerk from St. Stephen, was sent from England back to Canada and examined by a medical board in Quebec, which found one lung infected with tuberculosis. They recommended treatment in a sanatorium, and he returned to New Brunswick, where he likely entered the Jordan Memorial Sanatorium in The Glades, near Petitcodiac. Other men left the unit with honourable discharges because they could not meet medical requirements for general service. Table 5 shows that 269 of the sample of 1,026 originals, or 26.2 percent, were medically unfit. Some, like Private Robert Crilley (#69132), could not pass the final medical examination in England prior to the battalion's going across the Channel in September 1915. A teamster from Saint John, Crilley failed the eye examination due to a serious myopia astigmatism in his right eye that was improved only slightly by glasses. In November, he arrived back in Saint John, where he had enlisted a year earlier, regretting that he would not see action with the unit.

The strength of the battalion was diminished in many other ways. Both officers and other ranks periodically received a leave of absence for varying lengths of time. Typically, a soldier received ten days' leave about once a

Table 5: Disposition of a Sample of Original Members, 26th Battalion

Disposition and Reason		Individually (number)	Individually (percent)	While Serving in Unit (number)	While Serving in Unit (percent)
Irregularities and behaviour		99	9.6	98	9.6
	rejected	12		12	
	undesirable	18		18	
	service not required	1		1	
	misconduct	5		4	
	inefficiency	3		3	
	irregular enlistment	2		2	
	cashiered	1		1	
	desertion	55		55	
	minor	2		2	
Transfers		21	2.0	160	15.6
	commissioned	8		8	
	resigned	1		1	
	surplus	1		1	
	transfer	7		146	
	compassionate grounds	4		4	
Casualties		538	52.4	491	47.9
	medically unfit	304		269	
	drowned	1		1	
	died	20		18	
	died of wounds	56		52	
	killed in action	141		135	
	missing	16		16	
Demobilization		364	35.5	273	26.6
Unknown		4	0.4	4	0.4
Total		1,026	100.0	1,026	100.0

Source: Survey of a sample of 1,026 original members of the 26th Battalion
Curtis Mainville.

year. During that time, they remained on the unit's nominal roll, but were temporarily unavailable for duty. Officers and other ranks also attended training courses in schools of instruction. Lieutenant Graham McKnight explained to his sister that these proved "most beneficial. You will begin to wonder what all the courses are for, but in this game there is something to learn every day, and an officer is always a picked one for them."

Many other soldiers were temporarily attached to other units, especially within the brigade — including the 5th Field Company, Canadian Engineers, and 5th Canadian Trench Mortar Battery — but would remain on the unit's rolls, or "on command," until they returned. Sometimes these postings became permanent: as Table 5 shows, 146, or almost 14 percent of the sample, transferred out of the battalion. Among them was Private Alexander Methot (#69556), a twenty-year-old deck hand from Dalhousie, an original who was wounded at Courcelette. In October 1916, after recovering, Methot transferred to the Canadian Machine Gun Corps, where he served until the end of the war. In February 1917, Private Hugh Wright, after being at the front with the 26th for seventeen months, transferred to the artillery, joining the 4th Canadian Siege Battery, where his brother Clarke was already serving. For Wright, it was a positive change. On February 12, he recorded: "I am writing today in a much happier mood than I was the last time I wrote.... I have got my transfer at last and have been with the Battery several days and like it fine. It is some change after being in the infantry so long." A month later, he noted that "I have had more time to myself since I came here than I had all the time I was in [the 26th]."

Some soldiers from the 26th were transferred to posts better suited to their civilian skills, especially those with trades needed for special services within the army, such as tool makers, lead burners, chemical plumbers, and coppersmiths. Lance Corporal Silas Wright (#70068) from Hopewell Hill, in Albert County, was hospitalized in London after developing blood poisoning in a finger. After recovering he was transferred to the headquarters staff at the base at Shorncliffe. According to an article in the *Daily Telegraph*, "Wright's experience as a station agent and former bank clerk at home no doubt assist in making him an efficient man in his present work."

Several men also went back home to join new units. In January 1916, Lieutenant Arthur Legere left to help recruit the 165th (Acadian) Battalion, while in mid-1916, Lieutenants Frank Easton and Edward Sturdee and Sergeant Earle M. Scovil (#444091) returned to New Brunswick to join the

Table 6: Offences among Sample of Original Members, 26th Battalion

Charge	Number
Absent	42
Absent & insolence	1
Absent & neglect	1
AWOL	237
AWOL & breaking	2
AWOL & disturbance	1
AWOL & drunk	3
AWOL & drunk & neglect	1
AWOL & escape	1
AWOL & refusing	2
Breaking	6
Breaking & absent	2
Breaking & drunk	3
Desertion	1
Drunk	46
Drunk & absent	10
Drunk & breaking	1
Drunk & disturbance	1
Drunk & insolence	2
Drunk & neglect	1
Drunk & resisting	3
Falling	6
Gambling	1
Insolence	5
Misconduct	6
Neglect	10
Refusing	11
Refusing & insolence	4
Self-inflicted wound	3
Theft	8
Unspecified	93

Source: Survey of a sample of 607 original members
of the 26th Battalion Curtis Mainville.

236th Battalion (New Brunswick Kilties - Sir Sam's Own). Others transferred to aerial combat, including Lieutenant Percy Sherren, an original officer from Crapaud, Prince Edward Island, who served with an RFC day bomber squadron, rose to become a major and command a squadron, and was awarded an MC for his exploits.

Men were also removed from duty through punishment. Discipline was an important battalion matter that was largely handled by the company and unit commanding officers, who had summary powers for dealing with numerous infractions without referring to a higher authority. The battalion commanding officer set the standard for discipline, and could impose a range of punishments, including stoppage of pay, fines, confinement to barracks, and Field Punishment No. 1. Lieutenant-Colonel McKenzie had a reputation for being a strict disciplinarian. In a letter home in early October 1917, not long after he joined the 26th, Lieutenant Graham McKnight noted that McKenzie had just returned to the unit to resume command: "He is a fine soldier, though very strict. I guess probably we will get used to him all right in time." Breaches of discipline ranged from minor offences, such as failing to salute, to drunkenness, insubordination, resisting arrest, and desertion. As Table 6 shows, based on Mainville's review of 627 records of original soldiers, 306 (48.8 percent) carried a disciplinary charge. Among them a total of 514 charges was identified. Some form of absence made up the largest proportion (304, or 59.1 percent), and covered a wide spectrum of offences ranging from being absent from parade and duty to overstaying leave, to being absent without leave, and desertion. In those cases where AWOL was indicated, soldiers went missing an average of 1.57 times. Drunkenness, the second most frequent offence, represented 71, or 13.8 percent, of known infractions.

A wide range of punishments could be imposed at the battalion level under the *Manual of Military Law*, many of which affected the soldier's standing in the unit. Company commanders dealt with minor offences by imposing extra duties or confinement to barracks for up to seven days. The battalion commander handled more serious infractions with reprimands and extra duties, fines, and pay forfeiture, confinement to barracks, detention, Field Punishment No. 1 and No. 2, and reduction of rank. Field Punishment

Field Punishment No. 1. Library and Archives Canada

No. 1 was one of the sternest options for punishment. It entailed the offender's being tied to a fixed post or wagon wheel in public view for a prescribed length of time. During his punishment, the prisoner was also limited to tea, biscuits, and bully beef unless it affected the efficiency of the prisoner as a "fighting man," when the scale of the ration could be adjusted at the discretion of senior commanders. The maximum time the battalion commander could invoke was twenty-eight days. Field Punishment No. 1 was used for many offences, including absence and drunkenness. In March 1916, the scale of punishment for drunkenness became the source of disagreement when the general officer commanding 2nd Canadian Division informed battalion commanders that he had noticed the incidence of drunkenness was increasing and, believing they were acting too leniently, directed them to remedy the problem: "It must be appreciated that drunkenness on active service is a most serious offence from a military point of view, and it is therefore necessary to deal with it with greater severity than is customary under peace conditions." He continued: "[W]hile not wishing to question or interfere with the discretionary powers of Commanding Officers, the following is suggested as a guide in dealing with offences of drunkenness unconnected with other offences.

1st offence — 14 days Field Punishment No. 1
2nd offence — 28 days Field Punishment
Subsequent — trial by Field General Court Martial"

Among the sample of 26th originals, the average length of Field Punishment No. 1 for drunkenness was 19.3 days. More serious crimes were dealt with outside the battalion by field general courts martial. Historian David Campbell's study of discipline and punishment in 2nd Canadian Division shows that the incidence of courts martial in the 26th fell among the lower half of the formation's infantry units. A total of seventy-six soldiers from the 26th faced courts martial, the majority in 1917 and 1918 (twenty-six and thirty-three, respectively). Fourteen were tried for desertion, thirteen for insubordination and disobedience, eleven for absence, ten for drunkenness, and fifty-seven for a range of other crimes (see Table 7).

Reinforcements

The Canadian Corps' reinforcement system evolved to become efficient at keeping units up to strength and making the corps a potent force on the Western Front. Over time, large numbers of replacements joined the 26th Battalion (see Table 8).

After many of its battles, the 26th had to be virtually rebuilt. Reinforcement drafts usually arrived in comparatively large numbers, especially in comparison to the reduced size of the battalion. For example, after the Somme in 1916, the 26th received 290 reinforcements over about

Table 7: Summary Average Punishments among Sample of Original Members, 26th Battalion

Offence	Forfeiture		Detention		Fine		Field Punishment No. 1		Field Punishment No. 2		Confined to Barracks		Extra Duties	Reduction in Rank	Reprimand
	Cases	Days	Cases	Days	Cases	Amount	Cases	Days	Cases	Days	Cases	Days			
Absent	20	5.2	3	8.3	4	$6.25	14	13.2	10	4.6	7	6.9	1	2	2
AWOL	192	5.3	30	12.8	38	$6.16	25	12.1	15	13.4	24	6.2	1	10	9
Breaking Arrest	4	4.0	5	9.0	4	$6.75	5	17.4	0		2	10.0	0	0	1
Desertion	1	144.0	0		0		0		0		0		0	0	0
Drunk	8	6.5	10	8.4	12	$4.83	23	19.3	9	11.4	12	9.2	0	6	2
Falling Out on March	0		0		0		2	14.5	2	7.0	0		0	0	2
Insolence	0		2	10.5	2	$6.00	3	15.0	3	12.3	1	5.0	0	2	0
Misconduct	2	5.0	0		0		4	11.8	2	4.0	0		0	0	0
Neglect	1	7.0	2	40.0	3	$5.67	2	21.0	1	5.0	1	2.0	0	2	4
Refusing an Order	5	5.8	3	8.7	0		3	11.7	6	10.0	0		0	0	1
Self-Inflicted Wound	0		0		0		3	41.7	0		0		0	0	0
Theft	2	20.0	4	537.8	0		3	11.7	1	90.0	0		0	0	0

Source: Survey of a sample of 607 original members of the 26th Battalion Curtis Mainville.

Lieutenant Alexander G. Gunn, in London to receive the Military Cross. Mikan no. 3216409. Library and Archives Canada

three weeks from the 106th Battalion and another large contingent from the 140th Battalion during October to bring it up to strength. After Hill 70 in 1917, the battalion received almost 280 reinforcements in just two days—one draft numbering 191 and the other 189 other ranks from the 64th and 132nd Battalions, which revived the reduced companies. In that sense, by 1917, the system was able to resuscitate the battalion's numbers in fairly short order, especially compared with 1916 after the Somme, when reinforcements arrived more slowly.

Many unit histories describe briefly how these reinforcement drafts arrived shortly after battle and were absorbed into the unit while it rebuilt, usually on a quiet part of the front and often in preparation for another battle. Behind this all too brief narrative, however, is a complex story that raises a host of important questions: who were these new troops, how well

Table 8: Partial List of Reinforcements, by Source, 26th Battalion

Source of Reinforcements	Location of Unit	Number	Date of Draft
35th Battalion	Ontario	60	
39th Battalion	Ontario	60	
40th Battalion	Nova Scotia	85	March 1916
55th Battalion	New Brunswick & PEI	172	May 1916
59th Battalion	Ontario & Quebec	76	
64th Battalion	Maritimes	150	August 1916
104th Battalion	New Brunswick	588	December 1916
105th Battalion	Prince Edward Island	545	mid-1917
106th Battalion	Nova Scotia	319	October 1916
115th Battalion	New Brunswick	418	December 1916
132nd Battalion	New Brunswick	256	August 1917
140th Battalion	New Brunswick	428	October 1916
145th Battalion	New Brunswick	36	
165th Battalion	Maritimes	122	
236th Battalion	New Brunswick	13	

Source: Author's compilation

trained were they, and what effect did their arrival have on the character of the unit?

During the war, of the more than five thousand seven hundred men who served in the 26th Battalion, enough to refill it four and a half times over, over four thousand five hundred were reinforcements, who came from different sources, and initially there was little attempt to maintain the battalion's New Brunswick identity. At the Somme, the battalion began replacing some of its junior leadership losses by promoting its senior NCOs. Commissioning from the ranks ensured that the wealth of knowledge and experience acquired at such terrible cost would continue to serve the unit. At least eight NCOs became lieutenants in the 26th, including Alexander Gunn, the company sergeant major who had been in the forefront of the Crater fight, was later wounded at Regina Trench, and then mentioned in despatches in early 1917.[12] Gunn was commissioned in May 1917, became the battalion scouting officer, and in January 1918 was awarded the Military

---

12 The others were William H. Buddell, James W. Corey, Ralph L. Eaton, Charles S. Jenkins, Amos A. Pickard, Hugh R. Simms, and Roland J. Smith.

Cross. The chances of surviving unscathed for those commissioned from the ranks were not good: of the eight, two were killed in action or died of their wounds, one died of pneumonia, and two were wounded, including Gunn, who was hit again in April 1918.

Other officer replacements came from several of New Brunswick's disbanded battalions. For example, in late August 1917, following Hill 70, four lieutenants from the 132nd Battalion (H.W.S. Allingham, A.L Barry, J.G. McKnight, and J.E. White) joined the 26th. It had been a long journey to France for these men. Barry was born in Oromocto, and had gone to school at Fredericton High School and the Provincial Normal School. In 1913, he became vice-principal at the Harkins Academy in Newcastle, where he organized the first Army Cadet Corps. At the outset of the war, he was a lieutenant with the militia's 73rd Northumberland Regiment, which was mobilized to guard the Newcastle Wireless Station. He remained there for many months, then in November 1915, Barry became the first of five brothers to enlist in the CEF when he joined the 132nd (North Shore) Battalion. In October 1916, the 132nd went to Britain, where it was quickly broken up for reinforcements. Subsequently, Barry joined the 13th Reserve Battalion, where he took command of the drafting company that provided reinforcements for the 26th in France. By then, he had grown frustrated with his slow progress toward the front. As he wrote in his memoirs, "I now had three years of service and to the point where I was fed up with training and being trained. My name was always scratched off the list of officers when drafts were being prepared as indispensable. After a serious interview with Colonel [George] Fowler [commanding officer of the 13th Reserve Battalion][13] I was told he would allow me to go on the next call for officers." When Barry joined the 26th on August 25, 1917, however, it was at a reduction in rank: "I was again a lieutenant as all officers and NCOs reporting for duty on the battlefront for the first time had to start on the bottom rung of the ladder." All four of these lieutenants fought as platoon commanders at Passchendaele two months later. On November 6, Allingham was wounded during the attack on the village of Passchendaele,

---

13   Lieutenant-Colonel George W. Fowler was a New Brunswick senator who raised and commanded the 104th Battalion until it was disbanded in 1917, whereupon he took command of the 13th Reserve Battalion.

Uniform of Regimental
Sergeant Major Herbert Endall.
2009.008.01, New Brunswick Military History
Museum

followed by injuries to Barry in
April 1918 and White in October,
but they defied the odds, and all
survived the war.

Some senior NCO replace-
ments also had to revert to the
ranks to join the 26th in the
field. Herbert Endall, from War-
wickshire, England, was living in
Fredericton when he enlisted in the 64th Battalion in December 1915.
He had served for ten years in the Permanent Force, becoming a sergeant
in The Royal Canadian Regiment before leaving to become a mechanic
and father of four children. After joining the 64th, Endall was quickly
promoted to RSM before proceeding to England. In May 1917, he reverted
to the rank of private to join the 26th. He soon proved himself, winning
the Military Medal at Passchendaele and rising through the ranks rapidly,
becoming the 26th's RSM in May 1918. Later, he was also awarded the
Distinguished Conduct Medal.

A number of the replacements were returning wounded. Even some of
those who had suffered multiple wounds returned to the front after they had
recovered. Among the officers, Captain Reginald Major was wounded four
times. In June 1915, Major was a twenty-five-year-old civil engineer who
had served in the 62nd Regiment when he enlisted in the 55th Battalion as
a lieutenant. Major was a platoon and company commander with the 26th
and was wounded on the opening days of the attacks at both Vimy Ridge

and Hill 70, again while serving in the line in mid-May 1918, and a fourth time at Amiens. Among the other ranks, dozens received multiple wounds. One of the most notable cases was Private John W. Gallant (#70290) from Summerside, Prince Edward Island, who enlisted in the 55th Battalion in early 1915, was transferred to the 26th on May 1, and shortly afterwards left for Britain with the battalion. Gallant suffered four wounds of varying types and seriousness. On March 27, 1916, he received a serious "contusion" to his body from a shell, which likely meant he was concussed by a shell explosion. Shortly afterward, he was diagnosed with neurasthenia. He was wounded again on September 14, 1916, at the Somme, and for a third time on April 9, 1917, at Vimy Ridge. Finally, on August 28, 1918, he received gunshot wounds to the legs. Afterwards, he became dangerously ill, and on September 9 Gallant died of his wounds.

The bulk of these replacements were provided over time by numerous units. Initially, they came from the 12th Reserve Battalion, a First Contingent unit that remained in Britain as a reinforcing battalion, training recently arrived soldiers for the front. It had a large New Brunswick presence in its ranks, including many troops from the provincial militia's 71st York Regiment, and was commanded by Lieutenant-Colonel Harry F. McLeod, the pre-war commanding officer of the 71st. After the 12th was drained of its reinforcements, newcomers to the 26th came mainly from Ontario and Nova Scotia units, including a draft from the 39th Battalion, raised in eastern Ontario around Belleville. Their names began appearing in the 26th's casualty list in November 1915. Among the first of these to die in action was Private William A. Martin (#412277), a twenty-year-old farmer from near Brighton, England, who enlisted in the 39th in February 1915. In December 17, shortly after joining the 26th at the front, he was killed, and was buried in nearby La Laiterie Military Cemetery among his new comrades. Other early arrivals came from the 40th Battalion from Nova Scotia and the 59th Battalion from central Ontario.

Over time this trend changed, and the majority of reinforcements began arriving from New Brunswick battalions that had been raised for overseas service in 1915 and 1916 and broken up once they reached Britain. Notable among these were the 104th, 115th, and 140th Battalions, which among them provided over fourteen hundred troops. The 104th was raised in Sussex, New Brunswick, in 1915 and went overseas in 1916. In time, it joined 10th Brigade, 5th Canadian Division, and so was slated to become New Brunswick's second front-line infantry battalion. After 5th Division was disbanded, however, the 104th began furnishing drafts of men to battalions in France, including at least 13 officers and 575 other ranks for the 26th. The 115th Battalion was raised in December 1915 and stationed in Saint John. Commanded by Lieutenant-Colonel Frederick V. Wedderburn, a career army officer who had served in Egypt in 1884 and 1896, the Northwest Rebellion, and the South African War, and had commanded the 8th Hussars, the "St. John Tigers" sailed for England in July 1916. Over four hundred of them joined the 26th. Sizable contingents also reached the 26th from the 105th Battalion (Prince Edward Island Highlanders), which was amalgamated with the 104th in January 1917, and from the 106th from Nova Scotia; together, these units provided another 860 men.

Some of these troops came from diverse racial backgrounds. Among them were Fred and George Moore, Aboriginal twin brothers who were born near St. Andrews and lived on the Pleasant Point Reservation in Perry, Maine, until enlisting in the 115th Battalion in 1916. They joined the 26th in June 1917. Fred was wounded in early July and was absent from the unit convalescing when George went missing during the attack on Hill 70. Today, George's name appears on the Vimy Memorial. After contracting trench fever, Fred rejoined the 26th in August 1918, was wounded for a second time on October 9, 1918, at Cambrai, returned home to convalesce in 1919, and finally was discharged in July. He died in Eastport, Maine, in July 1966.

Private Rankin Wheary (#710017) was an African Canadian from Woodstock. He grew up playing baseball in school and for the Woodstock Federals. In January 1916, Wheary joined the 104th Battalion. After reaching Britain, he was transferred to the 5th Canadian Mounted Rifles and then in March 1918 to the 26th. He joined the regimental baseball team, became one of its star players, and competed in the corps championship. He was killed in action near Cambrai on October 7, 1918.

Behind these statistics are other important points that go some way toward explaining the overall success of the reinforcement system in helping to maintain the efficiency of battalions such as the 26th. First is the question of how well trained these reinforcements were when they reached the battalion. Most units arriving in Britain from Canada had received only a basic level of training. Over time, the training establishment in Britain expanded and improved so that, when reinforcements went to France, they had received a more uniform level of training. An important link in this system to prepare troops for the fighting was the reserve battalion system created at the beginning of 1917 as part of a major reorganization of Canadian troops in Britain. The 26th Battalion was served by the 13th Reserve Battalion, located at Bramshott, Hampshire. According to Major W.H. Laughlin, a doctor from St. Stephen and second-in-command of the 104th Battalion, in early January 1917 the remnants of the 104th and 105th, numbering about six hundred men, were amalgamated to form the nucleus of the 13th Reserve Battalion. The new unit also absorbed all New Brunswick men in England from the 115th, 132nd, 140th, and 145th Battalions, as well as those casualties from the 26th who were recovering from wounds in England. It came to number about thirteen hundred troops, and was initially commanded by Lieutenant-Colonel Fowler, the outgoing commander of the 104th Battalion.

The job of the reserve battalion was to provide more intensive training based on the British Army's fourteen-week syllabus[14] and physical hardening before the men went to France. Major Laughlin became the second-in-command of the 13th Battalion and the officer in charge of training and instruction. For a short time, he was attached to a British reserve battalion at Aldershot to "get the last method of training a Reserve Battalion in a short time, fourteen weeks at most," he wrote. Later on, officers from the 26th Battalion were sent back from France to the reserve battalion, presumably to inject a greater degree of first-hand battle experience into the training process. In August 1917, for example, Major John A. McKenzie, one of the unit's company commanders, left

---

14   By the end of 1915, British soldiers' training consisted of some nine weeks of recruit training, including squad and company drill, and preliminary musketry training. In the tenth and eleventh weeks, they would fire the full musketry course and receive five days' instruction in bombing. They then moved on to learn how to use field dressings and anti-gas helmets, and then final training in bayonet fighting, wire entanglements, and rapid loading and firing.

the battalion in France to join the 13th Battalion and did not return until December. He was followed by Majors Reginald Arnold, Walter Brown, Harold Wood, and Charles Leonard. And in late September 1918, Major Cecil G. Porter, another company commander, left the 26th to take command of the 13th.

Once the reinforcements proceeded to France, they were sent to the Canadian General Base Depot at Le Havre, which in time was transferred to Étaples, near Boulogne, and then, in September 1917, reorganized as the Canadian Corps Reinforcement Camp. Here the men received additional training that more closely conformed to the way the BEF's formations and units did things at the front. The curriculum consisted of basics such as drill, route marching, musketry, gas drill, and rudimentary tactics. This modicum of training allowed reinforcements to be assimilated more quickly and efficiently into their field units without great loss of efficiency. Inevitably, a period of training within the unit followed the arrival of reinforcement drafts, where more advanced training took place and the new men absorbed into the front-line ranks. Initially, the reinforcements were held in divisional entrenching battalions in the rear until they were sent forward to join their battalion. In December 1916, a brigade training battalion was set up behind the lines, with the 26th having its own company. Four lieutenants from the 26th were seconded to the company to train the newly arrived replacements. Lieutenant Bayard Coster of Saint John, a replacement officer from the 55th Battalion, commanded the company. Once these new troops reached the front lines, they got "hands on" instruction by, among other things, being attached to scout patrols, where they gained experience moving across no man's land at night. They received additional training while the unit was in brigade reserve. As can be well understood, the arrival of so many "strangers" made it important to fit them in as quickly and effectively as possible.

Another important issue linked to reinforcements was unit cohesion, so necessary for success on the battlefield despite heavy casualties and the influx of so many new soldiers into the ranks. In 1916, units began leaving some troops, including senior officers and NCOs and usually one platoon per company, out of battle to provide immediate reinforcements and continuity while replacements were absorbed. There is no doubt, however, that the character of the 26th changed dramatically over time as the originals were lost through attrition and the ranks filled up with reinforcements from different places and units. The replacements had mixed feelings about their new circumstances. Most were dismayed at the demise of their parent units, but often they admired their new comrades. For example, Corporal Francis H. Everett (#742236), a farmer, originally from England but living in Saint John, had joined the 115th Battalion in December 1915. After the unit was broken up, he went to the 26th. In early January 1917, he wrote that "there are still several of the original 26th men here, and one cannot help feeling proud of them, the way they have stuck it out." He was disappointed at the practice whereby NCOs from the drafts had to revert to the ranks "and start again at the bottom," but he accepted his lot, stating that "this is only fair to those who have been here some time." Everett was killed in action a few months later, on March 22.

It is more difficult to say how this transition affected the "originals," but the change within the 26th was unmistakable. The battalion war diary contains a copy of the nominal role of troops entering the line in late October 1917 in preparation for their part in the Passchendaele offensive. The battle force numbered 563 all ranks. A sampling of their regimental numbers shows how reinforcements now dwarfed the originals. The preponderance of the battalion's troops came from myriad reinforcement units, including the 55th, 70th, 104th, 105th, 106th, 115th, 132nd, and 140th battalions. During the middle years of the war, unit leaders became concerned about the effect of these changes on the battalion's provincial identity. In late February 1916, Lieutenant Arthur Legere acknowledged that, up to that point, "we have not received any easterners as reinforcements, officers and men coming from the western battalions." Although this began to change by the end of 1916, when more Maritimers joined the battalion, some remained frustrated by the wider issue of the apparent underappreciation shown to troops from the region. In a letter written in May 1917 to Lieutenant-Colonel McAvity, Lieutenant-Colonel McKenzie complained that "the old units…have been getting our New Brunswick men who should have gone to us [but] have been sent over [by] the hundreds to Montreal and other battalions. The

Major Frederick May.
Author's collection

Maritime provinces have been made the 'hewers of wood and drawers of water' for other battalions when we have got reinforcements from everywhere except where we should have got them. It seems to me that Canada does not extend beyond Montreal or Quebec — the Maritime provinces are only places to get fighting men from, not staff officers. You realize we are 'fed up' with our treatment but it does not concern us much except in the abstract." But he did go on to write that "conditions as to reinforcements are improving as we are now getting New Brunswick men, and we got a fine draft yesterday of which only five were not from New Brunswick but P.E. Island."

Presumably this change was brought about by the new territorial system, which aimed at ensuring overseas battalions were reinforced by troops from their own local areas. During 1916 and early 1917, hundreds of New Brunswickers from nine other CEF units raised earlier in the war were channelled into the 26th. This local link was further extended in March 1917 when the army introduced a regimental territorial system: reserve battalions in Britain and their affiliated fighting battalions in France would now be linked into territorial regiments bearing provincial designations. Then, in August 1917, the army began creating depot battalions back in Canada to take in reinforcements within their recruiting areas to be sent on to Britain and France. At that point, a New Brunswick Regiment was formed for New Brunswick and Prince Edward Island military district No. 7, headquartered in Saint John and consisting of three battalions: the

1st Deport Battalion in New Brunswick, the 13th Reserve Battalion in England, and the 26th (and later the 44th) at the front.

The 1st Depot Battalion, originally called the 1st Training Battalion, was formed in late 1917, and commanded by Lieutenant-Colonel McAvity, the original commander of the 26th. It was located initially at Saint John and later at Camp Sussex, where it trained recent volunteers and men called up under the *Military Service Act*. (During the Hundred Days campaign, these soldiers made their way to the front, and their names began appearing on the 26th's casualty lists beginning in September 1918. By the end of the war, at least eight conscripts had been killed in action and another twenty-one wounded.) The Depot Battalion used returned soldiers as instructors and staff, including many from the 26th, among them Major Douglas P. McArthur, who was sent home to Saint John in May 1917 on furlough to recover from a fever he had contracted in France. He did not return to the front, but in time became McAvity's second-in-command. Similarly, Major Frederick F. May of Saint John was wounded while serving with the 26th in France and invalided home, where he became a company commander with the Depot Battalion.

This new system went a long way toward delivering a constant flow of local reinforcements to the 26th, ensuring that it retained its provincial identity and also remained an efficient, full-strength battalion. It was this system that sustained the Canadian Corps during the great offensives of 1918, when it made a distinguished contribution to the fighting that ended the war. During the Hundred Days campaign, the 26th was engaged in almost constant combat and suffered some of its heaviest losses.

Chapter Seven

1918: Year of Victory

In late 1917, the Canadian Corps returned to the Vimy/Lens front, where it mostly remained for the next several months. In March 1918, a great German offensive to the south drove a deep salient into the British lines, and Canadian troops, including the 26th Battalion, helped to stem the advance. During the summer and fall, the rejuvenated corps was drawn into intensive and almost continuous mobile combat operations that drove back the Germans, culminating in the Armistice on November 11. Throughout this period, the 26th fought in some of the largest battles of the war, taking serious casualties that had to be replaced quickly if the unit was to maintain its efficiency during the fast-paced advance to victory.

As 1917 drew to a close, the men of the 26th found themselves in familiar trenches east of Vimy Ridge. On December 21, they moved into Army Reserve and had their first Christmas out of the line since reaching France over two years ago. In January 1918, they returned to front-line duties. Early in the month, the weather was so wet that water covered roads and the trenches became very muddy. Periodically, heavy snow storms swept across the region. Under these conditions, the troops entered into a routine that at times became monotonous, which they found ways to relieve whenever possible. Beginning around 5:30 p.m., everyone in the forward lines, with the exception of those on sentry duty the next day, would stand to throughout the long winter night until about 7:00 a.m. Sections would take turns at two-hour intervals going out into no man's land to patrol and repair wire. The soldiers looked forward to the arrival of rations and mail shortly after standing to. About 10:00 p.m., hot tea would come in dixies from the field kitchens. Then, about half an hour before standing down in the morning, the rum ration, known to the troops as the "nose-cap," would be served out, giving them a chance to share mail and comforts from home. A short time later, the men would eat breakfast, clean their rifles in preparation for rifle inspection, and then turn in. The daytime sentry details would take over watching the enemy's line, often through periscopes, until the evening when the routine would begin again.

Sometimes it was difficult to get the weary men to clean their rifles properly before going to sleep, but Lieutenant Arthur Barry found ways to encourage them. On one occasion, he observed members of his platoon sitting on the lower steps of a captured German dugout, probing a dead enemy body lying in about thirty centimetres of water. When the question was asked about who would be detailed to bury the corpse, the answer came back: "The owner of the first dirty rifle." After that, Barry had little trouble motivating his troops to clean their weapons. He reported that, at the end of their trench tour, the body was still there; he turned it and their trench stores over to the in-coming relief.

The battalion's routine was periodically enlivened by visits from out-siders. Beginning in late January, soldiers from the US Army were attached to the unit for instruction. Initially, they came as individual officers, the first being Lieutenant R.W. Love, who stayed for four days. According to the war diary, when he departed on the twentieth-eight, he was asked what impressed him most during his visit; his reply said much about the character of the unit and its soldiers: "Your conversation is all about War. There is no doubt that you take war as a serious business, but the humour you get out of it and the cheerfulness of all ranks under adverse conditions has impressed me the most." Later, small numbers of officers and NCOs from US infantry regiments underwent instruction.

The unit also received visits from New Brunswick civilians. In early February, the Anglican bishop of Fredericton, the Most Reverend John A.

Richardson, and several other clergymen met the troops. Richardson was on a fact-finding mission for the House of Bishops of Canada, investigating accusations made against the character of Canadian soldiers serving overseas. He visited hospitals and units at the front, including the 26th. During his stay, the bishop preached part the unit's church service held in the Chaplain Service Cinema Hut, and then had lunch at the battalion headquarters' mess. After returning home, Bishop Richardson toured the province speaking about his visit and criticizing what he thought were scurrilous slurs against Canadian troops.

In April, after the German offensive had overrun many British units, the battalion welcomed new faces from an unexpected direction. Three British soldiers from the 63rd (Royal Naval) Division, taken prisoner a month earlier on the southern flank of British Third Army around Flesquières, had escaped and entered the 26th's lines during the night. Unfortunately, the war diary does not record details about how this chancy return was carried out.

The unit also broke the routine with entertainments. In July, while in reserve, the battalion attended concerts at the YMCA given by its famous entertainment group, the Y-Emmas, and 2nd Canadian Division's troupe, "The See Toos." Sports were also popular. Colonel McKenzie, an outstanding athlete—while at the University of New Brunswick he had set a shot-put record—understood the importance of sports in maintaining morale. He was especially proud of the battalion's baseball team, which made a name for itself in 1918. During June and July, the team competed for the corps championship during a series of games that were well attended by the men; it won the divisional championship, but was defeated in the semi-finals for the corps title.

Enemy Encounters

During the winter months of 1918, the Canadian front was generally quiet, but skirmishes with the Germans still occurred. Throughout this period, the battalion adopted a policy of offensive patrolling in no man's land. Small patrols consisting of an officer and a dozen battalion scouts armed with Lewis guns would cover the battalion's front in relays from dusk until dawn. Although their forays usually passed without incident, they occasionally encountered the Germans doing the same thing. On the night of January 21, a large German force worked its way around the flanks of a 26th patrol, presumably planning to cut off and capture the Canadians, who used their skill and training to extricate themselves from a dangerous situation. Advancing in a crescent formation, they were ordered to shift into a wedge-shaped configuration once the Germans were detected, giving them "a splendid field of fire on either flank." The Lewis gunners took up position at the front of the formation, but according to the war diary, "unfortunately owing to mud causing a stoppage, the Lewis Gun was found to be useless." It was imperative that none of the patrol be captured for identification by the Germans, so the 26th men withdrew gradually, drawing the enemy toward a machine-gun post. As soon as they fell back to the position, a Lewis gun opened fire, both sides threw bombs, and the Germans hurriedly retired. The Canadians later searched for German identification but found none. The battalion war diary recorded: "The Corps Commander [Currie] commented that this situation was well handled."

The Germans also raided the 26th's lines. On the night of February 2/3, an enemy battle patrol numbering between four and seven soldiers penetrated the three belts of Canadian wire, cutting only the lower strands, and causing the 26th's wire patrol to miss their approach. They split into two parties and lay up against the Canadian parapet, then jumped into the trench in a bid to capture two stragglers from a ration party. The 26th's war diary described the ensuing action: "[O]ur men dropped their rations and fled towards the right yelling for help. One man threw his steel helmet in the nearest bosche's face. One of the enemy threw a cylindrical stick [grenade]. Two more of the enemy were seen running along the parapet. The right post heard the cry for help and opened up rifle and Lewis gun fire immediately, which was taken up by the left post." Parties from both positions searched the area after the firing had died down, but neither found any sign of the German intruders.

In February, the battalion returned to the Lens area to the east of Liéven, where the front lines were located among shattered villages.

Forward company defences were arrayed around several posts manned by garrisons numbering about a dozen men each. During the day they were lightly held, but at night everyone stood to. The troops were billeted in cellars in nearby buildings.

In March, the battalion was taken out of the line to rest and refit. Its stay was cut short, however, by the German offensive that began on March 21 to the southeast of Arras. On the twenty-fourth, the 26th moved southward, and soon entered the line near Neuville-Vitasse when 2nd Canadian Division was transferred to the British VI Corps, where it remained until the German assaults abated in July. The rest of the Canadian Corps remained around Vimy.

Shortly after arriving in the sector, brigade asked for raids to capture prisoners for interrogation, so the 26th carried out many patrols and raids to harass the enemy. The job fell to Lieutenant Barry, who became the new battalion scout officer after his predecessor, Lieutenant Gunn, was wounded on April 15. While probing the German lines, Barry put his training to good use. He had been instructed to lower his head to shield his face and stand still if sighted in no man's land — it was movement that gave away one's presence. On a moonlit night in late April, he was illuminated in the open during one of his forays:

> Then happened one of those few moments when the outcome depends on nerves, and mine were always good.... The sentry must have looked our way and sensed things didn't look the same. My head and shoulders were in full view and he was only 30 to 35 yards away. He stopped rocking. After about 15 seconds he leaned down and another soldier stood alongside him. They both stared and I stared them back. I had my tin hat pulled down to shade my face. It seemed a minute but I know it couldn't be more than 30 seconds. The second man stepped down and the sentry resumed his rocking side to side.... He thought he saw something — and did — but my failure to get out of sight fooled him.

Having failed several times to get into a German position near the Arras-Bapaume road, Barry decided on April 24 to mount a raid that once again brought them into close-quarters combat with the enemy. The objective, a post occupied by about eight Germans, was located near the end of an old communication trench and protected by a wire block across the trench about thirty metres in front of the position, and then by a stretch of tin cans strung from wire. Leading a force of three battalion scouts and seven men from D Company, Barry planned his attack for 4:00 a.m. When the Germans saw the approaching party, however, he decided to wait until daylight, hoping the enemy would go back to sleep. At 8:00 a.m. Barry and his three scouts crawled over the block, but the sound of one of the men rattling a can alerted the Germans. Barry then ordered the whole party to rush the post with grenades and revolvers. According to an account of the action published in the Campbellton *Graphic*, "[t]he Germans scrambled from the funk holes yelling and with arms up. Had they stayed in this attitude they would now probably be enjoying the same rations as others of their breed in our prison camps, but those who did not offer fight, turned to run towards the rear. There was some close-up revolver work, and our chaps got all but one whom they brought back as a sample." When German reinforcements bombed and machine gunned the Canadians, Barry and another soldier were wounded. The raiding party quickly returned to their trench with their captive, suffering no further losses. The battalion had its prisoner, but Barry had to be evacuated to hospital at Rouen, where he was operated on twice and would not return to the unit until mid-August. For his actions Barry was awarded the Military Cross, and two other ranks, Acting Corporal Joseph A. Biddiscombe (#742320) of North Forks, Sunbury County, and Private Alfred R. Coultas (#69109), an original from Scarborough, England, received the Military Medal.

As it turned out, the day's action was not yet over. Captain Robert B. Campbell, commanding D Company, organized a patrol with three other ranks to check the same post to see if it had been reoccupied and to inflict more casualties on the Germans. At 2:00 p.m. they left the front line, hoping the unlikely timing in broad daylight would surprise the enemy. When they reached the wire block, however, it became clear the Germans were present and alert. From his position, Campbell could see a sentry looking over the top of the trench. "As he remained motionless, it was difficult to be sure his head was not a dummy. To prove this, the officer carefully reached for a rifle, but on a slight movement was detected by the enemy, who shouted in a very loud and terrific voice, 'Kommen heraus.' (Patrol report no shortage of lung power in enemy troops.) Thus alarming the post, 8 enemy appeared over the top of the parapet of post as if by magic." Throwing bombs at the New Brunswickers, they rushed forward along the communication trench. The patrol dropped back, hurling Mills grenades as they went, then engaged with rifle and pistol fire. A Lewis gun firing from the front line covered them until they returned safely. In a postscript to his report, Campbell added scornfully: "If the enemy had had the 'guts of a louse' they could have made it a hand to hand fight and as weight of numbers would have told, our party would have fared badly, perhaps been wiped out."

Other raids were larger and much more elaborately planned, including an operation carried out on May 7 that aimed to inflict casualties on the enemy and take prisoners. At Zero Hour, an artillery hurricane bombardment crashed down on the German positions and the Canadian flanks along with trench mortars and machine guns. Flanking brigades also made demonstrations to mislead the Germans about the true location of the raid. The attacking party, commanded by Captain Albert E.L. Shand from B Company, consisted of four officers and eighty-four other ranks organized into four parties. During an exceptionally dark night, the raiders inflicted many casualties, including an estimated forty enemy killed by bomb or bayonet, and captured two enemy soldiers and a light machine gun. In his after-action report, Shand made clear the cold-blooded nature of fighting during raids: "The enemy exhibited very little desire for a fight. Two or three posts threw a few cylindrical sticks [grenades] at our parties as they approached, but on being rushed, after a few bombs from our men were quite ready to give in. Here the bayonet was freely used by our men and very little quarter given, hence the small number of prisoners taken." The 26th's casualties were one killed and fourteen wounded, mostly caused by bombs.

Throughout this time, the 26th underwent much training. In most months the battalion spent about a week training, but two lengthier periods occurred in March and July, the latter lasting about three weeks in preparation for the coming Allied offensive at Amiens. During the first round in March, the 26th spent a week in corps reserve at Niagara Camp at Château de la Haie, to the west of Vimy Ridge, undergoing a range of activities: shooting on the rifle ranges, passing through gas huts to test their respirators, and attending lectures on "Tanks in Offensive and Defensive Action," followed by a tank visit. They then moved to Raimbert, where they went into army reserve and began a two-week training syllabus where, according to a war diary appendix, "the general object is to train Section Commanders to realize that, in action, their section is the UNIT OF COMMAND, and to demonstrate to him his power of command." During the first week, they engaged in section, platoon, and company training and close-order drill, and paid special attention to musketry, including rapid loading, loading from standing, kneeling, and prone positions, aiming practice and trigger pressure, fire control, and target indication by section commanders. They also carried out box respirator drill and bayonet fighting. During the second week, they practised platoon and company schemes for trench, semi-open, and open warfare, and heard lectures on raids, scouting and patrolling, and attacking in both trench and semi-open warfare. They also carried out a route march; as the war diary proudly declared, "battalion in splendid condition and was highly spoken of (as usual)." The second week's training in March was cut short by the German offensive that began on March 21.

In early July, 2nd Canadian Division left British VI Corps and returned to the Canadian Corps, whereupon it went into reserve for a month and undertook another period of intensive training in preparation for the upcoming "show" at Amiens. Once again, the men began with the now "usual training": demonstrations in guard mounting and inspection, deploying platoons, and specialist training. This was followed by a demonstration with tanks, firing practice on the rifle ranges, and a day at the gas school to test and exchange their respirators. After almost two weeks of this program, the division had a short break, then training resumed by participating in a special demonstration of the "platoon in attack," followed by platoon training for the next several days.

By now the platoon in battle consisted of forty-one, all ranks: a five-man headquarters group consisting of the commander, platoon sergeant, two scouts, and a runner, and four nine-man sections, two rifle sections, and two Lewis gun sections. Each man was issued weapons and equipment designed to maximize the platoon's integral firepower and enhance its manoeuvrability against enemy positions. Almost half of the men in each rifle section were trained to act as rifle bombers or grenadiers; they carried one hundred rounds of rifle ammunition, four rifle bombs in a sandbag carried over the shoulder, and a cup discharger that fit onto to the end of their rifle to fire the grenades. The other men in the rifle sections carried 170 rounds of ammunition and two Mills bombs in their coat pockets. In the Lewis gun sections, one man armed with a revolver carried the gun, while the others carried their rifles and fifty rounds, and either spare parts for the gun or four machine-gun magazines in carriers. This system gave the platoon potent firepower: a total of 6,250 rounds of rifle ammunition, 48 magazines for the two light machine guns, 48 bombs, and 24 rifle grenades.

Training for a platoon in the attack consisted of a simple exercise that illustrated how all weapons in the platoon could be used in cooperation to gain fire superiority on an enemy strongpoint. The attack was carried out in several phases. First was the identification of the objective and reconnaissance by scouts while the rest of the platoon waited, followed by personal reconnaissance by the platoon and section commanders, who made the plan of attack and issued orders. The platoon then advanced toward the objective in small columns that worked their way forward through the barrage, using ground to avoid casualties, all under covering fire from Lewis guns set up in advanced positions on the flanks. After a pause for further reconnaissance by the platoon sergeant, the advance resumed under Lewis gun fire, assisted by rifle fire and rifle bombers who laid down a smoke barrage. The sections continued moving forward, assisting each other with fire until superiority had been achieved by converging fire, whereupon a vigorous attack by rifle sections using the bayonet took the objective. In the final phase, the position was secured against counterattack by sending out the Lewis guns and patrols. These small-unit tactics were used with much success during the last two and a half months of the war. In the final stages, they also trained for working with tanks, where horses represented the tanks and flags the enemy strongpoints and trenches.

While the Canadians trained in the spring and summer, the Germans launched a series of powerful attacks along the Western Front, driving the Allies back but failing to deliver a strategic knockout blow. By July they were spent, and the Allies, now reinforced by the Americans, resumed the offensive, forcing the Germans to retreat, bringing them to the point of collapse, and compelling them to ask for an armistice. The 26th Battalion became heavily engaged during the early stages of this campaign, known as the Hundred Days, fighting in the decisive Battle of Amiens and the first phase of the Battle of Arras—yet another costly battle that included the loss of their commanding officer. The battalion was less heavily involved in the capture of Cambrai in October and in the final advance through Valenciennes to Mons by November 11. Nevertheless, it remained in action from early August to the Armistice, paying the price of victory in a steady loss of men that added up over the final weeks of the war.

The Battle of Amiens: "a Great Wallop We Handed Fritz"

In early August, the Canadian Corps moved to Amiens to join the coming Allied offensive. After a long, fatiguing march, made worse by congested traffic on the roads and heavy rain on the evening of the fifth, the 26th Battalion reached the assembly trenches at Cachy, to the east of Amiens. Allied troops were poised across a wide front to push rapidly through the Germans, who were defending the salient created by their spring offensive. The Canadian Corps, deployed between the Australian Corps to the north and French forces to the south, attacked with brigades from 1st, 2nd, and 3rd Canadian Divisions along a seven-kilometre front between Villers-Bretonneux and the Amiens-Roye road. On the left, 4th Brigade spearheaded 2nd Canadian Division's attack, its objective the Green Line beyond the village of Marcelcave. Using 26th and 24th Battalions, 5th Brigade would continue the attack to the Red Line near Caix, while 6th

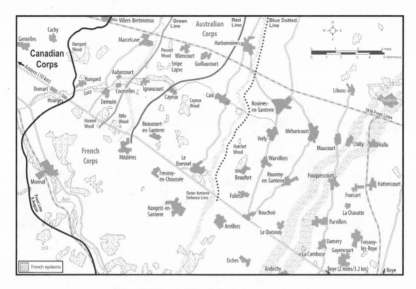

Map 6: The Battle of Amiens. Mike Bechthold

Brigade would carry through to the day's final objective near Méharicourt. The plan called for a highly organized, all-arms assault, using infantry, artillery, tanks, and cavalry, along with low-flying aircraft strafing enemy positions. If successful, the offensive would force the Germans to abandon their deep salient.

The attack began at 4:20 a.m. on August 8 with a shattering bombardment across the Allied front. 4th Brigade led off to the south of Villers-Bretonneux, followed by the troops of 5th Brigade. The 26th Battalion's C and D Companies advanced in the first wave, with two lines of platoons in file behind 4th Brigade troops. B and A Companies followed them forward. Early in the advance, heavy fog made it difficult to keep direction. They also met stubborn resistance, and suffered significant casualties at the German front line from enemy troops missed by the lead attackers in the fog. According to Captain Shand's B Company afteraction report, the German machine gunners they encountered proved to be fighters, "as they almost invariably remained at their guns until the last."

At 5:20 the 26th passed through 4th Brigade at the Green Line, and

British tanks advance at Amiens, 1918. Mikan mo. 3395384, Library and Archives Canada

shortly afterwards came under heavy fire as it approached Snipe Copse, a small wooded area that held German 77-mm field guns firing at ranges as close as four to six hundred metres—troops reported being able to see the crews working the guns. The infantry advanced in section rushes following tanks, the likely targets of the German guns. The tanks played an important role in overcoming enemy resistance, with the 26th battalion's after-action report recording that they "rendered valuable assistance, particularly around Snipe Copse where the battalion was held up and suffered heavily from machine gun and rifle fire." In A Company's report, Captain Charles A. Moore wrote that "too much cannot be said about the work of the tanks [at Snipe Copse] and at many other points during the attack. Helped silence a German 77 battery along with company Lewis guns."

Once past this resistance, the battalion advanced more rapidly over level wheat fields and through a deep ravine in front of Caix. By 12:30 p.m. it had reached the objective, the Red Line, near Caix, having advanced more than eight kilometres, a distance that would have been inconceivable six months earlier. 2nd Canadian Cavalry Brigade and 6th Infantry Brigade then pushed through to continue the attack a total of thirteen kilometres eastwards, the longest single-day advance by the Canadians in the war. Meanwhile, the 26th dug in for the night.

During the attack, the New Brunswickers captured large numbers of machine guns, a few field guns and howitzers, and many prisoners. But success had been costly: casualties totalled almost 250, all ranks. C Company had entered the battle with 138 soldiers and lost 68, almost half its strength. Casualties among junior leadership were again heavy: C Company's commander and three platoon leaders were wounded, leaving Lieutenant Robert B. Murray of Chatham, commander of No. 11 Platoon, to bring the company through to the objective. Among the dead was Lance Sergeant Fred Woodbury from St. George.

The attack left a strong impression on some of its participants. An unnamed member of the unit from Saint John described the early phase of the attack in a letter he wrote on the thirteenth: "It was certainly a great wallop we handed Fritz this time. Before zero hour Col. ----- of the office staff, a signaler and myself went up front as a forward headquarters. We just got up in time to see the fight. There was just a short and sweet bombardment and then our boys went over with the tanks. Shortly after there occurred one of the finest sights I ever witnessed; guns were going over the top after the infantry, and squadrons of cavalry and lancers were going over on the double." He described how German prisoners began streaming back to the Canadian lines soon afterwards, including staff officers and colonels, as well "a lot of very young chaps among them and they were scared to death until they found they would not be ill-treated." The exception was one who did not go quietly: "One Fritz came in with a bomb in each pocket, a few of us suspected, and we proceeded to search him. We took one bomb from him and a big 'Yank' who was on the job with us found the other and started to remove it. Fritz objected and tried to retain possession of it, but the 'Yank' handed him a left hander that made him change his mind. The Hun was lucky at that, for if it had been one of our boys in German hands he wouldn't have lived long."

The 26th resumed the advance the next day, moving toward Hallu to the east in the wake of the corps' attack. The troops came under fire two or three times, but did not encounter serious resistance. By the time they reached Méharicourt, they had advanced about nineteen kilometres. Over the next few days, they came under periodic heavy shelling and withdrew to Vrély, where they were relieved on the eleventh, moved back into reserve, and received about two hundred reinforcements.

The Battle of Amiens effectively ended on August 11. The corps was exhausted, having lost almost twelve thousand casualties, nearly four thousand on the opening day. Nonetheless, it had helped deliver the Germans a stunning blow, advancing almost twenty-three kilometres on a 9,100-metre front, capturing nine thousand enemy troops, two hundred artillery pieces, and more than a thousand machine guns and trench mortars. Amiens marked the beginning of the "Hundred Days" that culminated in the German army's eventual defeat.

On August 15, the 26th re-entered the line, and D Company made a local attack, advancing the front five hundred yards in places, with the loss of another fifty men. On the eighteenth, the unit was relieved, and the next day moved north by bus, train, and on foot to re-enter the line near its old positions southeast of Arras near Neuville-Vitasse in preparation for the next phase of the Allied attack.

The Battle of the Scarpe: The Death of Colonel McKenzie

As the Canadians travelled north, they passed dense lines of American soldiers who, according to Barry, cheered the Canadians and "threw heaps of smokes, gum and fruit to our boys." On the twenty-fifth, they reached assembly trenches near Beaurains as the Canadian Corps prepared to attack east of Arras through the Hindenburg Line toward the vital rail junction at Cambrai. The 26th's trenches were drenched by German shells containing phosgene gas, a deadly chemical agent that was difficult to detect because it was colourless and had only a faint smell. Barry recounted his first experience of sleeping in a trench with a gas mask on all night: "A clip was placed on the nose and breathing was done through a mouth-piece, the air passing through a decontaminator. Next morning my mouth was like a sheepskin which had been nailed to the barn door all summer." Despite the gas and the cold, wet weather, C Company's after-action report recorded that the troops were "in splendid spirits."

On August 26, the Canadians launched the opening phase of the attack against the Hindenburg Line, known as the Battle of the Scarpe, when 2nd

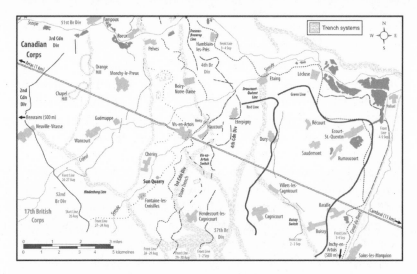

Map 7: The Advance to Cambrai. Mike Bechthold

and 3rd Canadian Divisions advanced on both sides of the Arras-Cambrai Road. To the south, 2nd Canadian Division opened its assault with 4th and 6th Brigades. In reserve was 5th Brigade, which would pass through 4th Brigade the next day and continue the advance toward the Fresnes-Rouvroy Line, the next heavily defended section of the German line. The 26th moved east across recently captured country for several thousand metres under light enemy shellfire, and incurred few casualties. The next day, 5th Brigade, with the 26th on the Canadian right, led the attack, jumping off at 10:00 a.m. C Company's report described the advance as "a walk-over at the start, the Boche putting up very little resistance outside of his artillery fire…. The Germans seemed to be terrified and were only too willing to be taken prisoner. In cleaning out the dugouts, we would find anywhere from twenty to fifty and sixty men. They would immediately throw up their hands and at a signal from us would 'beat it' to the rear as quickly as possible." The 26th reached its first objective, the valley of the then-dry Sensée River, with little interruption. As it moved eastward beyond the range of the supporting guns, however, it met heavy artillery and machine-gun fire at point-blank range from the opposite slope. By

4:30 p.m. the men were unable to go any further, so they stopped and dug in beyond a point called Sun Quarry.

At 12:30 p.m. on the twenty-eighth, the attack resumed, with the Fresnes-Rouvroy Line as the objective. The attack went well at first, with the Canadians following the barrage, but then they encountered intense machine-gun fire from various German positions. A Company gathered together the remnants of two platoons and moved forward in twos and threes, only to encounter heavy wire in front of Ulster Trench, which they got through with great difficulty. By the time they reached their immediate objective, the company had only fifteen men left and could not go on; it was later reinforced by British troops moving up on the right. D Company also encountered exceptionally heavy machine-gun fire and, with only light support from the barrage and no tanks, lost an officer and forty other ranks in about twenty minutes. The attack came to a standstill after advancing about 1,200 metres, but still short of the objective.

Among the casualties on August 28 was Lieutenant-Colonel A.E.G. McKenzie, the highest-ranking New Brunswicker killed in action during the war. Barry, who witnessed McKenzie's death, recalled waiting with the headquarters personnel for their turn to advance. "While we waited, one of our low-flying planes, aiding the attack with machine gun fire from the air, met a German 'Black Maria' artillery shell head on. In black smoke it folded and fell about 200 yards in front of us. None of us, the Colonel, adjutant, chaplain, regimental sergeant-major or myself...made a comment, but checking with the adjutant and chaplain after, they experienced a feeling similar to mine—a bad omen." The first wave moved out of sight over a rise to attack the German front line. One of the keys to British and Canadian success in 1918 was ensuring that the command element, including the CO, went forward to direct the fight. When the headquarters group of the 26th advanced, they were the only troops in sight. As they passed the crest and took shelter in a shell hole, they saw the German front, which had just been taken, at the bottom of the hill. Beyond that lay another rise, held by German heavy machine guns, and beyond that yet another ridge, from which German light artillery was firing at them over open sights. Colonel McKenzie stood to move forward, but after a

Lieutenant-Colonel A.E.G. McKenzie, killed in action, August 28, 1918.
Author's collection

few steps was hit in the groin by a burst of machine-gun fire and died instantly. Barry crawled out to check on him, then returned to the shell hole, where he told the chaplain, Captain R.C. MacGillivray, that the colonel was dead. "His answer was brief and to the point, 'A diamond in the rough.'"

MacGillivray recorded his own impressions of McKenzie's conduct during the two days of battle, and spoke of the critical importance of battalion COs leading from the front in 1918:

> His utter disregard for danger, his prompt and correct deci-
> sions in times of necessity and his presence in the hottest
> parts of the fight, inspired not only his officers, but all other
> ranks to deeds of heroism. On one occasion he personally
> took a number of prisoners, and again when several platoons
> took cover from intensive shell fire he calmly walked through
> the barrage and by his cool demeanor encouraged those men
> to advance. On halting he saw to the condition of his flanks
> and personally supervised the placing of his men, and, in the
> meantime, though the field was swept by Artillery, Machine
> Gun and Rifle fire, he repeatedly exposed himself and would
> not take cover until his Battalion was advantageously placed.
> On the 28th of August, he followed the immediate centre of

his Battalion, and seeing his men held up by most destructive fire of all kinds, he pushed forward to personally lead them and was killed while so doing. On the way, prior to his death, he showed an extreme coolness and an almost superhuman courage.

Lieutenant Alfred J. Brooks, commanding C Company, noted that the "whole company were deeply affected over the loss of their Colonel, to whom they were greatly devoted." New Brunswick newspapers reported that Brigadier Ross recommended McKenzie for the Victoria Cross for his actions on the twenty-eighth, but the award was not approved. He nonetheless was posthumously awarded a bar to his DSO. In early September, Lieutenant-Colonel Walter Brown assumed permanent command of the 26th.

That night the 26th was relieved and moved back to Neuville-Vitasse. The attack had been very costly. Including McKenzie, the battalion lost 73 killed and 250 wounded. Over the three days, C Company lost 70 men, almost half its strength. The battalion's dead were buried in mass graves at Wancourt, about eight kilometres south of Arras.

After a period of rest at the end of August, the battalion spent the first half of September rebuilding, receiving reinforcements, and undergoing training. On September 19, it re-entered the line near Inchy-en-Artois, close to the western bank of the Canal du Nord. By then, the Canadians had taken the Fresnes-Rouvroy and Drocourt-Quéant Lines, and were preparing for the next major step: crossing the Canal du Nord and advancing on Cambrai. While the other divisions prepared for the attack, 2nd Canadian Division occupied the front line, keeping pressure on the Germans and improving jumping-off positions. The Germans were mostly quiet, although occasional shelling continued to inflict a few casualties each day. Late on the twenty-second, this pattern changed when the battalion pushed two posts forward, precipitating heavy localized fighting on the twenty-fourth and twenty-fifth when the Germans mounted heavy counterattacks. At daylight on September 25, Lieutenant Robert B. Lloyd's post was driven in, and they fell back on a position defended by a platoon led by Lieutenant R. Chester Dean (#69220) of Dalhousie. Both Lloyd

(#69522), of Saint John, and Dean were originals who had enlisted as privates in November 1914, were commissioned in 1917, and rejoined the battalion as replacement officers. Lloyd, who had been awarded the DCM in 1917, was killed leading a counterattack. Two other German forays were driven off later in the morning, and things remained quiet until 3:30 p.m., when the Germans attacked again, preceded by a heavy bombardment. During this attack, Dean was killed, and the survivors were forced to abandon the other post and take up positions in nearby shell holes. Later in the evening, a counterattack by the 26th enabled them to recover one of the posts. During these operations, casualties were heavy: in addition to the deaths of Lloyd and Dean, eight members of the battalion were captured during the melee in what was the battalion's largest single loss of prisoners during the war. Among them was Sergeant Charles Campbell (#69143), an original from Blackville, New Brunswick, one of five brothers who joined up, all of whom served overseas. During the night of September 25/26, the battalion was relieved and moved to the rear.

The Battle of Cambrai
On September 27, the Canadians launched a bold and innovative attack across the Canal du Nord and pressed on toward Cambrai. The next day the 26th moved forward in the wake of the advance, reaching Raillencourt, east of Cambrai, on October 2, where it remained in brigade reserve until the eighth, providing working parties while the Canadian Corps prepared its attack on Cambrai. In early October, British Third Army resumed the advance south of Cambrai, and the Canadian Corps cooperated by carrying out operations to the north of the city. Second Canadian Division was ordered to secure bridgeheads across the Canal de l'Escaut and link up with Third Army to the east of Cambrai. Fifth Brigade would take Morenchies and Pont d'Aire, on the far side of the canal, and push east through Escaudoeuvres and beyond. The 25th and 26th Battalions would lead off on the right and left, with the 22nd in support, and push on to the railroad and road junction near Naves and hook up with 24th British Division. Special measures were taken to deal with challenges the Canadians faced, including having engineers

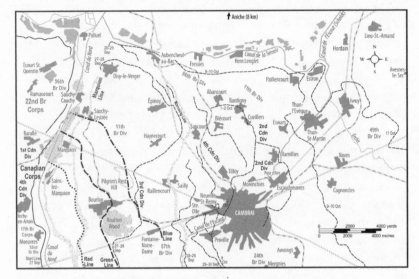

Map 8: The Battle of Cambrai. Mike Bechthold

follow the infantry forward, ready to throw portable bridges across the canal where needed.

According to the 26th's after-action report, the night of the 8/9th was "beautiful...dark. Hun Bombing Planes were overhead and an occasional shell was landing in the area, while away on the right Cambrai was burning furiously, lighting up the surrounding country for miles." The approach march in the darkness to the jump-off positions near Tilloy was made more difficult by German gas, "and what with wearing gas helmets, the lines of barbed wire, roads, and hedges, houses, and occasional shells, only good guides...[meant] that we ever found our way at all."

On October 9, Canadian and British troops captured Cambrai, and the 26th played its part in the operation, which marked its last set-piece action. A member of the unit described the early phase of the attack: "Our battalion and the 25th Nova Scotia Battalion with another battalion on our left [27th] jumped off at 1:30 am on the 9th/10th and took Cambrai. We flanked it by going around the N.E. of the city; took the suburbs and [Escaut] canal. Another platoon, together with my own, took the wood this side of the canal, which was full of gas and pitch dark. The Hun didn't

Canadian engineers bridging the Canal de l'Escaut.
Mikan no. 3405437, Library and Archives Canada

put up much of a show there. Ran into one machine gun. He opened one spurt, missing us. Our machine gunner spotted the flash, opened up and got them. There were three in a hole. He killed two and we got the other one." Farther on, they encountered the canal, a formidable obstacle eighteen metres wide and three metres deep, with a fifteen kilometre per hour current. The Germans had blown up most of the bridges, but the engineers erected a portable footbridge and the unit soon crossed. Sergeant Harris A. McGinley (#817801) of Saint John, the acting battalion bombing sergeant, was wounded as part of a storming party selected to take and hold two bridges across the canal. He described the action in two letters to his mother written on October 11 and 15:

> We made the first bridge, which Fritz had partially de-
> molished with a mine, protected the engineers while they
> repaired the gap. We then started for the second bridge, 200

yards ahead, but almost ran into our own barrage, and had to drop back until it lifted. Then we went on. When we reached the end of the bridge, the Germans were running for the other end to blow their mine, but we got there first and had a dandy scrap for about half an hour. [In the meantime the engineers cut the wires to the mine.] It was in that fight that I got hit…Sergt. Stevens of No. 1 platoon came up then with more men and the two sections managed to beat back three attempts of the Huns to retake the bridge. An hour after I was hit I was able to go back to Captain Moore [his company commander] and report that the bridges were safe, the wires cut and all ready for the passage of A Company. He then asked me if I could take a party into the town and bomb out any of the enemy lurking about alleys and buildings, but I told him my arm was too stiff and sore and he gave me permission to evacuate. Then I beat it for a dressing station….

I was hit in the left arm above the elbow with a steel rivet head blown from the bridge by machine gun fire. I had the piece cut out in the operating room last night. I am going on finely, but will probably be out of the show for the winter as the doctors tell me it will take my wound that long to heal. However, don't worry for it is all right.

Advancing in the darkness gave the troops protection, but it also presented challenges. The troops wore white brassards on each arm to identify themselves as friendly soldiers; any man not wearing them would be regarded with suspicion, arrested, and sent to headquarters for identification. After daylight the troops removed the brassards. The darkness might have saved Lieutenant Melvin C. Buchanan, who commanded C Company. He reported that, when he reached the canal, "I was halted by [an enemy] sentry who evidently thought I was a German. There were two in the post, and only about five yards away. I had my revolver in my hand, and dispatched them both." Barry also had a close call while scouting for a crossing place along

Lieutenant Graham McKnight.

the canal when a bullet fired by a German sentry in the dark about twenty-five metres away whizzed past his ear. As he ran for cover, the German shot at him three more times. He described the effects of being under such close-range fire: "My heart came up to my throat and cut off my wind so that when I got under [cover] I could do nothing but gasp for a minute or two."

Following a barrage "which was enough to blow all the Huns to H—l, which it did," the lead companies crossed the canal. The barrage then lifted onto the final objective, and the advance continued with little opposition through Escaudoeuvres around 4:30 a.m. and on to the railway. Patrols were sent forward to join up with British troops advancing from the south. Late in the afternoon, the battalion was ordered forward to Naves in pursuit of Germans fleeing Cambrai. The anonymous soldier described the final stages of the attack: "At 5 that afternoon we jumped off again. Only went a short distance and met terrific machine gun fire. Our company commander was wounded and a lot of our company as well. It got dark but we pushed ahead until we met a lot of Hun wire and machine guns; so held there for the night. Dug in and held our position. It started to rain; had no coat, so nearly froze all night. Of course we could not sleep as were next door neighbours to the Huns."

Once the fighting quieted down, French citizens began emerging from cellars where they had sheltered. According to C Company's report, many fled to the rear, "while others more hardy remained in the wrecks of their homes. One party consisting of a very old man and woman appeared with a wheelbarrow on which was loaded all their possessions and wheeled by one poor dejected looking little Hun."

Next day, 4th Brigade passed through the 26th, which remained in position until falling back on the night of the eleventh to the canal for a rest. The unit could take pride in this operation. As Lieutenant Graham McKnight noted in his diary on the ninth, "Cambrai fell and our battalion helped to do it." With the fall of Cambrai, the Germans lost their main logistical centre and rail hub in the north, and so began the general retreat toward Belgium. Casualties for the operation were four other ranks killed and seventy-eight wounded. Shortly afterward, the battalion was relieved and moved to the rear to clean up.

The Final Advance

Throughout the weeks of the advance beyond Cambrai, the Canadians had experienced a form of warfare new to them as they marched long distances over open terrain. One member of the battalion recorded that the country "is similar to Carleton County, NB, excepting that the hills are not so steep or high. It is very rolling country and rich in farming except the old battle ground between Arras-Cambrai which is part of the old Hindenburg line."

The nature of the fighting had also changed, and so had the battalion's methods. Movement had become more frequent and wide ranging. In early October they moved from the area around Bourlon to a position northeast of Cambrai (14 kilometres), then farther north to Bantigny (4.5 kilometres), back to the rear at the town of Marquion (10.5 kilometres), which only a short time earlier had been in the front line, and then north again to Épinoy and the town of Aniche (17 kilometres) in preparation for the Canadian Corps' final advance toward Valenciennes and Belgium. This represented some forty-six kilometres of marching. Then, during the first ten days of November, the men moved another forty-five kilometres from Aniche to Wasmes, in Belgium — a total of ninety-one kilometres in less than six weeks. Some of the movement was done by "bus" or lorry, but most was on foot.

This frequent movement over long distances had its challenges. To move across country, the unit marched by platoons on compass bearings. Some troops went astray, especially from the rear echelon. For example, the war diary recorded that, during the march back to Marquion in mid-October, "the mess cart got lost and the C.O. had to go to bed practically dinnerless, causing the Sub-Staff much grief." In the same humorous vein, it added that the second-in-command was "amused as he bummed dinner at Brigade." The pace of operations forced the troops to seek shelter in the open. Near the end of September, shortly after the opening of the Canal du Nord attack, while the battalion waited at Sains-lès-Marquion for its turn to move up, Lieutenant McKnight wrote: "made home in shell hole, had interesting time dodging long range gun firing every ten minutes." A few days later, he wrote that he spent the day in a funk hole awaiting orders to stand to. Under these circumstances, he got little sleep. He noted ruefully that another soldier piled into their position "making 9 in room for 3." The troops also had little opportunity for other kinds of amenities. McKnight recorded that, after they moved back to Marquion in mid-October, they had a bath parade—his first bath and change of clothes in four weeks.

These more mobile operations also offered a stark contrast to the earlier days of positional warfare. A member of the battalion wrote that "the Hun is doing 90 [percent] of his damage with machine guns, the remainder with gas and artillery." During the Germans' retreat, they came across thousands of empty gas shells marked with painted crosses of various colours denoting the kind of gas they contained: a yellow cross for mustard gas, green for phosgene, and so forth. He had great praise for the formations supporting the infantry during these all-arms operations: "Our artillery is the marvel of the war. It matters not how long an advance we make in a day, the artillery is always supporting us before daylight the next morning. Our transport is wonderful. Our mules and horses are better than in 1915. That is another point against Jerry: his transport is very poor." Even though the line was moving ahead daily, the engineers kept pace. As Barry reported, "[i]t is surprising how soon our Engineers could get these services set up right behind our advancing line but a hot bath and change of socks and underwear was a great booster to morale."

As the fighting became more fluid, the troops found new ways of holding the front line. In mid-October, while they were at Bantigny, to the north of Cambrai, all four companies were in the line covering a front over six kilometres wide. They maintained contact with the Germans by sending out daylight patrols. Later, the soldiers began to see towns and countryside much less devastated by years of continuous fighting. The war diary recorded that Aniche was "in splendid shape. To the weary soldiers after plodding 40 kilometres from Arras it seemed like the promised land. Good billets for all, needing however a great deal of cleaning, as the Hun had left the town in very bad shape." Ten days later, they reached the town of Anzin, to the north of Valenciennes, where they took up billets in some very fine houses.

On November 6 they crossed into Belgium, and on the eighth had their last day in action when they attacked the village of Élouges, just south of the Mons-Valenciennes Road, near Dour. By then the retreating Germans had stopped evacuating the local population, so the Canadians were warmly greeted by happy Belgian civilians. The unit after-action report noted that preparations for the attack on the eighth were slowed "by the barrage of Kisses, Coffee and Cognac put up by the good inhabitants of [Élouges], where it became the custom for all ranks to stop the war occasionally while they retired to enjoy a repetition of the aforementioned tokens of appreciation." As Barry commented, "this was war at its best." He was embarrassed, however, to be greeted as "the redeemer." He also slept between sheets on a spring mattress and "undressed for the first time in the front line or near it."

When the attack came off, the battalion advanced to the east more than eight kilometres, encountering determined enemy resistance at several places. Among the last 26th soldiers killed in action was Private Charles Clark (#709752) of Cornhill, Kings County. At the time of his enlistment with the 104th Battalion in November 1915, he was in charge of the Cornhill cheese factory and was one of three brothers to join up. He had been with the 26th less than three months when he was killed on November 8.

By November 11, the battalion had reached the village of Wasmes, a few miles to the southwest of Mons. In the morning they received an operations order to move forward toward Mons, but it was immediately followed by another directing them "to remain where we are until further orders, as an armistice would be signed at 1100 hours." The war diary recorded that "there was great rejoicing in the village." That night, the divisional commander dined at battalion headquarters located in the village château. "It is a beautiful place and Battalion Headquarters are treated royally. The dinner was followed by music and dancing and about 1600 hours the village band paraded in front and played the French, British and Belgian national anthems.... Lots of wine and cigars for everyone."

On the fifteenth, Barry took a platoon of thirty wounded and decorated men from all companies and headquarters to participate in the official Canadian entry into Mons. Then, on the eighteenth, the battalion joined the Canadian contingent of the Allied Army of Occupation in its march across Belgium into Germany and the first leg of the journey home.

General Sir Arthur Currie, commander of the Canadian Corps, takes the salute as 2nd Canadian Division troops cross the Rhine at Bonn, December 1918. 19930065-679, Canadian War Museum

Chapter Eight

Returning Home

The fighting ended on the Western Front with the Armistice on November 11, 1918, but for the soldiers of the 26th Battalion, service in Europe was far from over. It would be another six months before they sailed for Canada. During this time, they marched across Belgium to Germany, where they spent five weeks as part of the Allied Army of Occupation, followed by two and a half months in a small town in central Belgium, and then more than a month in Britain waiting for transport before finally heading for home.

The March to Germany

Shortly after the ceasefire, the Canadian Corps received word that it would be part of the Allied occupation force being organized to ensure that Germany honoured the terms of the Armistice and signed the coming peace treaty. This was something the troops understood. In a letter home, Lieutenant Fred Mowat of Campbellton wrote that "we are now on our way to the Rhine to impress the Hun that there is a peace treaty to be signed." The Canadians established bridgeheads across the Rhine between Cologne and Bonn from which they could advance into the interior if necessary. They also administered martial law among the local population.

On November 18, the 26th set out for Germany. Initially, its pace was slowed by logistical problems stemming from damage to the railway between

Valenciennes and Mons, which delayed the delivery of supplies and rations. The Canadians received a warm welcome from the Belgian civilians as they marched east. Lieutenant Arthur Barry recalled that they were showered with flowers: "It was like Caesar returning triumphantly from Gaul." At their first stop, Houdeng-Goegnies, the streets and houses were decorated with flags and signs proclaiming, "Welcome to the brave British soldiers." A large crowd cheered, grabbed the troops by the hand as they marched past, and handed out wine and cigars. Some citizens proudly exhibited the large stocks of brass they had hidden from the Germans during the occupation. According to a letter home written by Private John Urquhart (#817929), a lumberman from Covered Bridge, in York County, the troops were billeted with civilians, each family taking two or more men: "The night we came in they made us take off our boots and washed our feet in salt water, and made us sleep in the best bed in the house." But the Canadians also saw the deep scars left among the Belgians by the German occupation. "There were big riots in the town last night; the civilians destroyed all the houses belonging to German sympathizers or any one that had anything to do with the Germans when they were here; there were some beautiful houses destroyed and some valuable property too. I guess there is going to be some more tonight."

On the twenty-eighth, while still near Namur, the Canadians received word that they must reach the German border, over a hundred kilometres away, in four days, so they pressed ahead in cold, rainy weather. Two days later, they were informed that, "on account of an expected revolution in Germany," they would push on to the Rhine, which they must reach by December 8. Logistical problems persisted: on December 3, the war diary noted that they had "bought a cow to supplement Rations." Nevertheless, they marched on, crossing the German frontier on the fifth. Once they entered Germany the mood changed. Barry noted: "The first thing we noticed was the absence of flags which decked every house in the Belgian towns and villages, also the cheering crowds and showers of flowers. Now the blinds were drawn and the people kept out of sight but when we took over our billets they were very civil. The countryside looked very much like New Brunswick. The towns and villages were tidy and the roads good."

As they moved farther into Germany, the country became more thickly populated. Officers stayed in hotels and the men in schools. On December 9, they marched through a very hilly area in the rain in fighting order, having piled their packs in lorries. Once they neared the Rhine, the going got easier as they crossed a plain that extended to the hills along the river, which they reached on the eleventh. According to the war diary, after a day's rest, the brigade made a "triumphal march through BONN and across the Rhine with Colours flying and Bayonets Fixed. The Corps Commander [General Sir Arthur Currie] took the Salute near the East end of the Bridge. It rained during the whole day and everyone got very wet, since Overcoats, etc., were not allowed to be worn."

Occupation

The next day, the 26th moved on to Menden, a town numbering about two thousand people, located a few miles northeast of Bonn. There they remained until the thirtieth in brigade reserve, while the other battalions manned an outpost line and main line of defence centred on key terrain features. They had comfortable billets and a relatively relaxed routine. Each morning, a short parade was held to maintain discipline, but the troops generally had the rest of the day and evening free. Sports were organized to keep the men busy, and an educational program taught illiterate members of the battalion how to read and write. Barry, who had been a school teacher before the war, took on the role, first teaching them how to sign their name instead of making an X before a witness. Troops who travelled by train to Bonn saw the effects of the Allied blockade: shops were nearly empty of consumer goods, especially soap. At one restaurant, Barry was served horse steak. On Christmas Day, the battalion enjoyed a large dinner in two sittings, much of which was provided through donations from New Brunswickers, especially the Daughters of the Empire, who sent boxes of Christmas treats. According to the war diary, a German orchestra "supplied good Music."

Although the Canadians were courteous to the Germans, especially women and the elderly, they were also strict, fearing that familiarity might breed contempt, according to Barry. Fraternizing and walking out with

German women was forbidden, and the population, especially the men, was encouraged to show respectful behaviour toward Canadian soldiers. Officers went about armed, but no serious trouble occurred. The troops soon got to know the Germans, and some of the soldiers looked upon them sympathetically. At Menden, the troops passed out food to children who gathered around their field kitchens. According to Barry, "this kindness to hungry children...did more to break down the aloofness of the population than anything else." In a letter home written on Christmas Day, Lieutenant Hugh O. Morrison of Hampton, New Brunswick, reflected on the people and the occupation: "The German people are making merry in their own way, and try their best to be agreeable. Every little home has its Christmas tree highly decorated. The woman where I am billeted was at great pains not to let me get out without first viewing the tree. They had a plate of cakes for me." He found it difficult to understand the nature of their reception, "which is entirely different to what one would naturally expect in an occupied country. It seems that we made a good impression and are not the cut-throats we have been pictured to them."

Another officer from the battalion echoed this viewpoint, writing that "we were used fairly good by the Rhinelanders, who took our entry coldly at first, but without remonstration. They were agreeably surprised at our behavior towards them, which was just the opposite of their expectations. Several told me that their papers many times gave out that the Colonial troops were doing all of Britain's fighting, and they also told them we were all black." This unnamed officer also learned first-hand about what would later become known in Germany as the "stab in the back" — namely, the German army had never been defeated and the Kaiser had not been a bad ruler; they had lost because the home front leadership failed them: "The Germans speak very optimistically about getting another crack at England later on and when one starts to knock the Kaiser they all say, 'Good man the poor Kaiser; it was all the fault of Tirpitz [Grand Admiral of the German navy] and Bethmann-Hollweg [the chancellor].' They certainly have lost none of their love for him, the only complaint being that he should have stayed in Germany with his people and not flee to Holland like a coward."

Not all of the troops liked the Germans. Private Edward E. Jay (#712735) from Fanning Brook, Prince Edward Island, was hobbled by the long march to Bonn, and a few weeks after arriving was sent to hospital in France. On February 16, 1919, he wrote from his bed that "I see by the paper that Germany don't seem willing to sign the peace terms, damn them. One should start it up again and bombard the devil out of the towns—civilians and all." A few individual soldiers clashed with German citizens. On the night of December 13/14, the day of the march across the Rhine, two soldiers from the 26th absented themselves and were arrested the next day on charges ranging from striking a civilian in the head with a beer mug to stealing money and cognac from Germans, absence, resisting arrest, and drunkenness. At their field general courts martial, they were found guilty of absence and theft of the liquor, and each was sentenced to one year of imprisonment with hard labour. On January 12, another soldier was convicted of stealing money from a civilian, for which he received the same sentence. In all of the trials, German witnesses were called to testify.

On December 30, the 26th moved into the forward outpost line in 5th Brigade's zone, where they spent a quiet week mostly enforcing traffic restrictions on the locals moving between the German-controlled area and the occupied zone. On January 6, they joined the garrison in Bonn for a week. Most mornings were devoted to training, and the rest of the day to recreational activities such as attending the cinema and concert parties performed by the divisional troupe, "The See Toos." A few days after arriving, they were visited by the Prince of Wales, and the battalion band and colours arrived from England. The next day, "the Battalion made a triumphal march thro' the principle streets of BONN with Band and Colours, presenting a very fine appearance." The war diary added that two soldiers, whom Barry called bouncers, "walked on the sidewalks knocking off hats of all who failed to salute," part of their program to ensure respect for Canadian authority. On the thirteenth, General Sir Herbert Plumer, the British Second Army commander, visited to wish the battalion a Happy New Year. The next day, they returned to Menden, where they received a warm welcome. On the twenty-second, their service with the occupation force ended, and they entrained for Belgium. The war diary noted that "the inhabitants were very sorry to see the Battalion leave."

Belgium

On January 23, the battalion arrived in Tamines, in central Belgium, where it remained for the next two and a half months until the shipping needed to transport the men home became available. They followed a familiar routine of morning parades, training, route marches, and church services on Sunday. The educational program also continued, with lectures on subjects such as the work of the Royal Navy, "Canada," and the new League of Nations, the latter delivered by a US Army lieutenant. A group of twenty officers also travelled to the nearby battlefield at Waterloo. They also took in more highbrow entertainments, including a performance of Shakespeare's *Henry VIII* by an English concert party.

The unit found various ways to keep the troops active. Sports featured prominently in the men's routine. During the winter months, they played indoor baseball, football, and soccer, and the battalion soccer team competed against a civilian squad. Unit teams also participated in formation competitions, such as brigade tug-of-war matches. On March 22, about one hundred officers and men proceeded to Brussels by special train to attend a corps sports competition. The battalion came first in the shuttle relay race, while individuals won the high jump and half-mile race events.

The troops also interacted with the local population. At the beginning of the war, the town was the site of the second-largest series of atrocities committed by the German army in Belgium. As the war diary summarized: "This town was entered by the Germans on August 22nd 1914, and in revenge for the death of some of their men, they collected 500 men of all ages in the square, and turned machine guns on them killing 350 and wounding 83. They then burned dozens of houses throughout the town." On March 3, 1919, the battalion mounted a ceremonial parade with colours, "and took part in a celebration with civilians to commemorate the massacre of Tamines." On the thirteenth, Albert, King of the Belgians, made an unannounced visit to the town to view the large cross erected in memory of those who died during the massacre and to mourn with their families. Despite short notice, the regimental band turned out in the square and "serenaded him," whereupon the King met and shook hands with the bandmaster, thanking him for their courtesy.

Even though the fighting had stopped, deaths continued. On November 24, 1918, Private Frank J. Butler (#3255280) from Barnaby River in Northumberland County, New Brunswick, was killed in Luttre, Belgium, when he climbed a power pole to view the surrounding destruction caused by the Germans, and touched a live wire. He was buried the next day in the town communal cemetery. On February 4, 1919, Lieutenant William Buddell, the former RSM who had been commissioned from the ranks and appointed battalion adjutant, was buried in the Tamines Communal Cemetery with full military honours. He had been admitted to hospital in Namur on January 30, and died a few days later. An unnamed 26th officer described the sad circumstances of Buddell's passing. "His death was quite sudden. He and I were left behind on business when the battalion left Germany. We came down from Cologne in a freight train, the only accommodation available, and it proved too severe a trip for poor old 'Billy.' He caught cold, which developed into pneumonia, and he died within a week."

In Britain

On April 5, the battalion left Tamines in a freight train bound for Le Havre. The war diary noted that they received a "Great Send off by the people of Tamines." One officer left the following thoughtful description of their departure.

> We had quite a farewell on leaving Tamines. We hardly
> believed there were so many people in the town, but they
> answered the last muster in great numbers and were out in
> such force to bid us goodbye that it was with some difficulty
> we pushed our way through their ranks. Many eyes were
> damp (among the civies), there was a lump in many a manly
> throat as for the last time our band played La Brabacone
> [the Belgian national anthem] and saluted our colors

with O Canada. Loud and hearty were the cheers of these good Belgian people as we moved off from in front of the Hotel de Ville—good, honest cheers, regret and good luck intermingling in their meaning.

He wrote that they felt more like citizens of the town than guests: "We shall always carry with us kindest memories of our stay in Tamines. Quiet and slow it seemed, old-fashioned in its ways, and very often we were 'fed up' with the deadness of the place, but its people were the essence of kindness and did their best to make pleasant our stay. They have greatly suffered in the last four years, and perhaps the tranquility of their village is but the continuing sorrow of the massacre by the Huns in August, 1914."

Two days later, the battalion reached Le Havre, where they encamped for three days before sailing across the Channel to Southampton. From there they travelled to Witley Camp, in Surrey, to begin preparing for the return to Canada. The troops spent a few days parading before medical and dental boards and receiving their pay, then most proceeded on leave to different parts of Britain. By the twenty-third, most men had returned to camp, where they were joined by about thirty members of the 13th Reserve Battalion for the trip home. On May 1, a detail of 125 other ranks was selected to take part in the march of Dominion troops through London. Two days later, the march party and a large number of men travelled to London to watch the procession.

Over the next week, the 26th undertook company parades and recreational training until, on May 10, 1919, the long-awaited day arrived and the battalion entrained for Southampton, where, along with several other units, it boarded the RMS *Olympic*—sister ship of the *Titanic*. The next day, they sailed for Canada, to a boisterous send-off by a huge crowd lining the docks and numerous vessels in the harbour. The battalion numbered 35 officers, 75 sergeants and warrant officers, and 706 other ranks, about 200 men short of its establishment strength.

With mostly fine weather, the voyage went quickly. Troops passed their time attending the cinema, concerts, and sing-songs, and played deck

The 26th Battalion parading at the Union Depot,
Saint John, May 17, 1919. Harold Wright Collection

games and sports. In contrast to the wartime crossings, the ship's lights
glowed during the night, no sentries were posted to stop the men from
smoking on deck, and they did not wear their life jackets for the duration.
The sight of two icebergs stirred the most interest.

Home!

On May 16 the *Olympic* docked at Halifax, "a spectacular sight," according
to an effusive report in the *Daily Telegraph*: "On the shore, wharves and
all places of vantage thousands congregated and in the harbor was the
moving mass of a giant and noble ship with her decks teaming with
khaki-clad heroes. Cheers upon cheers were given the men and in return
they waved with frantic enthusiasm. Here and there the dark rough hand
of a stalwart tommy would be raised slyly and a tender tear that even
such a man could not keep back was swiftly brushed aside. That tear was
expressive of a feeling that has enchanted many Canadian soldiers as they
gazed on Canadian shores for the first time since going overseas." At 9:30

that evening, the 26th, along with 2nd Canadian Divisional Ammunition Column, left on two trains bound for Saint John.

Plans to welcome home the 26th had begun in early April, when a citizens' reception committee was formed to coordinate the event with the city of Saint John, the provincial government, and various patriotic societies. After numerous delays, the trains arrived at Union Depot in Saint John at two half-hour intervals beginning at 1:30 p.m. on May 17. Among the returning troops were four officers and 113 other ranks from among the 1,148 "originals" who had sailed away nearly four years earlier. A large parade then headed for Kings Square, consisting of the just-returned units marching with sloped rifles and fixed bayonets, several bands, returned soldiers and veterans from the 26th and Great War Veterans Association, various dignitaries, Brigadier-General A.H. Macdonnell—former CO, 5th Infantry Brigade—and his staff from No. 7 Military District, and members of various patriotic societies, the Salvation Army, Boys Scouts, and cadets. The reception committee had done an outstanding job of orchestrating what the *Daily Telegraph* newspaper reported was "the greatest crowd that ever gathered in St. John." The paper described the scene: "It was one continuous cheer from the time the men started from the depot until they reached Kings Square, and the shrill whistles of harbor craft and of factories added tremendously to the noise and general abandon of the populace. St. John had seen nothing like it before in all its long history. The bands of the procession added martial music to the cheers of the people, and the march was indeed one of triumph." In places, anxious relatives who had joined the parade were also cheered. The reports further recorded that "many of the men showed plainly in their faces that they had endured hardships unknown to those who stayed at home, and the bayonets on their shoulders were not the only war-like mark upon them." The soldiers waved to the crowd, and "smiled the simple smile of victors. They were home again, knew it and showed it."

On the reviewing stand at Kings Square, a number of dignitaries, including the Honourable William Pugsley, the lieutenant-governor, and Premier Walter Foster, welcomed them home. Lieutenant-Colonel Brown responded on behalf of the 26th, assuring the crowd that the wonderful reception "will remain a beautiful memory in the minds of all of the men." Afterwards, the

A Saint John business welcomes home the 26th.

Daily Telegraph (Saint John), May 17, 1919

parade reformed and marched to Barrack Green Armoury for a meal laid on by several patriotic societies and the Knights of Columbus, consisting of regular army fare—beans, bacon, bread, and coffee—supplemented by such delicacies as maple sugar, fruit, and two thousand eggs.

The troops began taking their discharges at the armoury. Standing in line waiting his turn, an NCO was heard to say, "getting out of the army is a darn sight harder than getting into it." His impatience was understandable, but in reality, between 4:30 and 8:30 p.m. the administrative staff of the dispersal station processed a record 805 soldiers, beginning with the out-of-town men so they could get away that evening. Some of the local men completed the process the next morning. During this long-awaited moment, the troops handed in their rifles and other equipment, signed their discharge papers, and received a discharge certificate, transportation warrant, and a cheque for any pay that had been saved for them; the cheque, which could be redeemed on the spot by two Bank of Montreal tellers, often totalled more than $500.

Some men spent the next few days in the city visiting the theatres and buying new clothes. Eager for their patronage, the Semi-ready Clothing Store on the corner of King and Germain extended a 10 percent discount for the "first civilian outfit" and free "'Bus" from all boats and trains to all returned soldiers.

Reintegration: "carry on"

During his welcome home speech, Premier Foster told the troops: "Many of you will now be entering civil life again, and while you have offered all you had in the great conflict, you can now say your life has not been lived in vain, and you have assisted in accomplishing much, yet I venture to invite you to participate in the work of solving the problem which now confronts our country. If you enter into that work with the same spirit and the same zeal which animated you when you enlisted in the services of your country, the solution of many problems will be speedily accomplished. In the language of the day — Continue my fellow men, to carry on!"

But, Lieutenant Barry acknowledged, "it is not easy to fit one's self into civilian life after wearing a military uniform continuously for five years." As he pointed out, the government wisely continued army pay to all ranks for six months to allow time to adjust. The downturn in the regional economy the following year, especially in the lumbering trade — the province's chief industry — did not help matters. Much had changed for these soldiers during their long absence, often in ways that no one could have predicted. Reflecting on those who had left years earlier, the *St. John Standard* reported: "They are not the same men who went away. They are older — not with added years, but with something else which has given to their faces an expression of knowledge that time alone does not bring. What they have done and what they have seen have left their mark, and now, experienced in the bigger things of life, with a knowledge that can only be gained through the performance of difficult tasks and through suffering, they come home better men than before, to receive the thanks of those who could not go." The challenge these ex-soldiers faced in reintegrating into civilian life had as many different stories as there were men to tell them.

Many men from beyond Saint John received rousing welcomes when they got home. Among them was Private Alexander Methot (#69556) from Dalhousie. An original member of the unit, Alexander was wounded at Courcelette, and, after recovering, transferred to the Canadian Machine Gun Corps. In October 1918, he was again wounded, and earned the Military Medal. He "rejoined" the 26th for the return to Canada. Methot was greeted in Saint John by his mother, who, on May 19, travelled with him on the train to Dalhousie Junction, where they were met by two automobiles and taken to the family home. Here family, friends, and neighbours enjoyed "a sumptuous supper," and his two sisters presented Alex with a beautiful grooming set. One of the sisters read an address from his family that captured the spirit of the moment: "How we missed you! Yet the noble impulses which prompted you to leave home and friends, to go forth and offer your services for your country, and the cause of human liberty, were known to us and, as consequence our humble yet devoted prayers went forth for your speedy and safe return."

Alex began working in the lumber camps. In December 1919, he was in the woods when the ceremony conferring his Military Medal took place in Saint John. He remained in the camps until 1921, when he moved to the United States to work on construction projects. In 1928, after hearing that International Paper was building a newsprint mill in Dalhousie, he returned home. For the next few years, he worked on the construction of the mill, and then was employed in the mill as an oiler and beaterman until his death in February 1958. His post-war life epitomized the contribution to community for which Premier Foster had called.

Alex became a member of the Dalhousie Branch of the Legion, and Remembrance Day was an important event for his family. His two eldest daughters attended ceremonies at the Dalhousie cenotaph. Later, his son Leonel would go with him to the Legion after the November 11 ceremonies "to have a beer and I a coke.... I was an Army Cadet during my high school and would participate in the Remembrance Day parade. My father

Alexander Methot after receiving his Military Medal in 1919.

Courtesy of Leonel Methot

would wear his Legion beret and medals, and I the cadet battle dress." Alex's medals, discharge paper, and certificate from King George VI were prominently displayed in their home. Leonel recalls that his father was "a believer in the benefits of army training and discipline," something that inspired Leonel to undertake military training and follow in his father's footsteps. "He did not hesitate when at age 13 I asked him for permission to go to Camp Aldershot for a seven week army cadet basic training course. I again went in 1957 for a seven week signals course." After Alex's death in 1958, his wife received a small pension from the Department of Veterans Affairs for their children until they turned twenty-one. According to Leonel, his mother used the money to help put him through university; the remainder of his university expenses were covered by the second lieutenant's pay he received as a member of the Canadian Officers' Training Corps at Mount Allison University. His training included three summer camps at the Armoured Corps School at Camp Borden in Ontario. In 1962, Leonel received his commission.

Others found their pre-war circumstances much changed when they went home. In fall 1915, seventeen-year-old Napoleon Williams (#817200) from Shediac enlisted in the 104th Battalion, was transferred to the 140th, and in 1916 joined the 26th, where he served until being discharged when the battalion came home. Tragically, by the time he arrived in Shediac, both of his parents had died in the great influenza pandemic that swept across much of the world. Williams moved in with his sister to start his post-war life.

Some veterans used government programs to upgrade their education and job skills. Among them was Lance Corporal Francis (Frank) J. McNamara (#742616), who had what might be considered a typical career with the 26th. Born in October 1896 in Coal Creek, Queens County, he worked on the family farm until January 1916, when he enlisted in the 115th Battalion. He joined the 26th in late June 1917 and was slightly wounded a month later, but remained with the battalion; he underwent a hernia operation later in the year, and rejoined the unit in April 1918. In early October, he received a gunshot wound in the left forearm, whereupon he was hospitalized in England, and in January 1919 returned to Canada. After undergoing further treatment for his left hand at the Military Hospital in Fredericton, he was discharged in May 1919 medically unfit for military service, and received a pension for his partially disabled left hand.

According to his daughter Christena, Frank, who had attended school only to about grade six and whose writing and grammar skills were limited, took advantage of a government-sponsored course offered at the Forestry School at the University of New Brunswick in 1919-20. There he learned about trees and plants, which greatly assisted him in his lifelong career as a trapper and guide in the backwoods of central New Brunswick. Along with his father and brother, he ran a guiding, hunting, and trapping outfit for years throughout Northumberland County. During the winters, he trapped sables and martens for their furs, which he sold in Fredericton and Woodstock; in the summers, he guided parties of trout fishermen.

Frank did not marry until 1948, at age forty-two. He and his wife Florence lived in Holtville, west of Boiestown, where they raised their five daughters. His eldest, Christena, described her father as a quiet man who "tended to be a 'loner.'" He ran his traplines throughout the winter during the 1940s and 1950s, returning home early in the spring. He never joined the Legion nor, like many veterans, did he talk much about the war to his family. Christena did recall his saying that he always dug a deep foxhole: "many others didn't and were dead by morning." And, again like many old soldiers, he might have had little time for uninformed civilian ideas about the war. Christena remembered an incident when one of her sisters mentioned to him that "a teacher had told the class that the

Francis J. McNamara, on enlistment in 1916 and later in life.
Courtesy of Christena (née McNamara) and Bernard Beukeveld

German soldiers were the evil bad guys: he took exception to that and said to my sister that they were just like the Canadian, English, etc. soldiers, only doing as they were commanded! She recalls his being quite upset, and angry with her teacher." In time, he was inducted into the Trapper's Hall of Fame. Frank died in November 1982, and is buried in Holtville.

Sergeant Clarence Gillies returned home to make an important contribution to the veterans of the province. Discharged on April 7, 1919, the first anniversary of his knee wound, Clarence made a fairly good recovery and was able to walk quite well with a cane, but was incapacitated from labour that required "stooping." Upon discharge, he moved to Fredericton and took a course in telegraphy, but found it impossible to obtain a job. Having grown up on a farm and being familiar with caring for livestock and working in the woods, in early 1920 he applied to the Soldier Settlement Board of New Brunswick for a position. His application was successful, and he spent the next twenty-five years working with New Brunswick veterans. Established in early 1919, the board helped ex-overseas soldiers to buy farms, equipment, and livestock through low-interest loans to be paid back over twenty years. Field supervisors such as Clarence visited the loan recipients two or three times a year to offer advice and encouragement at what could be a difficult time for veterans and their young families, especially during the economic downturn in the 1920s, or if they had little or no practical farming experience. After more than two decades of service with the board, Clarence finally left in October 1945, due to an illness. In a letter of congratulations, the district superintendent wrote: "Down through the years you have not failed to display those qualifications so necessary in the welfare and destiny of the ex-service man and his family. Your wise, yet firm counsel, has done much for many looking for re-establishment and the ownership of homes and know of the pride you take when a family repays their indebtedness in a venture you were instrumental in starting them out with. Your influence outside the organization has been marked and you have done much to help build up the good reputation we enjoy."

In January 1919, Clarence joined the Great War Veterans Association, and later the Legion. He also served for six years as a Fredericton city councillor. Around 1949, he moved to nearby Lincoln, where he became keeper of the Wilmot Bluff Lighthouse on the St. John River until it was decommissioned in 1967. In June 1968, Clarence died and was buried in the Lower Lincoln Cemetery; the Last Post was played at the graveside. His family headstone identifies him as a sergeant in the 26th Battalion, an indication of the enduring pride he felt in his service during the war.

Soldiering On

During the post-war period, many veterans of the 26th Battalion played important roles in the provincial militia's transition to peacetime service. Former soldiers of the 26th continued their strong connection with the 62nd Regiment (St. John Fusiliers) — redesignated The St. John Fusiliers in 1920 — the militia unit that helped to raise them in 1914.[15] Among the earliest returned soldiers from the 26th to join the Fusiliers was Captain

---

15   The new unit became a two-battalion regiment with active and reserve battalions. The active battalion perpetuated its close wartime connection with the 26th Battalion, being designated the 1st Battalion (26th Battalion, CEF) until 1936.

Gravestone of Clarence Gillies, Lower Lincoln Cemetery. Author's photo

Reginald Major. After receiving his fourth wound at Amiens, he was evacuated to England and, following a lengthy convalescence, returned to Saint John in December 1918, where he took charge of the dispersal station. In September 1919, Major rejoined the Fusiliers as adjutant. Other 26th veterans followed, including Gordon Holder (#742204) from Saint John, who had served with the 62nd before the war, enlisted in the 115th in 1915, and was promoted to company sergeant major. In mid-1917, he joined the 26th in France after reverting to the rank of private. In time, he regained his CSM appointment and was awarded the MM and DCM at Passchendaele and Amiens, respectively. Holder was commissioned from the ranks late in the war. After the war, he rejoined the Fusiliers and eventually rose to command the regiment in the 1930s. His RSM was William Abell (#69028), a 26th original from Fairville, New Brunswick, who had served with Holder in the 62nd before the war. Abell became a sergeant in early 1916, and was seriously wounded in the leg in May. Many of the NCOs Abell commanded in the post-war Fusiliers were also veterans of the 26th.

Veterans of the 26th also had a strong presence in the militia on the province's North Shore. In 1920, the Northumberland Regiment — soon to be renamed the North Shore (New Brunswick) Regiment — re-formed. Its first three commanding officers, Lieutenant-Colonels Cuthbert Donald,

Herman S. Murray, and Arthur Barry, had all served with the 26th. Major Donald was attached to the battalion for a short time in early 1917 before returning to Britain and then Canada; Lieutenant Murray served with them for several months before being seriously wounded at Vimy; while Lieutenant Barry remained the longest, from August 1917 to March 1919. Barry also had the longest connection with the militia following the war. After returning to Newcastle, where he worked as an accountant, he joined the federal Department of Fisheries in 1924, working progressively as director for Newcastle, New Brunswick, the Maritimes, and eventually the eastern fisheries, by which time he was living in Ottawa. In 1920, Barry resumed his militia career, rejoining the local unit and serving as adjutant. During the 1921 nine-day summer camp, he noted a major change from the pre-war days: they "now had a cadre of trained and war tested officers and NCOs as well as many men in the ranks." Between 1929 and 1933 he served as the commanding officer of the North Shore Regiment during the lean years of the Depression. Although there were more recruits than the training establishment called for—Barry believed the high rate of unemployment contributed to this trend—the officers agreed to pool their allotments, and turned out for eight days of summer training for only four days' pay. From 1935 to 1938, he commanded the 16th Infantry Brigade. After the Second World War, Barry became the honorary lieutenant-colonel of the regiment. In 1956, Barry left government service in Ottawa and returned to New Brunswick, where he worked in an insurance company in Moncton until he retired in 1963 and returned to Newcastle. In 1964, following the death of Lord Beaverbrook, Barry became the honorary colonel-in-chief of the North Shore Regiment. Like many veterans of the Great War, he also joined the Great War Veterans Association and then the Legion, serving as president of both the Newcastle branch and provincial command. According to a report in the *North Shore Leader* in March 1929, he "worked untiringly for the relief of disabled ex-service men and their dependents." On April 26, 1972, Colonel Barry died and was buried in Newcastle.

Commemoration and Remembrance

After the war, the memory of the 26th and its soldiers was kept alive in many ways. The Saint John Cenotaph was unveiled on June 10, 1925, almost ten years to the day from the sailing of the *Caledonia*. In this way, the city's memorial to its fallen soldiers became closely associated with the anniversary of the departure of the 26th, whose ranks were filled so heavily by men from the community. Then, in September 1928, veterans of the battalion formed the 26th Battalion Overseas Club to keep the memory of their fallen comrades and the spirit of the unit alive, and to stay in touch with and watch out for surviving veterans around the province. The club met on or near June 13 each year for the next seven decades. In this way, June 13, 1915, became a landmark event in New Brunswick's collective memory of the Great War and of the contribution made by those five thousand seven hundred soldiers who served with the 26th. The first annual banquet, held on June 13, 1929, marked the fourteenth anniversary of the battalion's departure.

Not unlike on Remembrance Day, the veterans attending annual re-unions sometimes paraded to the Saint John Cenotaph, where they laid a wreath and then adjourned to the Legion or local hotel for a banquet. Representatives of the city of Saint John, the province, local clergy, the serving military, and such organizations as the Legion and Red Chevron Club usually sat at the head table. The program featured guest speakers, toasts, and a ceremony to remember recently passed comrades. The dinner menu was often presented in ways that recalled where the unit had served and the battles it had fought. During the forty-fifth anniversary banquet supper, for example, they ate roast turkey à la Somme, creamed potatoes du Courcelette, and Vimy creamed peas, followed by Amiens apple pie and Passchendaele cheddar cheese. The meal concluded with a tot of rum, which the men called "SRD."[16] In the early years, attendance could number two hundred or more, especially on important anniversaries. Although most members lived in the province, some came from farther afield, including the United States — among them Harvey M. Powers (#69750), who travelled from Orlando, Florida, for many years.

---

16   At the front the rum arrived in jars stamped SRD. Although there is now wide disagreement about what SRD stood for, during the war the troops agreed it meant "Seldom Reaches Destination."

26th Battalion Overseas Club banquet. Harold Wright Collection

On major anniversaries, like the fiftieth in 1965, the club's events stretched over two or three days. That year, members also attended the opening of a special exhibit at the New Brunswick Museum entitled the "Great War Show," and drove to Camp Gagetown and then Fredericton for a wreath-laying ceremony. On two occasions, special commemorative plaques were unveiled during their reunions: at the Royal Canadian Legion Branch No. 14 on Charlotte Street in 1965, and at Market Slip in 1975. In October 1991, the 26th Battalion Overseas Association — a successor to the original club — unveiled a new plaque at the old Pugsley Wharf near Water Street, where the *Caledonia* departed. Unfortunately, the park was later removed to make way for a parking lot, leaving the monument isolated and virtually inaccessible to visitors. In November 1992, the original plaque was rededicated at the newly established Ross Memorial Park on Loch Lomond Road.

These reunions received almost continuous coverage in local newspapers such as the *Evening Times Globe* in Saint John. On major anniversaries, the reporting was extensive: in 1975 it covered three days and featured a full page of articles and photographs that offered detailed information about the 1915 departure and more general information on the history of the battalion. In this way, the memory of the men of the battalion was kept before the public, both in Saint John and in the rest of the province.

Occasionally, the club held other kinds of events, including Grand Midnight Frolics for their members. On April 26, 1935, the second frolic took place at the Capitol Theatre and featured a presentation of the motion picture made of the battalion prior to its departure in 1915, a high-bar and tumbling act, and a musical program that included songs of the day.

With the passage of time, the number of veterans attending reunions declined. In 1965, only sixty-five members from the original battalion were still alive, and in 1970 only about one hundred of those who had ever served with the unit attended the reunion. Among them was seventy-eight-year-old Watson Baird (#69055), an original from Moncton, who was seriously wounded at the Crater fight in October 1915, when he received shrapnel wounds to the leg, arm, and face, fracturing his lower jaw. He remained in hospital until June 1916, when he was discharged, but never again saw front-line service. After the war, he lived in Campbellton, Toronto, and finally Vancouver. He travelled from British Columbia to attend at least two reunions. By the later 1980s, the veterans' gatherings had ceased.

The memory of the 26th Battalion has been perpetuated in many other ways. After its return to Canada, the colours loaned to the 26th by the 104th Battalion were returned, and a new set donated by the Imperial Order Daughters of the Empire (IODE) was presented by the Prince of Wales during his visit to Saint John in mid-August 1919. Since the unit had already been disbanded, a colour party composed of 26th veterans received the colours, while upwards of three hundred other veterans looked on at Barrack Green Armouries. In May 1922, the colours were laid up in Trinity United Church, where they remained until December 1972, when the originals were replaced by a new set, again donated by the IODE.

Another vivid reminder of the 26th is a carved piece of chalk that has its own unique history. In spring 1918, two soldiers drafted into the 26th in France, Privates Harry L. Little (#709393) and William C. McKiel (#817306), arrived at the reinforcement camp at Étaples to find the battalion's lines unmarked, unlike the other units within the corps. Deciding to do something about it, the two soldiers found a large slab of

Plaque commemorating the 26th New Brunswick Battalion, Jervis Bay-Ross Memorial Park, Saint John. Author's photo

chalk, which they spent three weeks decorating with carvings featuring the battalion crest and several of its battle honours. Two days before going forward to join the unit in the field, they placed the marker within the lines. Sometime later, when the lines were moved, the slab was left behind, whereupon Private Samuel G. Barter (#817889), who was recovering from wounds suffered at Hill 70, claimed it, saving the section with the carvings, which he arranged to send to his daughter living in Saint John. The marker never arrived, however, and when Barter returned to the site in November 1918 he found it still sitting on the shelf where it had been left. Once again, he arranged to send it home; this time it was waiting for him when he reached Canada. In 1932, Barter presented it to the Overseas Club at its annual banquet, with both Little and McKiel in attendance. Sometime later, the club presented it to the New Brunswick Museum, where it still resides.

Memorials for fallen soldiers of the 26th Battalion can also be found in cemeteries and churches around the province in the form of headstone engravings and stained glass windows. One example is the memorial for Private Stuart M. Adams (#70191), in the Campbellton Rural Cemetery. A twenty-two-year-old plumber from Campbellton, Adams tried to enlist in the 55th Battalion in early 1915, but was found medically unfit. After undergoing an operation, he joined the 26th in April 1915, went

Memorial for Private Stuart M. Adams, Campbellton Rural Cemetery. Author's photo

overseas a few months later, and was reported missing in action on September 15, 1916, during the Battle of Courcelette. His name appears on the Vimy Memorial. The arresting red granite gravestone in the Campbellton cemetery takes the shape of a large-calibre artillery shell, complete with a driving band around its lower end. Beneath his name and birth and death dates is the traditional entry, "Somewhere in France." These family memorials to sons, brothers, and fathers lost overseas can be found in cemeteries all over the province. Their names also appear on church and school honour rolls, among them the University of New Brunswick's roll, in Memorial Hall, which includes fallen alumnae Lieutenant-Colonel Ernest McKenzie, and Lieutenants Charles Lawson and Fred Foley.

Various steps were taken to commemorate Colonel McKenzie's service with the 26th. In July 1920, a brass tablet remembering McKenzie was placed in the Albert School in Saint John, where he was principal from 1905 to 1907. In December 1921, the Reverend Major R.C. MacGillivray, the former chaplain of the 26th, while speaking at the Canadian Club in Saint John, paid tribute to McKenzie's leadership and courage, and called on the people of New Brunswick to erect a monument to his memory. Shortly afterward, it was suggested that Sugarloaf Mountain, located in

Honour Roll, Memorial Hall, University of New Brunswick, Fredericton, including fallen alumnae Lieutenant-Colonel A.E.G. McKenzie, and Lieutenants Fred Foley and Charles Lawson. Author's photo

McKenzie's hometown of Campbellton, be renamed Mount McKenzie; in this way, everyone passing through the province via the Canadian National Railway would be reminded of his service. The *Campbellton Graphic* took up the cause, recommending that a road be built to the summit, where a small park could be created. Unfortunately, the suggestion was never acted upon. Then, in October 1939, the Association of Former Officers of the 26th Battalion honoured McKenzie by presenting an oil portrait of him to the province. The large painting was unveiled in the Legislative Assembly chamber by Mrs. McKenzie in the presence of some one hundred former officers. During the ceremony, Lieutenant-Colonel Charles Leonard stated that McKenzie "represents to us the soldier and leader of the New Brunswick military." Also speaking was the Hon. J.B.M. Baxter, chief justice and administrator of the province, who described McKenzie as an outstanding and promising figure in both civil and military life. To all who knew him, "he was an ideal soldier. It was a tragic day for his regiment when he fell." The portrait continued to hang in the assembly for many years; in 1967, the officers of the 26th Battalion Overseas Club donated it to the New Brunswick Museum. In the early 1960s, when Colonel Art

Portrait of Lieutenant-Colonel Ernest McKenzie
donated to the Province of New Brunswick by
former officers of the 26th Battalion, October 1939.

1967.53, New Brunswick Museum

Barry wrote his memoirs, *Batman to Brigadier*, he dedicated the book to
the memory of McKenzie: "the best soldier I ever took an order from."

The experience of the soldiers of the 26th Battalion and their successes
on the Great War battlefields hold a key place in New Brunswick's history
of the war. About one-third of all New Brunswickers who served at the
front fought with the 26th, and their memory lived on during the post-war
period. June 13, the date of their initial departure overseas, became a red-
letter date for commemoration. Many veterans of the battalion returned
to the province after the war, where they found work, married, and raised
families, often in the face of significant challenges. In various ways, they
kept the memory of their fallen comrades alive, and helped those who
struggled to reintegrate into civilian life. Their experiences were often

passed on to their families, many of which have preserved the stories, letters, diaries, photographs, and other objects, handed down from one generation to the next. These and other vivid relics in cemeteries, churches, and other sites around the province of soldiers who did not return remind us that the war reached into families and communities, large and small. Today, it is easy to forget the enormous effect the Great War had on Canada and its provinces, but tangible evidence of its tragic consequences can be seen everywhere once you begin looking. In New Brunswick, many of these historical artefacts commemorate the soldiers of the "Fighting 26th."

Courcelette

It was on the 15th of September, Sir,
Yes, I remember it quite well;
When the gallant boys from Canada
Charged the Huns, like very hell.
The sight of that fight was glorious,
And I never shall forget
How Jack Canuck smashed old Fritz
When we captured Courcelette.

We started out in the late afternoon;
Yes, right in the broad daylight,
And all of us were eager then
To get in and show a fight.
Their shrapnel killed a few of us,
But the rest paid off the debt;
For many Huns went down to hell
When we captured Courcelette.

Our 5th Brigade were in that day,
Their first trip on the Somme;
And knew that people waited
For their work's report back home.
Their wives' and sweetheart's and children's,
Pictures in their heart were set,
Fond mothers, too, were thought of
When we captured Courcelette.

The Huns, they got it hot, well, yes;
But we played the game quite fair,
And we took the Boches prisoners
When their hands went in the air.
Up went their hands, and down their guns,
And run? They're running yet,
Tom Longboat would not catch them
When we took Courcelette.

We stuck them with the bayonet, Sir,
And battered them with the butt;
Some bad ones, we treated good,
Their throats we nicely cut.
We certainly soaked them fine, Sir,
And earned a name, I'll bet,
For it nearly killed the Kaiser Bill,
When he heard we had Courcelette.

My chum was killed that evening,
And to me there fell the task
To let his dear old mother know;
One request he did but ask:
"Phil, tell my mother darling
That she must not cry nor fret,
But be proud to say her only boy
Was killed at Courcelette.

In closing I'd like to say, Sir,
A word for the Medical Corp,
Some folks think they are bomb-proof,
They once were, but no more;
For they went into the fighting mass,
Our wounded boys to get;
Yes, the C.A.M.C. did their share
When we captured Courcelette.

—Philip S. George Horne ((#444380)

Acknowledgements

During the several years it took me to research and write this book, I received invaluable help from many friends and colleagues:

Marc Milner for patiently editing the manuscript.

Curtis Mainville for sending hundreds of newspaper files and much, much more.

Harold Wright for providing copies of many of the photographs used in the book.

Gary Hughes at the New Brunswick Museum for patiently answering many questions about the museum's collections.

Alan Sheppard and Julie Scriver at Goose Lane Editions, who guided the manuscript through to publication. Freelancer Barry Norris for patiently copy editing the text and saving me from many spelling mistakes.

Bill Stewart for reading Chapter Four and recommending useful changes.

Bob Lockhart who kindly provided me with a copy of the ever-useful "New Brunswick's 'Fighting 26th': A Draft History of the 26th New Brunswick Battalion, C.E.F., 1914-1919," by S. Douglas MacGowan (1991).

Roger Gillies for giving me access to the Sergeant Clarence Gillies Collection.

Christena and Bernard Beukeveld for providing me with valuable information on Private Frank McNamara.

Leonel Methot for sending me information on Private Alexander Methot.

Karen Messer for sending me a photo of Private Fred Woodbury and copies of some of his letters.

Dawne McLean for the Private Hugh Wright letters and photos.

Arnie Kay for the research he carried out at Library and Archives Canada.

Thomas Littlewood for photographing the Gordon Holder Collection at Library and Archives Canada.

Roger Nason for patiently obtaining a copy of Private Ben Gaskill's diary from the Grand Manan Historical Society.

Jim Creamer for sending me a copy of Private Egbert M. Robertson's diary.

Janice Cook at the Provincial Archives of New Brunswick, who alerted me to several collections of documents.

David Smith at the Fredericton Branch of the Royal Canadian Legion for loaning a copy of Corporal Fred Howard's diary.

John Williamson for sharing his research and thoughts on Lieutenant-Colonel A.E.G. McKenzie.

Bill Clarke at the Restigouche Regional Museum for information on Lieutenant Harry Ferguson.

Greg Fekner, who sent photos of artefacts held by the New Brunswick Military History Museum.

Phyllis and Danny Crowe from Smith's Creek in Kings County for giving me access to the United Church and showing me the Venning Farm, where Private David Gibbons grew up.

Selected Bibliography

A) Primary Sources
Archival

Gaskill, Private Benjamin. Diary. Grand Manan Historical Society.

Kempling, Private George H. Diary. The Canadian Letters and Images Project. Vancouver Island University.

Knowlton, Lieutenant Charles D. Letters. New Brunswick Museum.

Lawson, Lieutenant Charles. Letters and Scrapbooks. Jessie I. Lawson Fonds, New Brunswick Museum.

Lawson, Captain Walter C. Correspondence. York Sunbury Historical Society Collection (MC 300), Charlotte C. Saunders Collection (MS68).

McIntyre, Lance Corporal J. Walter. Diary. Fonds MC 3837, Provincial Archives of New Brunswick.

McKnight, Lieutenant Graham. Diaries and Letters. J. Graham McKnight Fonds, Archives and Special Collections Department, Harriet Irving Library, University of New Brunswick.

Woodbridge, Captain H.F.G. Papers. York Sunbury Historical Society Collection (MC 300), (MS65), Provincial Archives of New Brunswick.

Printed

Barry, A.L. *From Batman to Brigadier*. n.p., n.d.

Campbell, Ian. J., ed. *The Personal Diary of Lieutenant Harry Wensley Ferguson, 26th New Brunswick Battalion (5th Brigade, 2nd Canadian Division), Canadian Expeditionary Force*. n.p., 2012.

Clarke, W.A., and Ashley MacKenzie. *Ten Miles from Nowhere: WW1 Letters from and about Restigouche Boys*. Dalhousie, NB: Restigouche Regional Museum, 2014.

B) Secondary Sources

Campbell, David. "Military Discipline, Punishment, and Leadership in the First World War: The Case of the 2nd Canadian Division." In *The Apathetic and the Defiant: Case Studies of Canadian Mutiny and Disobedience, 1812-1919*, ed. Craig Mantle, 297-342. Kingston, ON: Canadian Defence Academy; Toronto, ON: Dundurn, 2007.

Cook, Tim. *At the Sharp End: Canadians Fighting the Great War, 1914-1916*. Vol. 1. Toronto: Viking Canada, 2007.

Cook, Tim. *Shock Troops: Canadians Fighting the Great War, 1917-1918*. Vol. 2. Toronto: Viking Canada, 2008.

Gould, R.W., and S.K. Smith. *The Story of the Fighting 26th*. Saint John, NB: St. John News Company, 1917.

Holt, Richard. *Filling the Ranks: Manpower in the Canadian Expeditionary Force, 1914-1918*. Montreal, QC: McGill-Queen's University Press, 2017.

Hyland, Chris. "The Canadian Corps' Long March: Logistics, Discipline and the Occupation of the Rhineland." *Canadian Military History* 21, no. 2 (2015): 5-20.

MacGowan, S. Douglas, Harry (Mac) Heckbert, and Byron E. O'Leary. *New Brunswick's "Fighting 26th": A History of the 26th New Brunswick Battalion, C.E.F., 1914-1919*. Saint John, NB: Neptune, 1994.

Morton, Desmond. *Silent Battle: Canadian Prisoners of War in Germany, 1914-1919*. Toronto: Lester Publishing, 1992.

Morton, Desmond, and Glenn T. Wright. *Winning the Second Battle: Canadian Veterans and the Return to Civilian Life, 1915-1930*. Toronto: University of Toronto Press, 1987.

Nicholson, G.W.L. *Canadian Expeditionary Force, 1914-1918*. Ottawa: Queen's Printer, 1964.

Rawling, Bill. *Trench Warfare: Technology and the Canadian Corps, 1914-1918*. Toronto: University of Toronto Press, 1992.

C) Newspapers

Campbellton Graphic
Daily Gleaner (Fredericton)
Daily Telegraph (Saint John)
Kings County Record (Sussex)
Moncton Daily Times
North Shore Leader (Newcastle)
St. John Standard
St. Croix Courier (St. Stephen)

Index

The New Brunswick Military History Museum

The mission of the New Brunswick Military History Museum is to collect, preserve, research, and exhibit artifacts which illustrate the history and heritage of the military forces in New Brunswick and New Brunswickers at war, during peacetime, and on United Nations or North Atlantic Treaty Organization duty.

The New Brunswick Military History Museum is proud to partner with the Gregg Centre.

Highlighting 400 years of New Brunswick's history.

The New Brunswick Military Heritage Project

The New Brunswick Military Heritage Project, a non-profit organization devoted to public awareness of the remarkable military heritage of the province, is an initiative of the Brigadier Milton F. Gregg, VC, Centre for the Study of War and Society of the University of New Brunswick. The organization consists of museum professionals, teachers, university professors, graduate students, active and retired members of the Canadian Forces, and other historians. We welcome public involvement. People who have ideas for books or information for our database can contact us through our website: www.unb.ca/nbmhp.

One of the main activities of the New Brunswick Military Heritage Project is the publication of the New Brunswick Military Heritage Series with Goose Lane Editions. This series of books is under the direction of J. Brent Wilson, Director of the New Brunswick Military Heritage Project at the University of New Brunswick. Publication of the series is supported by a grant from the Province of New Brunswick and the Canadian War Museum.

The New Brunswick Military History Series

Volume 1

Saint John Fortifications, 1630-1956,
Roger Sarty and Doug Knight

Volume 2

*Hope Restored: The American Revolution and the
Founding of New Brunswick,* Robert L. Dallison

Volume 3

The Siege of Fort Beauséjour, 1755, Chris M. Hand

Volume 4

*Riding into War: The Memoir of a Horse Transport Driver,
1916-1919,* James Robert Johnston

Volume 5

*The Road to Canada: The Grand Communications Route
from Saint John to Quebec,* W.E. (Gary) Campbell

Volume 6

*Trimming Yankee Sails: Pirates and Privateers
of New Brunswick,* Faye Kert

Volume 7

*War on the Home Front: The Farm Diaries
of Daniel MacMillan, 1914-1927,*
edited by Bill Parenteau and Stephen Dutcher

Volume 8
Turning Back the Fenians: New Brunswick's Last Colonial Campaign,
Robert L. Dallison

Volume 9
*D-Day to Carpiquet: The North Shore Regiment and
the Liberation of Europe*, Marc Milner

Volume 10
*Hurricane Pilot: The Wartime Letters
of Harry L. Gill, DFM, 1940-1943*,
edited by Brent Wilson with Barbara J. Gill

Volume 11
*The Bitter Harvest of War: New Brunswick and the
Conscription Crisis of 1917*, Andrew Theobald

Volume 12
Captured Hearts: New Brunswick's War Brides,
Melynda Jarratt

Volume 13
*Bamboo Cage: The P.O.W. Diary of Flight Lieutenant Robert Wyse,
1942-1943*, edited by Jonathan F. Vance

Volume 14
*Uncle Cy's War: The First World War Letters
of Major Cyrus F. Inches*, edited by Valerie Teed

Volume 15
Agnes Warner and the Nursing Sisters of the Great War,
Shawna M. Quinn

Volume 16
New Brunswick and the Navy: Four Hundred Years,
Marc Milner and Glenn Leonard

Volume 17

Battle for the Bay: The Naval War of 1812, Joshua M. Smith

Volume 18

Steel Cavalry: The 8th (New Brunswick) Hussars and the Italian Campaign, Lee Windsor

Volume 19

A Neighbourly War: New Brunswick and the War of 1812, Robert L. Dallison

Volume 20

The Aroostook War of 1839, W.E. (Gary) Campbell

Volume 21

The 104th (New Brunswick) Regiment of Foot in the War of 1812, John R. Grodzinski

Volume 22

Till the Boys Come Home: Life on the Home Front, Queens County, NB, 1914-1918, Curtis Mainville

Volume 23

Letters from Beauly: Pat Hennessy and the Canadian Forestry Corps in Scotland, 1940-1945, Melynda Jarratt

Volume 24

The Endless Battle: The Fall of Hong Kong and Canadian POWs in Imperial Japan, Andy Flanagan

About the Author

J. Brent Wilson teaches military history at the University of New Brunswick and previously taught at CFB Gagetown through the Department of Continuing Studies of the Royal Military College. He was the curator of the York-Sunbury Historical Museum in Fredericton from 1978 to 1984 and worked at the Brigadier Milton F. Gregg Centre for the Study of War and Society at the University of New Brunswick until 2018. He is now Editor Emeritus of the Gregg Centre's New Brunswick Military Heritage Project.

Wilson has written on subjects as diverse as American counterterrorism policy and New Brunswick's military history in the nineteenth and twentieth centuries and conducted battlefield tours in France, Belgium, Canada, and the United States. Previous publications include editing *Hurricane Pilot: The Wartime Letters of Warrant Officer Harry L. Gill, DFM, 1940-1943*, and co-authoring *Kandahar Tour: The Turning Point in Canada's Afghan Mission* and *Loyal Gunners: 3rd Field Artillery Regiment (The Loyal Company) and the History of New Brunswick Artillery, 1893 to 2012*.